# Graham
# HILL

## Master of Motor Sport

Hill waits with characteristic concentration for the start of the 1966 German Grand Prix. *(PN)*

# Graham HILL

## Master of Motor Sport

# John Tipler

breedon **books**

PUBLISHING

First published in Great Britain in 2002 by
The Breedon Books Publishing Company Limited
Breedon House, 3 The Parker Centre,
Derby, DE21 4SZ.

ISBN 1 85983 279 2

Printed and bound by Butler & Tanner, Frome, Somerset, England.

Cover printing by Lawrence-Allen Colour Printers, Weston-super-Mare,
Somerset, England.

# Contents

# Acknowledgements

MANY thanks to all who assisted with the compilation of the Graham Hill story, including BRM technical director Tony Rudd, the legendary private-entrant Rob Walker, and former Team Lotus mechanics Jim Endruweit and Bob Dance. I am particularly grateful to those that raced against Hill for their invaluable insights into his character and techniques, including BRM teammate Jackie Stewart, his Brabham teammate Tim Schenken and Mario Andretti from the Gold Leaf Team Lotus days. Thanks also to John Surtees for agreeing to be interviewed for the book.

Photographs were supplied by Peter Nygaard/Grand Prix Photos *(PN)*, Ian Catt *(IC)*, Ted Walker/Ferret Fotographic *(FF)*, Roger Palmer, Andrew Weall, Vanna Skelley/Castrol Picture Library *(C)*, Fran Chamberlain/Ford Motor Company Photo Archive *(FMC)*, Clive Chapman/Classic Team Lotus *(CTL)*, Klaus Parr/Porsche AG *(P)*, Tim Wright/LAT *(LAT)*, myself *(JT)* and Jim Endruweit *(JE)*. Helen Tulloch and Mike Bennett provided photographs from Derek Jolly's *(DJ)* collection. Darren Galpin helped me with a photographic query. I am most grateful to all concerned.

Finally, a big thank you to Dianne Davies for compiling the results of Graham Hill's race record, a major endeavour indeed; my wife Laura for her incisive subbing; and to Susan Last and Graham Hales of Breedon Books for putting it together. And, last but not least, Rupert Harding for managing the project.

# Introduction

THE most significant aspects of Graham Hill's racing career are its duration and diversity. In an era which saw too many of his colleagues and friends die on the track, Graham was one of the greatest survivors. A dreadful irony then, that he should meet his end in a needless air crash when on the threshold of a promising new career as a team owner.

Hill made the Monaco Grand Prix his own, winning five times, an achievement bettered only in 1993 by Ayrton Senna and subsequently by Michael Schumacher. Here he drives the BRM P261 to third place in the 1966 event. *(PN)*

Graham Hill is still the only racing driver to win the Formula 1 World Championship, the Indianapolis 500 and the Le Mans 24 Hours, and as befits a national icon, his career is well documented in several books and at least one video. His autobiography *Life at the Limit*, which he wrote while recuperating from the accident in a Team Lotus 49 at Watkins Glen at the end of 1969 that smashed both his legs, tells much of the story in his own inimitable style. At the time, he was still reigning world champion. But although he made a strong recovery from that accident, going on to win the Le Mans epic with Henri Pescarolo in 1973, it was clear that the glory days in single-

seaters were over. Gone too were the meetings where he would drive anything from Porsche to Jaguar to Ferrari as well as an F1 or F2 car. Late in 1972 he followed the example of some of his contemporaries, like Jack Brabham, Bruce McLaren and John Surtees, and formed his own Formula 1 team.

Graham was supremely versatile, and during the first decade of his career he drove a wide variety of machinery, including a 7-litre Ford Mk II at Le Mans in 1966. *(IC)*

While not exactly coming from an impoverished background, Graham had to work mighty hard at getting on the bottom rung of the ladder climbed by aspirant racing drivers. While some were fortunate enough to have cars provided for them, Hill traded his services as a mechanic for drives. His motor-racing career started from literally nothing, with no training, just an exploratory outing at Brands Hatch which cost him five shillings a lap. His first race was a Formula 3 event at Brands Hatch in 1954, finishing second in his heat and fourth in the final. It's most unlikely that such a scenario could happen today, when the big teams eye the junior kart tracks for signs of precocious talent. Those were the days when such things were possible, a time of post-war austerity and ex-servicemen on the move and on the make. Hill's success says much about the man, his tenacity, single-mindedness and self-belief. He did not suffer fools at all, and was as hard on his mechanics and associates as he was on himself. As his former teammate Jackie Stewart affirmed:

> Everything that Graham did was determined, very focused, when he drove Jaguars for John Coombs and Tommy Sopwith and Ferraris for Maranello, and later on in Lotus Cortinas. He was a very versatile driver; in those days you had to be – you were a Formula 2 driver and a Formula 1 and Indy car driver. We did Indy together in the same team and had a wonderful time. We had great laughs together over there.

As well as winning the Monaco Grand Prix five times, as seen here in 1969, Graham Hill remains the only racing driver to win the Formula 1 World Championship, the Indianapolis 500 and the Le Mans 24 Hours. *(FMC)*

Sardonic humour was certainly at the forefront of the Hill arsenal, almost his stock-in-trade. By the early 1960s, Hill the celebrity was in the ascendant, and as his unofficial role as motor racing's leading personality – its ambassador, even – coalesced, fostered by successes at Monaco and Indianapolis, he was in a position to acquire the sponsorship necessary to go his own way in 1973. BRM (British Racing Motors) designer and team manager Tony Rudd confirmed: 'He was a very good ambassador for the sport, a very strong personality. If you came into a room it wouldn't take you long to sense he was there.'

But Hill's skills as a racing driver have been veiled to a great extent by his celebrity status. Invariably the last to leave a party, and never likely to turn down an invitation to be guest speaker or judge the Miss World beauty contest, Graham's social adeptness brought greater prominence in the media, and his cult standing as racing hero snowballed to showbiz proportions.

His loquacious gifts were well known. 'I always thought of Graham as one of the funniest people I've ever known,' said Rob Walker. 'I used to go to functions with him, and once I had to speak before him. I said to him, "do you get nervous before you give a speech?" and he said, "I can't eat a thing before I make one!" And he was probably making a speech practically every day. The toastmasters of London declared him the best speech maker in the whole of London, including prime ministers and the Lord Mayor of London.' The establishment took note too, and he was awarded the OBE in 1968.

His first F1 world title in 1962 made Graham Hill a household name and, given his natural humour and charisma, he grew into the role of motor racing's ambassador. Here he is interviewed by well-known reporter and commentator Barry Gill at Silverstone in 1967. *(FMC)*

The proposition in this book is to re-examine Hill's career as a racing driver rather than regurgitate the various accounts of Hill the talented raconteur, dead-pan wit, *bon viveur* and party animal. In the following chapters, I record his career in fairly strict chronological fashion, because that projects more starkly the depth and variety of events he competed in, and the cars he drove.

It is sometimes said that, while Clark and Stewart were sublime natural talents in the cockpit of a racing car, Hill was a grafter. Of that there is no doubt. But the situation is not quite so cut and dried. To be F1 world champion twice, as well as winning many races in most of the other formulas, requires a good deal of race-craft and natural car control. So I suggest that Graham occupies the middle ground. He was not the magician that was Clark, but he was superior to a journeyman driver like Jo Bonnier, and with more than enough ability and gutsiness to place him in the Nigel Mansell category or, indeed, to come even more up to date, that of his son, Damon. After all, to have lasted two decades, pretty much at the top of the tree, he must have been doing plenty of things right.

Throughout his career, Graham received the unstinting support of his wife Bette, who invariably compiled his lap charts from the pit counter. She is seen here with their daughter Samantha. *(PN)*

Friends, rivals and teammates. Some enthusiasts say that, while Clark was a natural, Hill had to work at it, but you cannot be world champion and win a lot of races in other categories without plenty of natural ability and tactical and mechanical knowledge. *(FMC)*

No one was more meticulous than Hill in diligently recording every suspension setting for every circuit under all conditions. He would spend hours doing this, considering set-ups, then compiling job lists for his mechanics. And few drivers rivalled him in the number of practice laps they did prior to a Grand Prix. They say that behind every successful man is a powerful woman, and it is significant that he enjoyed the devoted and unwavering support of his wife Bette throughout his career.

Many wondered why he did not retire earlier than 1975, when it was clear that his career as a top-line F1 driver was well and truly over. The answer is that he loved motor racing and kept on doing it for as long as possible. Had fate not overtaken him, it is easy to imagine him having a go in saloons or GTs just for the hell of it. And as the elder statesman, his dead-pan humour would have made him excellent value in the TV commentary box, where the Hill drawl and wry sound bites would have admirably complemented Murray Walker's effusions.

# Chapter 1
# Rowing and Racing Schools

LIKE many boys brought up in the middle of the 20th century, Graham Hill cut his mechanical teeth on a Meccano set. These consisted of a range of metal plates, nuts and bolts, and gears and wheels, with which it was possible to construct working model vehicles. Graham spent long hours beavering away with his Meccano, which testifies to an innate ability with things mechanical.

Born on 15 February 1929 in a Hampstead nursing home, Norman Graham Hill's scholastic career was not that distinguished, although he was an avid reader of books, as well as constructing Meccano models. He was aged 10 when World War Two broke out, and the Hills were evacuated to Hereford, where Hill senior was stationed, for a brief period during the Blitz, but they soon returned to Hendon. In his autobiography *Life at the Limit*, Graham recalls watching dogfights in the sky between English and German planes, selling bits of shrapnel and disinterring unexploded incendiary bombs from his back garden. He speaks quite nonchalantly of knocking these burning bombs off the roof of the house. They never slept in the underground stations, preferring the comfort of home with the attendant risks of bombing. He speaks of a huge bomb destroying rows of houses in the vicinity. A childhood accustomed to upheaval, risk and danger, then.

If Graham's father's work at the London Stock Exchange is a barometer of social status, then the Hills could be described as Home Counties suburban middle-class. While Hill senior was, according to Graham, a 'most unmechanical' man, who'd never driven a car in his life, his mother owned a 250cc Triumph motorcycle when she was 17, so there were certainly some vehicular genes in the family, even though they never owned a car. The closest that the young Graham came to anything to do with motor racing was seeing some photographs belonging to a neighbour called Edgar Fronteras who'd raced an OM in the 1930s.

In his book *Team Lotus: the Indianapolis Years*, competitions manager Andrew Ferguson recalls that he and Graham attended the Orange Hill Grammar School in Hendon, north-west London, although Hill was three years ahead of him. Ferguson reminds Hill about a girl from a neighbouring school who, for a few pence, would entertain an audience of schoolboys in an air-raid shelter by removing her knickers.

Aged 13, Hill attended Hendon Technical College, where his most successful contemporary was Harry Hyams, the archetypal 1960s property developer and creator of the West End's towering yet architecturally anonymous Centre Point. At the same time, Graham joined the Scouts, often spending six nights a week at the Scout group. For the young Hill, activities included PT (physical training or PE) and playing drums in the band. He enjoyed Scout camps and, although the Hill family were not church-goers, he was a server at the Scout group's monthly Sunday service. Aged 16, he embarked on a five-year apprenticeship with Smith's Instruments, whose dials occupied many a contemporary car dashboard. A natural aptitude for mechanical engineering probably prompted him to go this way rather than into higher education. But a lack of aspiration to academic qualifications suggests a certain mindset, and much of Hill's career trajectory can be explained by his background.

## Naval Base

Back in the 1950s, all young men were obliged to do National Service and, aged 21, Hill signed up for three years in the Royal Navy. He was sent on a petty officer's course, the equivalent of being an NCO in the Army, and a post absolutely ripe for aspirational middle-class types. The training involved assault courses and lectures, and it was here that Hill first discovered his aptitude for public speaking and how to issue commands. The naval discipline must never quite have left him, since Jochen Rindt's biographer Heinz Prüller refers to Hill as being 'like a soldier [who] obeyed orders and was prepared to drive any car Chapman allocated to him.'

With the rank of petty officer, Hill became an engine room artificer (engineer) aboard a modern 10,000-ton cruiser, HMS *Swiftsure*. His job was to operate the throttles that governed the ship's four steam-turbine engines. The ship paid a courtesy visit to Monaco in 1951, but at that time, Graham, still a non-driver, had no idea that it was the setting for a Grand Prix, let alone the significance that the principality would come to have for him a decade or so later. He did win at the casino though.

While commuting from Smith's engineering college in Cheltenham up to London, Hill had an accident on his 1936 Velocette motorcycle. The teenage rider ran into a broken-down car, abandoned in the road in the Cotswold fog with no lights on, and the ensuing crash hospitalised him for three months with a broken left thigh. It was this incident that left him with a characteristic

bow-legged gait and a bad back. Hill was not deterred from riding motorcycles as a result of the accident, however, and replaced the Velocette with a 500cc Matchless 1947 competition model.

The characteristic Hill moustache was cultivated after he quit the Navy in 1952, and it was actually a bushy RAF-style arrangement, deliberately calculated to upset the naval establishment when he returned for the obligatory three-weeks-a-year reserve training. Beards are permitted in the Navy, but not moustaches. Graham's first car was also acquired at this time. It was a 1934 Morris 8 Tourer and, with virtually no driving experience, he steered an erratic course home across London. A fortnight later he took his driving test, but not long afterwards the Morris was written off by an errant laundry van. The case came to court but, because he'd not hooted at the van, the judge held that Graham was partly to blame for the accident! So no compensation, and no car.

Back at Smith's Instruments in 1953, and still with no clear career ambition, a colleague showed Graham an advert in a motoring magazine offering laps of Brands Hatch stadium (as it was known in those days) in a Formula 3 car for five shillings a lap. Out of curiosity, he decided to have a go and, in a borrowed helmet, invested £1 in four laps in an F3 Cooper powered by a 500cc JAP engine – 'a small torpedo with a wheel at each corner,' he said. It was enough. Hill was smitten, and from that point on he resolved to take up driving racing cars professionally. Hindsight tells us that he succeeded in re-inventing himself as a racing driver, and an immensely successful one at that. Stirling Moss was the obvious role model, a driver who started in the rough and tumble of the late 1940s 500cc F3 and, although he had yet to win a Grand Prix in 1954, he was a works Maserati driver by then and good enough to be hired by Mercedes-Benz for 1955. The era of the 1960s when all things seemed possible was some way off and, without private means, only the most determined would survive to reach the top.

The first step was to work for the race-driving school – the Universal Motor Racing Club – as a part-time mechanic in exchange for races in the car. Unfortunately the operation went bust and he never got to race. Not long after that, Graham approached a man called Weller who was keen to set up a racing drivers' school, and in early 1954 began preparing a couple of 500cc F3 cars – Cooper and Kieft – in Weller's barn at Westerham, Kent. To do this required him to leave Smith's Instruments – a move of which his father was not apprised, although his mother collaborated – and, resourcefully, he went on the dole to finance his commute to Kent. There was no payment from Mr Weller, just the promise of going racing.

## Race Debut

Weller's pledge was honoured on 27 April 1954, when Graham had his first race for the Premier Motor Racing Club in the Mk 4 Cooper JAP F3 car. He had never even spectated at a race up to that point, yet he managed to go quickly enough in practice to make the front row of the grid. At the start, he wound the revs up to 6,000rpm, dropped the clutch and, much to his amazement, found himself in the lead. Eventually second in this heat, he came fourth in the final, having been pipped for third place on the finishing line. It was an auspicious beginning, and Graham could now tutor the school's novice pupils with genuine authority.

Hill's second race was something of an anticlimax, as the newly rebuilt Norton engine expired while he was running second. Abandoning the car, Hill got into a conversation with some spectators in the Brands Hatch infield, who turned out to be Colin and Hazel Chapman and Mike Costin (Lotus's technical director since 1953). It was the sort of casual meeting that anyone with a track pass might have had, yet it was a pivotal moment in Hill's life.

At around this time, the labour exchange had explained to Hill that, since there was no prospect of them finding him an opening as a racing driver, they would no longer pay him the dole. And when Mr Weller declined his request for a weekly salary of three pounds, the impecunious Hill was left with no option but to hitch a ride from Brands

Hatch back to London. Showing the kind of nerve that would characterise his racing career, he asked Colin Chapman for a ride in his furniture-van transporter, on the basis of their brief encounter. Chapman, who assumed that Graham was a friend of Mike Costin, readily agreed. And of course, Costin thought Hill must have been a friend of Chapman's.

Back at Colin Chapman's north London base at Tottenham Lane, Hornsey, Graham offered his services to repair the team's bent Lotus Mk 8 sports racer. Chapman took him on for the princely sum of one pound a day, which was a vast improvement on his earlier circumstances. Despite the modest brick-built workshops, output was prolific, with a succession of aerodynamic sports racing cars emerging from 1954 onwards. Hill worked on the austere Mk 6 production cars during the day and the sports-racing Mk 8s in the evening, while at the weekend he worked on customers' racing cars. As a result of hanging around at the august Steering Wheel club in Shepherd Market, Mayfair, the regular haunt of motor-racing people, Graham met garage proprietor and racer Danny Margulies. They became friends and he went along as riding mechanic and co-driver in Margulies's C-type Jaguar on a European tour, taking in races at Spa, Bari, Sardinia, Sicily and the Nürburgring. An exciting itinerary even today, and pretty exotic for the mid-1950s.

## Rowing Clubs

Meanwhile, Graham had not been neglecting his other sporting interest, which was rowing. While in the navy he had met his future wife Bette at the Auriol Rowing Club in Hammersmith. She became a member of the Stuart Ladies' Rowing Club, and Graham coached her eight as they won their category in the European Games. He rowed stroke in the London Rowing Club's winning first eight in the Henley regatta's Grand Challenge Cup, and maintained his membership of that club. It was their distinctive dark blue and white cap insignia that Graham – and subsequently his son Damon – wore on his racing crash helmet. Significantly,

Hill looks on as Chapman offers some advice to King Hussein of Jordan, who was having an outing at Goodwood in a works Eleven in 1956. *(FF)*

Graham attributed his resilience in getting through the difficult times in his motor racing career to 'the self-discipline required for rowing, and the never-say-die attitude it bred'. 'It taught me a lot about myself,' he said, 'and it's also a great character-building sport. You not only get to know about yourself but you get to know about other people – who you'd want to have with you in the boat over the last quarter-mile of a race when you're all feeling absolutely finished. With seven other fellows relying on you, you just can't give in.'

Graham's relationship with Bette would be crucial to his career, since she allowed him to race wherever and whenever he chose, loyally supporting him as timekeeper in the pits. Initially their romance was sustained by a difficult cross-town commute from north-west to south-east London, since Hill had little money and only a bicycle for transport. After they were married in

August 1955 they honeymooned at Bognor Regis, close enough to the Goodwood circuit for Hill to be able to drive for Team Lotus in the Nine Hours race as co-driver to Keith Hall. It was a major event, with many of the top names racing, including Stirling Moss, Mike Hawthorn and Tony Brooks, and it was Graham's first real taste of the big time.

The newly-weds rented a little flat in Belsize Park, north London, for five guineas a week, which meant sharing the bathroom with nine other people, and Bette continued to work as a secretary, which, at £12 a week, was more lucrative than being a racing-car mechanic. It was not until 1962 that the Hills' fortunes improved dramatically, enabling a move to a substantial detached family house in Mill Hill, north London. Back in 1955, Graham's personal transport was a 1929 Austin Chummy, bought from Hazel

Chapman for £25 with the proviso that she could borrow it to take part in the annual Wrotham Cup trials. Battered and well-worn, the car owed the Chapmans no favours, since it had recently carried them over the Grossglockner Pass in Austria, which is one of the highest in the Alps. It was fundamentally lacking in the braking department, had to be bump started because the starter didn't work and, although pretty reliable, it drank fuel, oil and water in equal amounts. Hill sold it three years later for £25, a reflection of the care he bestowed on it – photos in *Life at the Limit* show he fitted a new hood and 'tarted it up'.

Hill was one of the first people to benefit from Colin Chapman's quasi-philanthropic DIY race-car deals, whereby he gave you the makings of the car, you built it and raced it, while he got whatever start money, bonuses and winnings accrued from it. And he still owned the car. Aspiring drivers like Hill and Trevor Taylor benefited from being able to go racing in a state-of-the-art car that they knew

inside out, and Lotus gained the exposure of on-track publicity. Hill entered the Ford 100E-powered Lotus Eleven that Chapman had thus loaned him in the *Autosport* Championship series of 1956, and he won his first event in it, the up-to-1200cc sports car race at Brands Hatch on 29 April. At the same meeting, he placed second in the up-to-1500cc race, setting fastest lap. Hill had laid down a marker.

The Lotus Eleven was the Chapman-designed car with curvaceous Frank Costin-inspired, all-enveloping bodywork by Williams and Pritchard. Hill's Eleven was the road-going version, which came with a two-seater wraparound windshield, unlike the race versions that had a more stream-lined single-seater screen and a fairing behind the driver. Hill's car was painted bright yellow and, predictably, was nicknamed the Yellow Peril. He fitted it with a hood and drove it to and from circuits. On one occasion at Brands Hatch in August 1956, he spun four times on four

Driving the 1100cc Lotus Eleven, Graham won the up-to-1200cc sports car race at Brands Hatch in April 1956, and came second in the 1500cc version in the up-to-1500cc class, setting fastest lap and a new class record of 72.23mph. *(FF)*

consecutive laps, and was black-flagged by the officiating RAC steward who assumed that there must have been something wrong with the car for him to spin so often. A deflated Hill was forced to retire, but became reconciled to the fact that a cooling-off period following a racing mistake was actually prudent.

During 1956, Graham drove Elevens entered by Equipe Endeavour, Jack Richards and Tommy Sopwith, and by virtue of more wins and high placings at circuits like Brands, Mallory Park and Aintree – plus a hillclimb at Prescott – was leading the *Autosport* Championship before the start of the final round, a three-hour race at Oulton Park. But a con rod bolt had been over-tightened as Hill prepared the engine, and it snapped.

Although Chapman didn't discourage Hill from racing, he wasn't that keen on him going off every weekend, since Lotus was steadily expanding. Responsible for modifying Austin A30 gearboxes into racing format, mating them to Coventry Climax engines and sourcing MG J-type gearboxes for use with the 2-litre Bristol-engined Lotus Mk 10, Graham was in charge of the Hornsey transmissions department by 1957. Chapman's eye for talent suggests that Hill was a skilful mechanic, and he was not alone, since other colleagues in these early days were Keith Duckworth, (who went on to design Cosworth racing engines), and Jim Endruweit, who became Team Lotus chief mechanic and racing manager.

During the 1957 season Graham was gradually getting noticed, enabling him to trade his services as a mechanic in return for drives in other people's cars. He scored four wins in Dr Manton's Climax-powered Eleven, and drove Tommy Atkins's outdated F2 Connaught to fifth place at Goodwood, having stalled on the grid. Also at Goodwood, he drove Atkins's Aston Martin DB3S, and spun at Fordwater, the fast right-hander, leaving skid-marks 180 yards long. Tommy Atkins then got Aston Martin expert Roy Salvadori to try it, but after one lap the car was pronounced undriveable. It transpired that the front dampers were bereft of oil, so it was effectively lacking front suspension. Hill was vindicated, and it was another lesson learned. He was once observed by Team Lotus driver Cliff Allison hurling the Aston around Brands Hatch in a test session, spinning some five times. The Hill technique was to 'take the car by the scruff of the neck', which takes bravery and commitment in a big sports car like an Aston Martin.

He also drove John Ogier's 3.5-litre Tojeiro-Jaguar at Brands Hatch, and while practising, he lost the right-hand front wheel when a stub-axle broke, luckily without hitting anything. He was also entered for another race that day in a 1500cc Willment special, and during practice for that car's race, it too shed the same right-front wheel when the hub carrier broke.

His rivals at these meetings were some of the up and coming drivers of the day, including Alan Stacey, Peter Ashdown and Tom Dickson, as well as established stars such as Ivor Bueb, Roy Salvadori and Cliff Allison. When Hill started racing most of his contemporaries, at club level at least, were owner-drivers who were not particularly interested in helping anybody else. Motor sport was becoming more professional though, and by 1957 men of means like John Ogier, Tommy Atkins and John Willment were regularly entering new talent. They generally bought the best cars available, prepared them properly and employed good drivers. The usual arrangement was that the driver received half of the start money, bonuses and prize money. As a result of winning the 1100cc class in the British Empire Trophy in Dr Manton's Lotus Eleven, Graham earned £125. This was subtracted from the car's total earnings of £255, made up from £30 starting money, £20 from Esso, with whom Dr Manton had a contract, £150 for a class win, £20 bonuses from Esso and Dunlop, and £5 bonuses from Ferodo brake pads and Champion plugs.

## Works Lotus Driver

When Graham revealed to Colin Chapman that he wanted to quit to go and build a Formula 2 car for John Willment, his boss's immediate response was that Hill should drive for Lotus. Having committed to Willment, Hill declined what he

Graham's one and only drive in a Connaught was in the Lavant Cup race at Goodwood in April 1957, driving the F2 A-type of Tommy Atkins into fifth place.

considered to be a long-overdue offer from Chapman. But plans changed, and instead, John Willment arranged a works Formula 2 drive for Hill with the Cooper Car Company, as third driver to Jack Brabham and Roy Salvadori. Graham was astonished to be offered £100 starting money by John Cooper. Needless to say, he was allocated the third and least desirable car. At the International Trophy at Silverstone in September, Graham spun on oil, unseen by his new teammates, and rejoined the race just after Salvadori went by in a comfortable lead. Anxious to unlap himself, Hill made as if to pass the astonished Salvadori, who assumed, wrongly, that Hill was challenging him for the lead. After the race, Cooper's senior driver remonstrated with his new colleague, but was pacified when the real state of affairs was revealed.

Soon after this race, Esso competitions manager Reg Tanner arranged a meeting at the Steering Wheel club between Colin Chapman and Graham Hill, at which it was agreed that Graham would drive for Lotus for the remainder of the 1957 season and the whole of 1958. Into the bargain, Esso offered him a retainer of £1,000 for 1958, on the strength of which he bought his first brand new car, an Austin A35.

The Team Lotus seat meant that Hill got his first taste of up-to-date single-seaters, driving the Climax-powered Lotus 12 in two late-season events that had been postponed because of petrol rationing in the wake of the Suez Crisis. At Goodwood he jousted with Jack Brabham for the lead, and despite losing his exhaust, took the lead on the last lap, only for Brabham to regain it by driving across the grass on the final corner. At Oulton Park for the Gold Cup meeting in October, Hill raced the Mk 12 again, setting fastest lap and finishing 11th.

The 1958 season began with a couple of races at Goodwood in April, Hill driving the Lotus 12 Formula 2 car, where he posted second place in the Lavant Cup and a retirement in the Glover Trophy for F1 and F2 cars. Hill's first outing in the new Mk 15 at the same meeting was bedevilled by problems with the Lotus 'queerbox'. This new gearbox, designed by Chapman, Harry Mundy and Richard Ansdale, was similar to the modern sequential pattern, with the lever slotting into a series of shallow niches with each shift. The 15 was designed to take Lotus into a bigger capacity class at Le Mans. While customer cars were fitted with 1.5-litre Climax FPF engines, Team Lotus cars were powered by the 2-litre motor, subsequently replaced by the full-blown 2.5-litre Climax FPF unit.

The 15's first success came in the 1500cc sports car race at Silverstone in May in the hands of Hill. The pair of Team Lotus 15s that went to Le Mans that year also sported more aerodynamic tails, and this time Chapman's ingenious inflatable tonneau covers were fitted, running from the top of the windscreen across the passenger side of the cockpit to the rear panel. In practice, Cliff Allison/Graham Hill's 2-litre 15 showed much promise and, since it was quicker than all the Ferraris, there was even the prospect of outright victory. But in the race the head gasket blew on the fourth lap before Hill could have a drive.

A works 15 S3 was campaigned regularly on the British club scene by Graham Hill, most notably notching up victories in a club race at Mallory Park, the sports car race at the British Grand Prix at Aintree, Brands Hatch on August bank holiday Monday and the International Brands Hatch meeting at the end of August. At the time, Cliff Allison was Team Lotus's number one driver, and although his car was ready for the British Empire Trophy at Oulton Park on 12 April 1958, Hill's was still back at Hornsey being built. Allison's car was put through scrutineering, then back in the paddock, the scrutineers' pass and the racing

numbers were removed, Hill's numbers substituted and the same car was presented to the scrutineers again, where it received another pass ticket. The same procedure was adopted for practice, with first Allison and then Hill driving the car, with race numbers surreptitiously swapped. Hill's 15 duly arrived on race morning, driven up from London to Oulton Park by Mike Costin, with just a quarter of an hour to spare. Sadly, due to an errant spark plug, it was all for naught, although Hill did have the satisfaction of having set fastest lap and a new outright lap record, in a completely unproven car.

While Graham regarded Formula 1 Grand Prix racing as the ultimate form of the sport, he liked to drive in any other category simply for the fun of it. His racing was still carried out on a hand-to-mouth basis, and he never harboured any specific ambitions about driving in Grands Prix, as his career was down to the people who were giving him drives. He made a point of being available to drive any car at any time, helping with its preparation if required. Moreover, he never attended a meeting simply as a spectator, since that would not further his own career as a racing driver. Although he admired Fangio and Moss, he did not place the Grand Prix stars on a pedestal. So when Team Lotus broke into Grand Prix racing in 1958, Hill viewed it all rather matter-of-factly.

Jim Endruweit, who was a Team Lotus mechanic, then chief mechanic and racing manager during the period 1958–68, recalls meeting Hill at the time. He remembers, too, how casual and amateurish the Lotus organisation was in those days:

Graham and I weren't introduced. It was a bit weird, really. Let me tell you first how I came to be at Lotus and you'll see how casual things were, on the surface at least, in those days. Bit like how Graham came to be there. When I was due to leave the Fleet Air Arm in 1957, I phoned up Lotus and got through to Mike Costin, and he said 'Oh, come and have a chat.' He was an ex-serviceman, so we talked aeroplanes as much as anything. They put me in the development section, assembling the 'queerboxes'. Over in the racing shop, they were getting 15s ready for Oulton Park. So as I'd built the gearboxes, they said I'd better come to Oulton Park as well. And as I'd only done one all-nighter, and they'd done two, I got to drive the transporter. It was always a bit like that. I did another all-nighter, doing the gearboxes for practice, and then I went to bed in the hotel to try and get some kip. And at 2am there's a knock on the door, and this bloke introduces himself, with 'I'm Graham Hill'. So I shook his hand. 'Right,' he said, 'let's go down to the cars.' And he took me down the garage, and I spent the rest of the night modifying the gearboxes. Not really a very memorable meeting – but it was the first time I'd clapped eyes on him, and I had no idea who he was, really. He was OK. I'd never met him before. I was so used to dealing with pilots, who are not only pilots, they're officers, and had to be treated with proper respect, and I tended to regard racing drivers in the same light. They were like the officer class. When they said jump, you jumped.

So Hill's demeanour was that of the petty officer. Jim continued:

Sometime in 1959, Lotus entered a 16 in an F2 race at the Charade circuit at Clermont-Ferrand. I remember all sorts of odd things, like, one problem that we had was that the hot air couldn't get out of the 16's engine bay. So I cut chunks out of the back of the engine bay, which apparently helped, but later when the Old Man [Chapman] saw it, he said 'what have you done?' Panic! But Graham was pretty calm about it. And that was typical Graham.

I can't remember whether or not we finished. [Hill came sixth.] He and I got along all right on that occasion, and obviously I did all right as far as he was concerned. He had to have respect for you as a mechanic. All drivers did. As the driver, he was giving the orders. We didn't talk about that. We weren't mates; I was never mates with any of the drivers, even with Jimmy, though we'd been together a long time. I'd flown with him in his aeroplane, gone with him in his road car. But we were never quite mates. Obviously you got to know them as drivers, but you didn't necessarily know the man.

Hill was not yet a public figure, and at Clermont, we had a few drinks, because that was probably the first and last time it was just the two of us together. Chapman had said, 'he'll tell you what to do.' So he was in charge. But you had to get along with each other, so he must have decided that I was an OK bloke, so that was good for 1959. But then he left at the end of the season. He was fed up because something went wrong at every race. Team Lotus was hardly a force to be reckoned with in 1959.

The forays into Formula 1 may have been fruitless, but Hill was still getting results in sports cars. He developed a keen sense of his own value as a driver, and when he resigned from Team Lotus it was quite possible that they could have fallen by the wayside as far as Grand Prix racing was concerned. It was not so surprising that he accepted an offer from a more established concern, BRM, at the end of 1959.

## Grand Prix Debutant

There were 11 events counting towards the 1958 World Championship. During that decade, the Indianapolis 500 was one of them, but from the world of Formula 1, only Alberto Ascari ever qualified for the Indy 500, retiring his Ferrari V12 early on in the 1952 event. The second event on the 1958 F1 calendar was the Monaco Grand Prix, traditionally held in May. Whereas the teams and drivers were travelling to races by F1 charter aircraft by the end of Hill's career, back in 1958 he drove there himself, accompanied by Bette, in the A35, taking 13 hours to do the journey down through France. His teammate was Cliff Allison, a veteran of three seasons with Lotus, mostly driving the works Elevens, whose record included winning the Index of Performance in the 1957 Le Mans 24 Hours. Allison ended up having to weld up the tube-frame chassis of Hill's car after it broke when he hit a kerb in practice – none of the mechanics present was prepared to do it. The Mk 12 single-seaters had first raced in 1957, and in F1 guise were powered by 2-litre four-cylinder Coventry Climax FPF engines, which were bored-out versions of the F2 engine. Transmission was by way of the 'queerbox' transaxle, operated by the sequential shift gate, which was a good idea in theory but often troublesome in practice. While the Mk 12 was a relatively advanced design, it lacked the full-on power of the 2.5-litre BRM, Ferrari and Vanwall opposition. Indeed, the state-of-the-art car was probably the mid-engined Cooper T45 that was powered by the same Coventry Climax engine as Lotus. Stirling Moss had already won the first Grand Prix of 1958 in Argentina driving Rob Walker's Cooper T43. In those days only the fastest 16 qualifiers could start at Monaco, and Graham shared the last place with Swede Jo Bonnier's Maserati 250F.

On lap 75 out of 100, Hill's steady drive looked

Graham made his Grand Prix debut at Monaco in 1958 in a Lotus Mk 12, powered by the 2-litre four-cylinder Coventry Climax FPF engine. Here he takes the brick-paved harbour section (with a remarkable dearth of boats) pursued by Trintignant in the Rob Walker Cooper T45 Climax. *(PN)*

as if it had paid off. He was lying fourth due to retirements, but as he turned into Portier corner just before the tunnel a halfshaft snapped and a rear wheel came off. Hill got out of the car and promptly collapsed with exhaustion – 'I was as weak as a kitten,' he said. So the marshals came to his aid and moved the car off the track. Not too surprisingly the team visited the casino that evening and it was some consolation for Hill that he won £120, no mean sum in 1958.

Almost from the outset, Hill was rubbing

With only 25 laps to go in the 1958 Monaco Grand Prix, Hill was running fourth when a drive-shaft snapped and a rear wheel came off. He got out of the car and promptly collapsed due to exhaustion. *(FF)*

shoulders with members of the motor-racing establishment. Rob Walker remembered: 'I knew Graham from the first time he got into a Formula 1 car. The first time we really got to know him was in 1958 when we were staying near Monaco. We asked Colin and Hazel Chapman and Bette and Graham to come over and have a bathe with us, and we got to know them then.' That was the year that Trintignant won Monaco in Rob's Cooper.

Graham had one race in the pretty Mk 16, the car often described as the 'mini-Vanwall'. This was a Chapman-designed space frame car with a streamlined body inspired by Frank Costin, and was driven by Hill to fourth place in the F2 category at the Aintree 200 in April. The next race was the Dutch Grand Prix, where the 12's head gasket went after 41 laps.

A second place driving the Mk 15 in the Rouen Sports Car Grand Prix followed, and then came the Belgian Grand Prix at Spa-Francorchamps. This was always mighty fast, far longer then than it became in later years, and daunting for a relative novice. Initially the straight-line speeds scared Hill, but after a few laps of high speed acclimatisation he felt he had the measure of it. The 2-litre Lotus could probably reach 160mph, some 20-30mph quicker than anything he'd achieved previously. The Climax engine, however, failed after 12 laps.

Graham drifting the works 2-litre Lotus 15 during the 1958 Tourist Trophy at Goodwood. He shared the car with Cliff Allison, and they were in among the 550A and 1500RS Porsches, until Hill pitted for a driver change and the engine was reluctant to restart. The car was eventually retired. *(JE)*

The French Grand Prix, held on another high-speed circuit at Reims-Geux, threw up a problem of a different kind when Graham was driving the Mk 16, now with 2.2-litre Climax power. This was a very low-slung car, an attitude achieved partly by canting the engine over on its side and routing the car's driveline between the driver's ankles with the propshaft passing diagonally under his left knee to

The starting grid for the sports car race that supported the 1958 British Grand prix at Silverstone, with Hill in the 1.5-litre Lotus 15 on the right, flanked by Salvadori in the Coombs 2-litre 15, with the two works Lister Jaguars of Moss and Hansgen alongside. Considering the field also included Ireland's 3.8 D-type and Bueb's Tojeiro-Jaguar, Hill did well to qualify on the front row. *(FF)*

DAILY
EXPRESS
From start to finish... DAILY EXPRESS ...always in the lead
SHELL
20
18

another universal joint, and a short shaft to the mid-mounted gearbox. The F2 variant had the engine mounted at 17 degrees to the left, and this was known as the upright engine, although of course it wasn't. With such a low bonnet line, the driver was thus positioned low down in the car, not stuck up in the airstream. In mid-race, the 16's gearbox became so hot that the solder attaching the oil filler cap melted, and boiling oil sluiced onto Hill's thigh as he passed the Reims pits flat out. In order to distract himself from the pain he levered his backside out of the seat, rising out of the cockpit, and retained control of the car as he negotiated the 160mph right-hander after the pit straight. The race was won by Mike Hawthorn (sporting a bow tie) in a Ferrari, and it was also Juan-Manuel Fangio's last Grand Prix. Although Hill did not race directly against 'El Chueco', his presence in the same event meant that Hill's career spanned three generations of racing drivers. BRM team manager and designer Tony Rudd recalled, 'I don't know if Graham looked up to Fangio. He was in Fangio's last race in 1958, but he wouldn't have been up against Fangio exactly, and there was no wheel-to-wheel stuff. If Graham saw Fangio

coming, he would most likely have got out of the way.'

At the British Grand Prix staged at Silverstone in July, Hill was forced to retire due to overheating when contesting fifth place with Harry Schell's BRM. A depressing pattern was beginning to be established in Hill's Grand Prix race record. He started the German Grand Prix at the Nürburgring from the back of the grid, but after four laps of the Nordschleif, an oil line split and the Lotus 16 expired in a cloud of white smoke. This was the event in which the personable Peter Collins was killed, battling with Hawthorn and Brooks.

Round 9 was the Portuguese Grand Prix, held on the city streets of Oporto, with roads criss-crossed by tramlines. These steel furrows caused Cliff Allison to lose control of his Mk 16 right in front of the pits, and it was written off in the ensuing accident. The same obstacle also caught out Hill in the race, getting his Lotus sideways and mounting the straw bales opposite the pits. Part of the problem was the cramped cockpit of the Mk 16, in which Hill found it difficult to operate to the full. Back at Tottenham Lane, Colin Chapman had the car's dashboard relocated by a couple of

Graham drove the works' 1.5-litre Lotus 15 in the sports car race supporting the 1958 British Grand Prix at Silverstone. As well as driving a Mk 16 in the Grand Prix, Hill also drove an A35 in the saloon car race, but retired from all three events. *(FF)*

inches so Hill could opposite-lock the steering wheel more easily.

Graham scored his first World Championship point at Monza, coming in sixth in the Italian Grand Prix in September. It was a dramatic race, including brake failure, a small fire and three pit stops to replenish the water radiator. In a display of typical Chapman brinkmanship, Hill's car ran out of fuel as it crossed the finish line. The final round was the Moroccan Grand Prix at Casablanca's Ain-Diab circuit, where Graham finished 16th and last, eight laps behind the battling Moss and Hawthorn.

Driving a Lotus Seven powered by a stage 1 Climax engine, Hill won the 15-lap Christmas Trophy on Boxing Day at a damp Brands Hatch, 1958. In so doing, he beat much more fancied runners, including Peter Ashdown's Lotus Eleven, Les Leston's Elva Mk IV and Peter Gammon's Lola. This was the meeting where Chapman's Elite narrowly beat Clark's in the GT race. Hill, meanwhile, went on to win the Silver City Trophy in the works F2 Lotus. *(LAT)*

Starting his 2.2-litre Lotus 16 from the fourth row of the four-three-four grid for the 1958 British Grand Prix at Silverstone, Graham battled with the Coopers of Salvadori and Brabham, the Ferrari of Von Trips and Behra's BRM. He had to retire on the 17th lap suffering from low oil pressure and a burned backside from the proximity of the gearbox. *(FF)*

It had been a year of mixed fortunes with the Lotus 15 in sports car races. But at the popular Boxing Day meeting at Brands Hatch, as 1958 drew to a close, Graham drove the first Lotus Super Seven, demonstrator '7 TMT' powered by a 75bhp Stage 1-tuned 1100cc Climax engine, and beat a top-class field of Lotus Elevens and Lolas in the up-to-1100cc race.

## Speedwell Conversions

Between race meetings, Graham worked at his Speedwell Conversions business, based in a mews garage in Golders Green, north London. Hill had formed the company toward the end of 1957 with up-and-coming rally star John Sprinzel, Len Adams and George Hulbert. Speedwell specialised in hotting up Austin A35s and Morris Minors, offering engine modifications including polished cylinder heads, modified combustion chambers, bigger valves and stronger valve springs, and suspension tune-up kits with anti-roll bars, anti-tramp bars and harder brake linings. Reflecting on Hill's preferred suspension set-up, Jackie Stewart commented: 'Apart from the fancy carburettors and camshafts, Speedwell also did suspension changes with stiffer anti-roll bars. It would have been Graham who thought up a stiffer roll bar!'

To prove the point, Hill (and Sprinzel) raced the Speedwell A35. Once wound up, it did not require brakes to go round corners like the old Woodcote or Stowe at Silverstone. With the right foot buried to the floor, it could be cornered at almost unreduced pace. Hill was third in the saloon car

The winning team in the 750 Motor Club's 1958 Birkett Six-Hour Relay at Silverstone was the Speedwell Stable, with its trio of mildly-tuned Austin A35s, driven by the company's partners, Len Adams (still wearing the relay sash), Graham Hill, George Hulbert and John Sprinzel *(right)*. Team manager Lutz Arnstein is at far left. Reliability and slick change-overs were their forte, and they still beat faster Morgans, MGs and Lotuses. *(LAT)*

race supporting the 1958 *Daily Express* International Trophy, but retired in the Grand Prix support meeting with overheating. A year later, Hill drove the A35 in a saloon car race at Brands Hatch. He was lying third and leading the 1-litre class on the final lap when he came up behind the leading duo of Les Leston and Ron Hutcheson in Riley 1.5s. They were so engrossed in their private battle that they failed to mark the flying A35, and Hill slipped by at Druids hairpin to take the win.

For Graham, the 1959 season kicked off with the International 100, an F1 race at Goodwood, in which the Lotus 16's brakes gave out, although in F2 guise he came fourth in the supporting Lavant Cup race. Engine vibrations put paid to his efforts in the F2 British Empire Trophy at Oulton Park in April, with a fifth in the Formula 1 Aintree 200

later in the month. Graham was also handling type 17 sports racer, a car that Lotus had to recall because of its dire understeering characteristics – designer Len Terry cured that at a stroke by fitting double wishbones at the front instead of the Chapman strut. In fact, Graham scored a fourth place at Oulton Park and came second at Aintree in the works 2-litre type 17.

The 1959 World Championship began with the Monaco Grand Prix. Fourteenth fastest in practice in the Lotus 16, Graham's race lasted 21 laps, at which point an oil pipe that had worked itself loose and rubbed against a red-hot rear brake disc caught fire under the fuel tank. Petrol is one thing, but these were the heady days of 100/130 octane Avgas. Hill stopped and tried to lever himself out, but the car rolled forward and he jammed it against a kerb. The on-board fire-extinguisher failed to operate, so, conscious that his appearance at the next race depended on saving the car, he grabbed a proper one from a diffident fire marshall and smothered the fire.

Hill then drove three Lotus sports racers in quick succession, coming third at Crystal Palace in the type 17, third at Mallory Park on the May bank holiday in the 1100cc Eleven, and first in the over-1100cc race at Mallory in the Mk 15. A few days later he was at Zandvoort for the Dutch Grand Prix. Here, Graham was fifth fastest in practice, putting him on the second row of the grid among exalted company including Jo Bonnier in a BRM, Brabham and Moss in Coopers and Jean Behra in a Ferrari 246 Dino. He got the jump on Moss at the start and pressured Behra's less wieldy Ferrari. The veteran Frenchman rebuffed his challenges, so Hill allowed Moss through, and the pair of them slipped by Behra. Hill's car immediately displayed symptoms of being on fire again, so he stopped, ripping his overalls in his haste to exit the car. When it became clear that there was no fire, he rejoined the race, only to discover that it was the brake fluid evaporating on the discs that had caused the smoke. He carried on with just front brakes operational to finish seventh, while new teammate Innes Ireland came fourth in his first Grand Prix.

Although Hill had been to Le Mans in 1956 as a Team Lotus mechanic and reserve driver for local drivers Masson and Héchard – whom he beat in practice – he did not get a run there until 1958, when he partnered Cliff Allison in a 2-litre version of the 15. They retired after only three laps with overheating, but in practice Hill had been fifth fastest overall, lapping at 4min 12.7sec (119.15mph) – quicker than the 3-litre Ferrari. For the 1959 event he drove a 2.5-litre FPF-powered Mk 15, partnered by Australian Derek Jolly. Chapman had his sights set on the possibility of outright victory with this car. However, Jolly accidentally over-revved the engine when it jumped out of gear, and that put paid to their challenge. Reporting on the race for *Motor Sport* magazine, Denis Jenkinson remarked on the value

of unhurried pit-work over panic-driven refuelling and tyre-changing pit stops. He observed the Team Lotus pit stops, and pondered on the slow, almost ponderous motion of the fellow doing the refuelling. It was done with such deliberation, in such a calm and collected way, that Jenkinson thought the operator must be 'dozy'. After successive pit stops he realised that the refuelling had been accomplished not only without drama but also faster than the wheel changing, topping up fluids and other pit work. The 'mechanic' in question was Graham Hill, and he later revealed to Jenks that he had timed the other operations and knew that he could do the refuelling job some 10 seconds faster.

It was at this time that the whole of Lotus relocated to its new premises at Delamare Road, Cheshunt, Hertfordshire, which meant far more space for the racing team as well as the plant that was building the Elite road car. The factory was actually opened on 14 October 1959. Incidentally, it was mainly due to Hill's diligence that the Elite prototype was ready for its launch at the 1957 Motor Show – he had led a dedicated band of workers through a series of all-nighters in the rented Edmonton workshop to finish it.

The French Grand Prix held in early July at Reims was preceded by an F2 race, from which Graham retired the Mk 16 with a blown engine. It was incredibly hot and, in addition to having to cope with flying debris caused by melting asphalt, many drivers suffered from heat exhaustion. Hill went out of the Grand Prix on the eighth lap when a stone pierced his 16's radiator.

Despite a shortage of 2.5-litre Climax FPF engines, Graham drove the Mk 17 in the sports car race that preceded the British Grand Prix at Aintree. A hard-fought duel between Hill and Jack Brabham lasted almost till the end of the race, when Brabham's Cooper-Monaco aquaplaned off the track, leaving Hill the winner. He was greeted by a delighted Chapman, who was promptly presented with the car's detached gear lever by its driver. In the Grand Prix, Hill started in ninth place, and was running eighth when he spun off. Rejoining the track, he traded paintwork with an

The curtain-raiser to the 1959 British Grand Prix at Aintree was the 51-mile, 17-lap sports car race and, in wet conditions, Hill's 2.5-litre Lotus 15 and Brabham's Cooper Monaco drew away from the more powerful machinery. Hill was hampered by the gear lever coming adrift, allowing Brabham through. But he retook the lead and went on to win, while Brabham spun, and Stacey in the 2-litre Lotus came second. Clark was fourth in the Border Reivers' Lister-Jaguar. *(FF)*

aggressive Salvadori until a slipping clutch dropped him back to ninth again.

The 1959 German Grand Prix was held on the Avus circuit instead of the Nürburgring. Originally the track consisted of two long, parallel straights connected by a pair of enormous brick-built banked bends. But since the original track was bisected by the Berlin Wall, with half in the east and half in the west, the race was run on just the west end, with a flat horse-shoe corner instead of the other banked bend. As with all such elevated corners, the surface was bumpy and the g-loadings substantial. Because of the length of the straights – almost two miles in each direction – lap speeds were extremely high. Tony Brooks's Ferrari's winning speed was 143.342mph. The Lotuses

were not so quick along the straights, being better suited to circuits with plenty of corners, and Hill's gearbox selector spring snapped during the first heat of the two-heat race.

It was the turn of the Team Lotus transporter to break down on the way to Lisbon for the Portuguese Grand Prix, and there was only just enough time for Hill and Ireland to qualify on the Monsanto Park road course. Aware of a leaking fuel tank prior to the race, Graham was nonetheless caught out when it dumped fuel all over his rear tyres and he spun to a standstill in the middle of the track. There was nothing that the fast approaching Phil Hill could do to avoid the stranded Lotus, and his Dino Ferrari caught the Lotus full in the rear suspension. Although neither driver was hurt, Graham Hill blacked out from the whiplash and suffered double vision for a while.

For the RAC Tourist Trophy at Goodwood, the works 2-litre Mk 15 was fitted with wire-spoke wheels with knock-off hubs instead of bolt-on Wobbly Webs for swift tyre changes. Although Graham and co-driver Stacey had been running third during the first hour, the Lotus was sidelined with slipped ignition timing.

Prior to the Italian Grand Prix at Monza, Graham's bent 16 was

At Aintree for the 1959 British Grand Prix, Hill shared the fourth row of the grid with Bonnier's BRM. He spun on lap 11, then duelled with Salvadori's Aston Martin, which knocked the Lotus in the rear more than once, its driver shouting ill-temperedly. Eventually Hill struggled home in ninth place, five laps down, with a sick Lotus. *(FF)*

cannibalised and the parts amalgamated with his Zandvoort car. As he was being pushed to the starting grid there appeared to be too much play in the steering; the steering column clamp had come loose, and the fuel tank had begun leaking. As it transpired, he could not even complete two laps, because the quill shaft between the clutch and the gearbox snapped. Ireland retired on lap 15 with no brakes, and there was real speculation that Team Lotus would disappear from Formula 1, so dire was its finishing record in 1959. Graham had certainly had just about enough, although he had the birth of his daughter Brigitte earlier that year to be cheerful about.

Fifth place in the Oulton Park Gold Cup was some compensation for the mechanical failings, but at Snetterton for the Silver City Trophy in October, the Mk 16's quill shaft broke again in exactly the same place. It was from the same batch as the Monza one, and had perhaps been incorrectly heat-treated. For Hill it was the final

straw, having finished just once and scored only two World Championship points in two seasons of Grand Prix racing. The parting was far from amicable. As Ian H. Smith tells it in his contemporary *Story of Lotus 1947-1960: Birth of a Legend*: '... by 12 December, the date of the first US Grand Prix, Graham Hill had signed to drive with BRM for the 1960 season, the circumstances of his parting unfortunately leading to a certain amount of friction, which, much to everyone's relief, was settled out of court.' Circumstances probably enabled a fairly swift reconciliation. Things were looking promising for Chapman – the mid-engined, multi-formula Lotus 18 was up and running, and the new Cheshunt factory had just come on stream. Hill's place was taken first by Alan Stacey, then by John Surtees (after Stacey was killed) and Jimmy Clark, in quick succession. Jabby Crombac says that 'Colin had made his peace with Graham quite soon after... although there always seemed a slight trace of bitterness.'

# Chapter 2
# The First World Title

WITH its origins in Raymond Mays's ERA concern, BRM became the competition arm of Sir Alfred Owen's Rubery-Owen Group in 1952, with the works racing cars entered and run by the Owen Racing Organisation. The Rubery-Owen Group made components for all kinds of motor vehicles, and included Shorrock Superchargers among its empire. After a slow start, the team had begun to get its act together by 1958, entering eight Grands Prix. BRM's first victory was in 1959, when Jo Bonnier won at Zandvoort in the Peter Berthon-designed front-engined P25. Like Ferrari, BRM always manufactured its own engines, unlike the new generation of 'kit car' teams exemplified by Cooper and Lotus, so inevitably life at BRM was more complicated, yet more controllable because everything was under one roof. The racing team was tightly controlled by Peter Berthon and Raymond Mays, and it was

There was a chance that Porsche could beat Cooper to the 1960 Formula 2 title, so for the Aintree 200 F2 race, Porsche sent two works cars for Graham Hill and Jo Bonnier (right), supported by the privateer entries of Stirling Moss and Masten Gregory. *(P)*

a very different style of operation to Chapman's Team Lotus.

Sir Alfred Owen was keen to have British drivers. Stirling Moss, a national superstar, had driven a British Racing Partnership BRM P25 to second place at Aintree that year, and Ron Flockhart had been on the BRM works strength fairly regularly since 1956. But Jo Bonnier was Swedish, while Frenchman Jean Behra had left at the end of 1958 after just one year at BRM, and the American Harry Schell left to join the Yeoman Credit team and was killed soon afterwards. So an approach was made to Graham Hill and Innes Ireland. Ireland turned the offer down, preferring to remain loyal to Lotus in spite of mechanical breakdowns, so Graham and Californian driver Dan Gurney were signed up by BRM team principal Raymond Mays. Things moved quickly. During the autumn of 1959, Hill was involved with BRM team manager and chief engineer Tony Rudd on a weekly testing programme at Goodwood. According to Tony, the sessions began

at 9am and carried on until something on the car broke or the light failed.

## Free Agents

The inability of current Grand Prix stars to drive anything other than a Formula 1 car is a relatively recent phenomenon, brought about by contractual ties and the heavy demands of testing and promotional commitments. And the modern F1 world championship calendar is twice as full as it was in 1960. Back in Graham Hill's day, the top drivers were more or less free to race whatever they chose. Being at a race-track every weekend was a way of life. His services were sought by Porsche, then an up-and-coming manufacturer, to drive its sports-racing and Formula 2 cars on an ad hoc basis.

A week ahead of the Argentine Grand Prix in January 1960, the season began with a round of the World Sports Car Championship, the Buenos Aires 1,000km, and Graham and Jo Bonnier drove a works Porsche 1600 RSK into third place behind

The 1960 Aintree 200km is about to start, and Moss (right) in the Rob Walker Porsche has pole, with Brabham's Cooper in the middle and Hill in a works Porsche to his right. Behind is Bristow's Cooper and Stacey's Lotus 18, with Ireland, Surtees and Salvadori among the fast runners. After a close race, reliability told, and the finishing order was Moss, Bonnier and Hill in the Porsches. *(P)*

Held on a 9.5km circuit comprising part of the Autodromo and an urban dual carriageway, the 1960 Buenos Aires 1,000km counted towards the World Sportscar Championship. On its way to third place is the 1600cc Porsche 718 RSK of Hill/Bonnier (30), following the Gurney/Gregory 2.8-litre Birdcage Maserati, while the Von Hanstein/Bohnen Porsche 356 Carrera (56) keeps out of the way. *(P)*

more risky and unpredictable. Spectators lined the roadside with no fear for their own safety, and a small boy ran out into Hill's car, which broke the child's leg.

Hill's method for learning this unique road circuit was to drive round again and again, taking an hour or so for each lap (72km, remember), picking out particular trees and houses as landmarks by which to calculate his approach speeds into the thousand or so bends. The smooth tarmac surface could be slippery in both wet and dry conditions, littered with stones churned up from freshly repaired potholes, and during the race itself there was the additional hazard of other competitors. The training paid off, and Hill and Barth finished fifth and won their class, the race being won by Bonnier/Herrmann's Porsche RS60 from Von Trips/Phil Hill's Ferrari Dino 246. Much to his chagrin, Graham was waved on by marshals

a couple of 3-litre V12 Ferraris. After over six hours of racing they were five laps in arrears. The Porsche pairing fared less well in the Sebring 12 Hours, held at the end of March, as the 1600cc engine threw a con rod. Hill liked driving for Porsche. He admired the RSK build quality and its smooth and generally reliable engines, but was less confident of the road-holding compared with conventional British cars.

Graham had his first taste of the ancient Targa Florio road race in May 1960, paired with Edgar Barth, father of Porsche's long-time 1970s and 1980s test driver Jürgen. Along with the rest of the works Porsche team, their car was a new RS60 Spyder, powered by a 1585cc engine, unlike the 1630cc unit in the other cars. Like most of the other teams, they travelled to Sicily a week ahead of the event to get in some practice driving regular cars, as the Madonie circuit was 72km long, much of it on twisting mountain roads flanked by sheer drops, and through normally sleepy villages. Due to the nature of the event and its rustic location, there was likely to be a laden mule or donkey cart around any corner, not to mention goat or sheep dung on the racing line, making cornering even

It was customary for drivers to spend the week before the Targa Florio trying to learn the Sicilian circuit's myriad twists and turns. Looking pretty casual in his check shirt, Graham waits among the Porsche enclave for his RS60 to be readied. Behind him is the 'bog-standard' 356 Carrera of Von Hanstein/Pucci. *(P)*

Which way to go? Out on reconnaissance for the 1960 Targa Florio, Graham ponders the signposts outside Campofelice in his Porsche RS60 Spyder. *(P)*

after the finish and was obliged to complete another hour-long lap, this time with failing ignition timing.

Graham Hill's first race for BRM was the Argentine Grand Prix, also staged at Buenos Aires,

Jo Bonnier gives Graham some words of encouragement before the start of the 1960 Targa Florio. Hill and Edgar Barth brought their 1585cc Porsche RS60 home in fifth place, behind the winning 1630cc version of Bonnier/Herrmann, the Von Trips/P. Hill Ferrari Dino, the Gendebien/Herrmann 1630cc RS60, and the Scarfiotti/Mairesse/Cabianca Dino Ferrari. Hill and Barth won their class after almost eight hours racing. *(P)*

alongside teammates Jo Bonnier and Dan Gurney. They were using the front-engined P25, which was reckoned to be well-balanced and good to drive. Hill soon found out how different the BRM regime was from the one at Lotus. Whereas Colin Chapman was open to trial and experimentation,

The Montlhéry 1,000km of 1960 was held for GT cars, and the 7.7km circuit incorporated a chicane at the start of the banked section to keep speeds down. Gendebien/Bianchi led a Ferrari 250GT walkover, but the Porsche-Abarth Carrera of Hill/Von Hanstein came a class-winning seventh. Here, the two teammates share a joke before the race. *(P)*

Peter Berthon controlled things at BRM much more strictly. Thus, when Graham asked for his front tyres to be pumped up to counter understeer, he was told that the car had been designed to run with a particular set of tyre pressures and no deviation was possible. Hill consoled himself with the prospect of a substantially better income than he had previously enjoyed. His retainer was greater and he would receive a bigger percentage of the start money. At Buenos Aires, however, Hill began to have grave doubts that he'd made the right decision to quit Lotus. Chapman had shown him the plans for the new mid-engined type 18 in a vain attempt to convince Hill to stay at Lotus. And here was the new Lotus in Argentina, driven by Innes Ireland and going quicker than Hill's BRM. He simply gritted his teeth and got on with

Hill prepares to do his stint at the wheel of the class-winning Porsche-Abarth Carrera at the 1960 Montlhéry 1,000km. Behind the pit counter, Bette Hill sets out her lap charts. *(P)*

Class-winners of the 1960 Montlhéry 1,000km Hill and Von Hanstein (also Porsche team manager) are presented with a bouquet by Michèle Behra, widow of Jean. *(P)*

the job in hand. His BRM's engine lasted 37 laps before overheating and succumbing to a broken valve spring, while Ireland's Lotus 18 went the distance and finished sixth.

## BRM Goes Mid-Engined

The mid-engined BRM P48 was introduced at the Easter Goodwood meeting, entered for the Glover Trophy at the International 100 meeting. Having tested at the same circuit, Hill knew the car's shortcomings and was far from optimistic about his chances. Indeed, Jo Bonnier elected to drive one of the old front-engined P25s, as the P48's handling could be violently unpredictable. Nevertheless, Hill managed a creditable fifth place, ahead of Bonnier.

Hill was still heavily involved with Speedwell Conversions, and in May 1960 the firm staged some high-speed runs on the closed-off Antwerp-Liege motorway at Jabbeke, using a pair of Austin-Healey Sprites. In one case, the standard car was fitted with a coupé body and faired-in headlight bonnet section, running a 978cc engine with twin Amal carbs. Graham Hill drove this car at an average of 110.9mph (178.48kph) holding a steady 7,500rpm during the two-way runs. The second Speedwell Sprite sported a rotund all-enveloping body with just a perspex blip over the driving seat. Its 978cc engine drank a heady cocktail of methanol and nitro-methane. Hill got this car up to 132.2mph (212.765kph) on a two-way run over the flying kilometre. Later that year, in July, Graham came second in class in the up-to-1100cc category at the Rouen sports car Grand Prix, carving through the field of smaller cars in a Speedwell Sprite. Had his car not stalled on the grid he might have beaten the faster French sports-racing DB of Jean Vinatier.

The 150-mile BRDC (British Racing Drivers' Club) International Trophy race at Silverstone on 6 May saw Graham put in one of his gritty performances in the BRM, finishing third behind Ireland's Lotus 18 Climax and Brabham's similarly powered Cooper. Nevertheless, he was over a minute behind them, which showed that BRM had a certain amount of ground to make up. In the supporting saloon car race, Graham in the Speedwell Jaguar Mk II mixed it with the regular front runners, including Moss, Salvadori and Sir Gawaine Bailey.

Hill's next outing in the BRM was the Monaco Grand Prix in May. Mediterranean weather can be notoriously fickle at that time of year, and by half distance it was raining, making the surface extremely treacherous. Later, as the track began to dry, wet patches were left under the trees, and this was to be Graham's undoing. As he and Phil Hill attempted to slip past Bruce McLaren's Cooper, he spun off and went straight into the steps of a radio commentators' wooden hut. The occupants were left stranded aloft, while the BRM's nose and radiator were completely removed by the pieces of wood. Hill was unhurt, but lost his watch, which was run over by another car.

With only a week separating the Monaco and Dutch Grands Prix, teams struggled to get their cars from the bottom to the top of Europe – in pre-autoroute days – and ready them for practice. To make matters more complicated, the BRM transporter broke its gearbox en route, while a new car was dispatched from Bourne for Graham in place of the one he had just crashed. Bonnier and Hill started from the second row. But Dan Gurney's car had a brake pipe split after only 10 laps and, as he ploughed off into the sand dunes at the Tarzan hairpin at around 120mph, the car struck and killed a youth who had crept under the barrier to get a better look. It was not immediately clear what had happened, so the other two BRMs were not called in, as might otherwise have been the case. Hill was harried by Clark's Lotus, but as more and more cars dropped out, Graham hung on to third place. Moss, still very much in the prime of his career, had started from pole in the Rob Walker Lotus, but had a puncture early on in the race and had pitted for a wheel-change. Twelve laps from the end of the race he was hauling Graham in at some two seconds a lap. Hill was fed information from the pits that he was 26 seconds ahead. For the first time, he was forced to calculate as he drove what he had to do to keep Moss at bay. Keeping a cool head, he finished just 1.1 seconds

Team Lotus's new recruit Jimmy Clark in his Lotus 18 challenged Graham for fourth place during the Dutch Grand Prix, swapping places a couple of times, and might have beaten him, but for a faulty gearbox. *(PN)*

Fifth quickest in practice for the 1960 Dutch Grand Prix, Graham had a brand new BRM P48 to replace the one he'd crashed the week before at Monaco. He drove an excellent race to fend off Moss, and finished third behind Brabham and Ireland. *(PN)*

ahead of Moss, who broke the lap record on the very last lap in his bid to catch the BRM.

As Tony Rudd recalled:

> In 1960 at Zandvoort, Moss lost an awful lot of time – he had a damaged wheel – and he was chasing Graham for third place. He

was gaining a hell of a lot, and we were quite worried that he was going to catch Graham for third by the end of the race and we kept giving Graham the pit signals. And afterwards, Graham said 'I don't know why you were worried about Moss catching me. I'd got the measure of him!' So you can deduce that Graham wasn't really looking up to him. He was much more objective about Gurney, because they were teammates and they drove Porsches together.

After the Dutch race the BRM hierarchy repaired to the Bouwes Hotel for a meeting, ostensibly to discuss drivers' starting money, but also to effect a restructuring of the racing team. Along with the three BRM drivers, who were threatening to go on strike, those present included Sir Alfred and Ernest Owen, their sister Jean Stanley – wife of Louis Stanley – Peter Berthon, Raymond Mays and Tony Rudd. Apart from the financial side, the drivers were not happy about the way Peter Berthon controlled the racing aspect with a mailed fist. Tony had just been propositioned by Chapman about joining Lotus, but he already harboured thoughts about going back to Rolls-Royce. Hill's political qualities came to the fore. He explained to Sir Alfred Owen that, as he and the other drivers saw it, the way forward was to elevate Tony Rudd to racing manager, to run the team and develop the cars, and make Peter Berthon focus solely on designing the cars. According to Hill's scheme of things, Raymond Mays, with whom he got on well, would continue as racing director, dealing with race organisers and drivers, administering starting money and travel arrangements.

According to Tony Rudd, the meeting at the Bouwes Hotel wound up at 5am, with Sir Alfred Owen decreeing that Tony Rudd would be in charge of building the racing cars and setting them up at circuits. Moreover, a new car would be built to Tony's design. Predictably, those sidelined in this new arrangement were less than delighted. However, the immediate crisis was to get cars ready to race at Spa, just eight days hence.

Three cars were transported to Belgium on board BRM's new transporter, which was based on a Leyland Royal Tiger chassis. The P48s handled well on the super-fast undulating circuit through the Ardennes pine forests, but in practice both Moss and Mike Taylor had nasty accidents in their Lotus 18s. Moss lost a wheel when a driveshaft sheared and suffered broken legs and back injuries, and Taylor got a broken collarbone and ribs, and a neck injury, when his steering column failed. It was incidents like these that earned Chapman a reputation for making fragile racing cars – one reason why Hill had moved to BRM. Graham's was the fastest of the BRM trio, and he started from the second row, circulating in among the leading bunch and rising to second place as cars retired. However, his engine failed on the penultimate lap, and he coasted into his pit, then located on the run down to Eau Rouge. To do this he actually crossed the start/finish line and, therefore, started his last lap. Had he stopped before the finish line and waited for Brabham and McLaren's Coopers to go by, and then crossed it, he would probably have finished third, as everyone else was a lap down. This race became infamous for its saga of tragic accidents, with up-and-coming Cooper driver Chris Bristow killed, and Team Lotus driver Alan Stacey taking a pheasant full in the face at the high-speed Malmedy corner and dying in the resulting accident.

Just a week later came the Le Mans 24 Hours, and Graham shared the number one Porsche RS60 with Jo Bonnier. Very early in the race they heard a clunk in the chassis or suspension, and after spending several minutes in the pits while the mechanics investigated the problem, the car was running almost last. Then, having recovered from 54th to 14th place, they were eliminated after 17 hours when a cylinder head joint blew.

When the F1 teams assembled at Reims for the French Grand Prix, BRM had just one car present on the Wednesday before the race, and that was Hill's. To make matters worse, the hydraulic clutch was playing up. Eventually the P48s of Gurney and Bonnier arrived, but it was Hill who made fastest

Graham Hill has a laugh with Porsche engineer Wilhelm Hild (left) in the Nürburgring pits prior to the 1000km of 1960. On the pit wall are Maurice Trintignant and Hans Herrmann, with Bonnier on the right. Hill was teamed with Edgar Barth and they dominated the 1151cc–1600cc category until the German driver tangled with a slower car and their RSK went off the road. The victors were Moss/Gurney in a Birdcage Maserati with the Bonnier/Gendebien Porsche RS60 second. *(P)*

time, putting his car on the front row alongside Phil Hill's Ferrari and Brabham's Cooper. Any hopes for a fine performance were dashed when Hill's clutch failed to depress, so he could not engage first gear, and at flag-fall he was left on the line, only to have Trintignant's Cooper-Maserati plough into his rear at around 70mph. The starter, Toto Roche, agreed that since Hill's BRM had actually crossed the start line, even if not of its own volition, the team could be paid starting money. So, in successive Grands Prix, Hill had retired on the last lap and the first lap, which was rather a strange accomplishment.

## Career Milestone

Paradoxically, Graham's performance at Silverstone in the Grand Prix was one of his finest races up till then, and a bitter disappointment. The

front row of the grid – four cars wide in those days – comprised the two Coopers of Brabham and McLaren, and the two BRMs, Hill and Bonnier, with Gurney in the third P48 in the middle of the second row. But when the recuperating Stirling Moss dropped the starter's flag, Hill stalled, and Tony Brooks ran his Cooper into his backside. It was a red rag to a bull and, after a push-start – legal then – Hill clawed his way through the entire field by 50 laps to challenge Brabham for the lead. By lap 55, Hill was the leader, Brabham tagging along in his wake as they lapped slower cars. But on one such occasion, Hill overdid things going into Copse, and spun out backwards into the earthworks at the side of the track. As well as the pressure from the reigning world champion, Hill was contending with a lack of brake adjustment, which meant he was having to pump the brake

The 1960 Le Mans 24 Hours was not a good race for Porsche. The lead RS60 Spyder of Hill/Bonnier was delayed early on when both drivers reported a possible broken chassis. They later climbed from 54th to 14th, when a cylinder-head gasket blew. Here, the mechanics dismantle the big-bore 1606cc engine in front of the pits to verify the trouble before wheeling the car to the dead car park. Hill and Bonnier on the pit wall look suitably fed up. *(P)*

pedal continuously to get the pressure up. The rear brake on the P48 was a single disc working off the gearbox and operating on the two rear wheels. When it was out of the airstream, it overheated, the seal melted and the brake fluid escaped. Nevertheless, Hill had the satisfaction of having set fastest lap, 1min 34.4sec (179.64kph) on lap 56, and the crowd gave him a rousing ovation as he walked back to the pits. Suddenly, here was an Englishman getting in on the act that Stirling Moss had made his own.

It was a milestone in Hill's career, and showed his considerable talent at its best. His performance sheds some light on that familiar proposition, that Jimmy Clark was a natural talent, but Graham had to work at it. Tony Rudd, who saw Hill in action at Silverstone, would not necessarily agree:

> That's not quite so. Jimmy was pretty consistent, and that was the great thing about him. He had this tremendous car balance, this sense of what the car was doing, and he was very consistent, whereas Graham, on his day, could beat Jimmy, but he wouldn't have those days very often. At the British Grand Prix in 1960, Graham

started last and he came first. That was a once-or-twice a year performance, while with Jimmy it was very nearly 9 races out of 10. He didn't have an off-day and he weighed the risks up and if he decided the risk was too great for James Clark he wouldn't try it.

A couple of Formula 2 races followed, and Graham, Bonnier and Gurney drove for Porsche in their works F2 models. At the Solitude circuit at Stuttgart (named after Solitude Castle that dominates the valley), Porsche fielded five cars to give themselves the best shot at a home win, with Surtees and Herrmann in the other two cars. However, Jimmy Clark led briefly in a Lotus 18, but Taffy von Trips in the new rear-engined Ferrari F2-60 emerged the winner, with three Porsches in hot pursuit. Graham was fourth. The German Grand Prix that followed a week later at the Nürburgring was dogged by rain and thick fog. This too was a Formula 2 race, and Graham started from the four-car front row, along with Brabham's Cooper and Von Trips and pole-man Bonnier in Porsches. The result panned out exactly as the front row grid positions, with Hill fourth again.

Just after the start of the Formula 2 race at Solitude, Bonnier's F2 Porsche leads the similar cars of Hill and Herrmann, with Von Trips's Ferrari followed by Ireland's Lotus, Lewis's Cooper, Gurney and Surtees in Porsches, Clark's Lotus, Phil Hill's Ferrari and Brabham's Cooper. *(P)*

The August bank holiday meeting at Brands Hatch featured the Silver City Trophy 50-lapper for F1 cars, which was the first race meeting to be held on the long 2.65-mile Grand Prix circuit. A full grid of 23 cars started the F1 race, with Brabham nursing his Cooper home to victory ahead of a closing Graham Hill in the single works BRM. In the saloon car race that traditionally rounded off such meetings, Graham set fastest lap and then promptly crashed the Speedwell Mk II Jaguar coming out of Druids. Unusually for those days, he was wearing a seat belt, which undoubtedly saved him from injury.

The 1960 Portuguese Grand Prix reverted to the city streets of Oporto. With a start/finish line and pits on the Atlantic promenade, the 7.407km circuit included two long dead straight uphill sections, a winding uphill gradient, followed by a serpentine downhill rush to the sea side again. The average lap speed was over 110mph. Four BRMs were present – the three regular cars for Hill, Bonnier and Gurney, the latter being the fastest BRM driver in practice. Hill shared the second row with Moss, who was having his first race since the Spa crash. Prompted by Graham's creeping BRM, almost the entire grid jumped the start, pressuring the starter to drop the flag several seconds earlier than scheduled. Hill then had a fine dice with Brabham, the BRM and Cooper Climax engines being identically matched for top speed going up the long Boa Vista straight. But on lap 9, Hill's gearbox cried enough, and he was out, leaving the win to the Coopers of Brabham and McLaren, with Jimmy Clark's Lotus third.

A couple of races followed with Graham driving for Porsche, netting fourth place overall both times. These events were the Tourist Trophy at Goodwood, where he drove a Carrera with an Abarth body to a class win, and the Formula 2 Kentish 100 at Brands Hatch. At this stage, BRM were trying fuel injection on the Mk 2 P48, but there were several problems including burned valves, broken valve springs and flat batteries. Tony Rudd wisely elected to use four-cylinder Climax FPF units until the new BRM engines were sorted. It was while Hill was driving a BRM in the Lombank Trophy race at Snetterton in September that his son Damon was born. In *Life at the Limit*, Hill wrote, somewhat unkindly, of his visit to see Bette and baby in hospital the next day: 'Imagine my horror upon finding him a bright yellow with little slit eyes – for all the world like a Chinaman.' However, he was quick to concede that Damon, like his sisters, 'grew into a lovely baby too.'

The UK-based F1 teams – BRM, Cooper and Lotus – boycotted the Italian Grand Prix in 1960, because the race was run on the combined road circuit and banked oval, and the cars received a terrible pounding on the poor surface of the banking. So the final race of the 1960 season was the US Grand Prix, staged on 20 November at Riverside, California. According to Mike Tee's report in *Motor Sport* magazine, Graham was 'lacking his usual verve', and was down the grid on the fifth row along with Jim Hall's Lotus and Phil Hill's Cooper – the latter released from his Ferrari contract for the race, along with Von Trips. Graham appeared not to like the circuit, having had difficulty learning some of its spectacular turns in practice, and went out at half distance with timing gear failure. Once again, everyone else was left to chase the flying Moss in Rob Walker's Lotus 18, and only Ireland in the works Lotus was anything like close to him. Thus ended the last race for the 2.5-litre Formula 1, with Brabham once again world champion.

## 1961 – A Year of Mixed Fortunes

The BRM team flew its cars direct from Los Angeles to New Zealand for the Grand Prix at Ardmore. This was the opening race of the Tasman Series, and was Graham's first venture 'down under'. It was difficult to separate the social aspect of motor racing from the competition side, and drivers and mechanics from rival teams were much more matey than they are today. After the New Zealand race, in which Hill finished third, he felt that the racers should repay some of the hospitality they had enjoyed. He accomplished this at a nocturnal party by diving naked into a swimming pool, illuminated by the headlights of Tony Rudd's hire car. Apart from shooting deer in the mountains with Innes Ireland, Hill also learned to waterski in the interim between the New Zealand and Australian races, with the presence of sharks an understandable incentive to stay upright on top of the water, rather than beneath it.

At the International 100 meeting at Warwick Farm, BRM were legitimately using BPK 50 percent methanol fuel, but it was so hot that the methanol dissolved the joints of the rubber fuel cells, and Hill retired when the tank split on lap nine and jettisoned all its contents onto the track. They reverted to regular petrol for the two-heat Victorian Trophy Formule Libre race at Ballarat airfield circuit, which Gurney won (after his car had been found – it had been hidden under straw bales by prankster RAAF aircrew.) Hill, whom Dan erroneously assumed to have been the villain of the piece, won the first heat and came second in the other. It was Dan's only win for BRM, and also his last race for the team.

## Bourne Reshuffle

Not only was the 1961 season the first for the incoming 1.5-litre Formula 1 rules, there had also been some reorganisation back at Bourne, and Wilkie Wilkinson was appointed team manager. Wilkinson thought, like Berthon, that once a car had been set up, that was how it should stay, whatever the prevailing circuit conditions might suggest. This did not sit well with Graham Hill, who wanted to try a range of suspension and roll bar settings to obtain the optimum handling, while Tony Rudd was expected to get on with designing a new car and not attend race meetings.

John Surtees cast light on the influence Hill wielded at BRM, even then: 'When I first started in motor racing in 1960 and Shell wanted to put me at BRM, he stopped that happening. But I never held any grudge about that. It's a standard thing which happens in teams.'

The new formula, with its upper limit of 1500cc and no supercharging, had been announced as far back as late 1958, and had met with objections from the British constructors, who were tasting the first fruits of success in Grand Prix racing using Coventry Climax engines. Both Lotus

and Cooper had received 2.5-litre Climax FPF units in 1959 and 1960, powering Cooper to the world championship title two years running. However, as engine builders, Climax and BRM were unprepared for the new formula, and all the British constructors were obliged to use the four-cylinder 1475cc Coventry Climax engine that scarcely developed 150bhp, while arch-rivals Ferrari had their 120-degree V6 engine pushing out nearly 180bhp. To make matters worse, these 1.5-litre Climax engines were in short supply, having being used in Formula 2 until then, and Hill was now sufficiently well-off to buy a couple of units from Tasman teams just to be sure of having an engine for F1.

BRM built lightweight versions of the P48 chassis and fitted the 1.5-litre Climax engines while they worked on a new V8. Coventry Climax too were hard at work developing the FWMV V8. Graham's new teammate was Tony Brooks, who had driven for BRM at Monaco and Silverstone back in 1956. A veteran of two seasons with Vanwall and one with Ferrari, Brooks had just had a mediocre season with the Yeoman Credit Cooper team. Hill's former teammates Bonnier and Gurney had both gone to drive the new Porsche F1 cars, which would run with their old flat-four F2 engines while Porsche developed their new flat-eight. The Porsches were good enough for Gurney to take pole at the high-speed Sicilian circuit of Enna-Pergusa in April – he and Bonnier came second and third in that race.

After the Antipodean races, Graham's season kicked off with a shared drive with Moss in the Sebring 12 Hours sports car race, but the Camoradi-run Tipo 61 Birdcage Maserati went out with a cracked exhaust manifold before Hill got to race it. The Easter Goodwood meeting found him in a variety of machinery, including a BRM P48 with 2.5-litre Climax engine, plus Tommy Sopwith's Equipe Endeavour Mk II Jaguar, picking up a couple of second places and a third. The big Jaguars were much less sensitive than single-seater cars, but more forgiving. There was a great deal of sliding in corners, and in closely fought racing, opposing door-handles would frequently clash. Graham gave the E-type Jaguar belonging to the same team its competition debut victory at Oulton Park in April, beating Roy Salvadori in John Coombs's E-type and other luminaries such as Jack Sears's Ferrari 250GT and Ireland's Aston Martin DB4.

The first hint of trouble between Wilkinson and Rudd came at the Monaco Grand Prix, when a less-than-delighted Wilkie discovered that the racing cars were accompanied by a plentiful and varied supply of anti-roll bars and suspension components. Wilkinson forbade nearly all alterations to the cars' set up after they left the factory, an attitude which Rudd disagreed with. The BRMs were powered by the stop-gap four-cylinder Mk II Climax units, and the main excitement of the race was the battle between Ginther's new 120-degree V6 Ferrari and Stirling Moss in Rob Walker's Lotus 18, with Moss triumphant in a car that was some way less powerful than the Ferraris. Hill, meanwhile, had retired early on with fuel pump failure.

At Zandvoort, Tony Rudd was banned from the BRM pits by Wilkie Wilkinson, and it took the intercession of the Stanleys to restore harmony. It was decreed that Tony could attend races whenever he chose, but his instructions to the mechanics would have to be vetted first by Wilkinson. There was a knock-on effect, in so far as the old guard, Peter Berthon and Raymond Mays, did not often appear in the workshops. Graham came in eighth in the race, having gently slipped down the order from a second-row grid position, alongside Moss and behind the three works Ferraris.

At the Nürburgring 1000km, Graham was

Porsche contested Class 2 (1601cc–2000cc) at the Nürburgring 1,000km in 1961. The Hill/Moss RS61 was running second, with Hill driving steadily and Moss doing the sprinting. At half distance the engine blew so, under team orders, the English pair were drafted in to co-drive the experimental Carrera of Linge/Greger. The car finished a class-winning eighth, hence the rather muted smiles on the podium from Herbert Linge, left, Sepp Greger, Moss and Hill. *(P)*

The F1 elite pose for the cameras at the 1961 German Grand Prix. In the front rank, from left, are Jim Clark, John Cooper, Innes Ireland, Stirling Moss, Graham Hill, Jo Bonnier, (seated, with Ferry Porsche's arm around his shoulder), Bruce McLaren and Dan Gurney. *(P)*

teamed with Stirling Moss in a works 1.7-litre Porsche RS61 Spyder. When that expired in Moss's hands while lying second, the British duo were promptly transferred into a German-crewed Carrera prototype to give it a better chance of success. They ended up eighth, 10 minutes behind the winning Maserati T61, after eight hours of racing. Then Graham was entered in the Le Mans epic alongside Moss again, but this time in the NART (North American Racing Team) Ferrari 250 GT. After running strongly in fifth place for some time, the engine gave out in the ninth hour.

Between sports car races, Graham went to Spa for the Belgian Grand Prix. Both BRM Climaxes

were on the third row of the grid, Graham a tad quicker than Brooks, and his race was spent largely dicing with Surtees's Cooper Climax. The BRM's exhaust split, and in so doing melted the HT leads. Although these were changed in the pits, the car soon developed an oil leak, and he was out, six laps from the end.

A couple of weeks later, Hill was back at the wheel of a Porsche RSK, entered by Camoradi for him and Moss in the Targa Florio. However, a broken differential put paid to their race.

It began to look as if Graham's ill-luck at Lotus had followed him to BRM. Despite freshly rebuilt chassis and engines for the French Grand Prix at

Along with other contemporary Grand Prix drivers, Hill took part in a kart race at Brands Hatch in 1961, driving a Villiers-powered Trokart. (FF)

Reims on 2 July, Graham managed a sixth place after a closely fought duel with McLaren's fifth-placed Cooper. The race was won by Ferrari's new recruit, Giancarlo Baghetti, who out-fumbled Gurney at the hairpin on the last lap after some close, high-speed racing. Despite the best efforts of Stirling Moss, the shark-nose Ferrari 156 was as good as invincible all season.

At a rain-drenched Aintree for the British Grand Prix, Graham circulated in sixth place, but had to retire on lap 44 with broken valve springs. Worse was to come. At the Nürburgring Graham was running fifth at the end of the first lap and made a move on Herrmann's Porsche on the inside at South Curve. The German veteran would have none of it, and Hill slid sideways and collected Gurney, who was attempting to pass on the other side. The force of the impact broke the BRM's steering and Hill flew over a bank into the long grass. The race result showed that Moss was still the master, beating the Ferraris of Von Trips and Phil Hill.

A couple of sports car races followed: the Peco Trophy at Brands, where he retired the E-type with a puncture, and the Tourist Trophy at Goodwood, where he drove a consistent race to finish sixth overall in a works Porsche 695GS Abarth, winning his class and lowering the class record several times into the bargain. There had also been a couple of mid-season races for the Intercontinental Formula, a short series intended to attract Indy cars and F1 machinery that could run with up to 3-litre engines. Graham finished third in both of these events, the British Empire Trophy at Silverstone and the Guards Trophy at Brands Hatch, driving a BRM P48 with 2.5-litre Climax FPF power. This race was a tussle between Moss, Surtees, Brabham, Clark and Hill. The first two dropped out, and Hill lost second place when he spun due to fuel starvation.

## Type 57

Having complete control over the Type 57 project – actually, 578 is the correct designation because of the V8 engine – Tony Rudd designed the tubular chassis to suit Graham Hill's physique (6ft tall and relatively large for a racing driver) and to carry sufficient fuel load to satisfy a 200bhp engine. Tony Rudd recalled that Graham had a significant input into the design of the car:

When we built the first BRM P48/57 in 1961, I discussed this in great detail with him. About how much he could recline and drive comfortably, and he spent quite a bit of time sitting in the tub. And of course he was much bigger than Jimmy, which was one of our problems. And he had broken one leg quite badly in a motorcycle accident years before, so he needed more room around his left knee. He gave me quite a lot of trouble with seat fittings and things like that. But you could talk to him about airflow. The first Monaco race we ducted the air round the side of his hips, and had the oil cooler behind the drive in the first car. We had rubber bag oil tanks on the sides of the monocoque, and he would be very interested in all of that sort of thing.

The 200-mile Silver City Trophy at Brands Hatch in June 1961 was won by Moss in the UDT-Laystall Lotus 18/21, although Surtees and Clark had outpaced him earlier in the race. Graham's BRM P48/57 Climax was not in the hunt, however, and he finished 13th. *(FF)*

Four months after the new chassis was ready, tests were completed on the new BRM V8 engine, and Rudd was in charge of the new car on its debut at Monza for the Italian Grand Prix. Wilkie supervised the Climax-powered cars. This was the first chassis and suspension that Tony Rudd had designed in its entirety, and hopes were high. The new car was taken to Monza ahead of the race for some testing. Again, the Grand Prix was to be run on the combined road circuit and super-fast banked oval, on which the cars circulated flat-out at over 160mph. To gauge how steep the banking was, Hill tried to run up it, and could only get to the top by removing his shoes to get a bit of extra grip. The banked oval was constructed in 1955 of concrete slabs, supported underneath every few yards by concrete stanchions, but by 1961, the slabs of concrete had sagged between the supports, to create a series of hollows and ridges that were potentially very damaging to a car travelling at high speed. In addition, the centrifugal forces tended to throw the car out of the corner, acting almost vertically and generating considerable downforce. The effect was to make the car twice as heavy and compress the springs to the extent that the chassis was riding on the shock-absorbers' bump rubbers. Thus the cars were effectively without suspension when they hit the concrete ridges and were thrown about in an alarming fashion, while drivers with blurred vision clung desperately to their steering wheels. Mercifully, the banking went out of use in 1968.

Although the pre-race testing did not reveal much about the BRM's road-holding abilities, it was a good test for the new engine, which was particularly smooth compared with the relatively rough four-cylinder Climax units. At one point when Hill was circulating on the banking at high speed, he became aware that the car was on fire. A fuel-line union had worked loose and fuel was being sprayed at full pressure onto the engine and exhaust pipes. Staying cool, Hill slowed the car to a standstill, the engine still aflame. When throwing earth on the flames had no effect, he stripped off his overalls and woollen vest to beat them out. Fire-retardant Nomex overalls and underwear were a long way off in the future, and Hill wore woollen undergarments as the best

thing available at the time, no matter how sweltering the climate. Although Graham managed to set a blistering time with the other V8 in official practice, despite a recalcitrant misfire, the BRM V8s were deemed to be too risky to use in the race, and they resorted to the Climax engines.

Tony Rudd recalled:

Graham used to like Monza. It was quicker than most places, and he was very intrigued when he found that I had got Monza worked out. For instance, if he wanted a quick practice time, the optimum time to do it was late afternoon, after 5pm, when temperatures are down and its just right, the sun is not in the driver's eyes. One time he came in at 4.30pm and said, 'the sun is right in my eyes,' and I said, 'yes I know, leave it for half an hour.' And he said, 'well why didn't you tell me before?' After that, he would always ask me about my knowledge of circuits.

The Italian Grand Prix itself was marred by the notorious collision on lap two between Jimmy Clark and Von Trips, when the German's Ferrari veered off into the crowd, killing 11 spectators. Von Trips died soon afterwards. Clark was uninjured, but his Lotus 18 was impounded and both he and Chapman faced manslaughter charges under Italian law, a shadow which hung over them for several years. Hill, meanwhile, retired on lap 10 with a dropped valve, and Americans Phil Hill and Gurney finished first and second, Phil's Ferrari being the only survivor of the five that started the race. It also secured for him the world championship title for 1961.

The Ferraris did not enter the US Grand Prix, the last Grand Prix of the season, staged at Watkins Glen on 8 October. Both Hill and Brooks had to make do with the Monza cars with their Climax engines, but nevertheless, Graham put his on the front row of the grid. In the second half of the race, he was challenging Innes Ireland's Lotus 18 for the lead, only to fall back with magneto trouble. The missing clip and cap were replaced in a pit stop, and he recovered to fifth place, a lap down, while Brooks came third in the other BRM. It was Team Lotus's first Grand Prix victory, but Graham had yet to score.

## Rally Challenge

Hill's varied motor sport calendar for 1962 began with the Monte Carlo Rally. Graham was hired by the Rootes Group to drive a Sunbeam Rapier with Peter Jopp as co-driver and navigator. Their performance was compromised by the team's failure to fit studded tyres to tackle a pass beyond Chambéry for the final run over the Col du Granier to Monte Carlo. The question of whether or not to fit studs depended on a report from the reconnaissance car, which in this case suggested that the road was clear. As it was, the sun had set, and the damp road surface turned to ice, and Hill did well even to stay on the road, let alone get a creditable time. The Rapier eventually finished 10th, and Sunbeam scooped the team prize.

The BRM team had to win in 1962, since Sir Alfred Owen had declared that he wanted to see results, or else he would shut them down. Hill was confident. 'Graham thought that the 1962 season was going to be his, right from the beginning,' Tony Rudd said. Graham's BRM team mate for 1962 was American Richie Ginther, erstwhile Ferrari sports car and Grand Prix driver and tester, noted for his wiry physique and trademark crew cut hairstyle. Early in the year, Ginther was burnt (and hospitalised) while testing a new fuel layout on a new P57 V8 at Witham airfield near Bourne when the fuel feed pipe to the injection control unit came adrift. In the wake of this incident, the future of BRM was even more on the line, but Mrs Stanley persuaded her brother to persevere since the prospects had never looked so good, with Hill and Ginther as drivers and the new engine on the verge of completion.

The two drivers got on well and their talents complemented each other. By this time Hill had a good reputation for being able to sort out a car's handling, while Ginther was seen as being more adept at engine and gearbox development. Thus, the American was entrusted with more of the power train development. He would be using a Colotti gearbox to begin with, while Hill would use BRM's own transmission.

At this point, another major milestone occurred in the BRM team's history. Tony Rudd was invited to take over as team manager, on the understanding that he secured two Grand Prix wins. The old guard was summarily dismissed. 'When we went to Brussels in March 1962 Graham knew that the BRM upheaval was in progress,' said Tony Rudd. 'I saw Sir Alfred Owen on the Thursday and he offered me the job, and I stayed the night with Graham so he knew that the fateful meeting would be the following Tuesday, and Sir Alfred was going to implement the changes, or maybe chicken out.'

Although his salary was increased by 50 percent, Tony Rudd was then told by the firm's accountants that BRM's budget for the year had already either been spent or committed. So he would have to complete the season on potential start money totalling £12,000, when more like double that would be needed to do a full season.

The first race with the new V8-powered type 57 was the non-championship Brussels Grand Prix, staged on 1 April in Heysel Park. Not only was Hill quickest in practice, he won the first heat ahead of Moss and Mairesse, despite wearing a steel corset, having slipped a disc a couple of weeks earlier lifting a crate of spares at Sebring, where he had been going to race the Scuderia Serenissima Ferrari. But for the second heat the starter motor failed, and Graham needed a push start, only to be black-flagged and disqualified. It mattered not that, when translated into English, the regulations allowed a push start. That was not the case in the French version.

At Snetterton for the Lombank Trophy meeting on 14 April, three of the cars present had new V8 engines: Hill's BRM, Moss's UDT-Laystall Lotus 21 and Clark's Lotus 24. BRM were running with stub exhausts as there were difficulties running the exhaust pipes through the suspension. The BRM

Graham was one of the more successful exponents of the Mk II Jaguar in saloon car racing, along with the likes of Salvadori, Parkes, Baillie and Chapman. Here at Aintree he won the supporting race at the 200 F1 meeting driving John Coombs's well-known 3.8-litre car 'BUY12'. *(FF)*

led initially, but Moss got through, only to fall back with throttle linkage trouble. Hill was then passed by Clark, and the two of them lapped everyone else who was still running.

Driving the BRM in the Glover Trophy race at Goodwood's Easter meeting, Graham took his first ever F1 victory and the first win for the V8-powered P57. However, this was the race that effectively ended the top-line career of Stirling Moss. Hill was leading comfortably while Moss was recovering from a couple of pit stops and was bent on unlapping himself in his efforts to get back into the hunt. He passed Hill under braking, but apparently went off the circuit and out of control, making no attempt to correct or slow the car before it ploughed into the bank. Being an on-the-spot witness, Hill believed that the accident had been caused by a mechanical failure. 'It was a terrifying sight and it gave me a fearful shock,' wrote Hill in *Life at the Limit*. 'What had happened to Stirling really took the gloss off, and everyone was dreadfully worried.' Whatever the

cause of the accident, it was an anxious time while everyone waited to see if Moss would survive.

'Graham was very worried about that,' said Tony Rudd, 'because he said Stirling was lining up to overtake him. He said, "do you think people will blame me for it?" So I said, "I don't know why they should." I was more inclined to agree that the car broke, but Graham was quite concerned about it.' A side effect of Moss's crash was to clear the way for a new generation of drivers like Clark and Hill to excel.

Graham won the support race in Coombs's Mk II Jaguar, repeating the achievement at Aintree five days later in the saloon car race that supported the Aintree 200. In this, the third national non-championship F1 race after Snetterton and Goodwood, Ginther fared better on carbs than Hill on injection, but both BRM V8s failed. Tony Rudd had this to say:

> Graham had quite a thing about throttle response. He was adamant that the throttle response of the injection engines was not as

good as the carburettor engines. We argued a lot about that, so we gave Richie a carburettor engine and he said it was slower. Richie was quite emphatic that the injection engine was more powerful. You could discuss that sort of thing with Graham, but what went on inside the engine was a closed book to him.

A bit severe, maybe, considering Hill's mechanical bent and two years in the Navy spent in the ship's engine room. Still, it was a relevant comment on the BRM drivers' respective talents. Rudd continued:

> Graham remarked at Monte Carlo that his initial acceleration out of the Gasworks hairpin seemed quicker than Clark's was on carbs. I said to watch the g-loads going round the corner. An injection system doesn't know its going round a corner. Then he said that, going down the straight in front of the pits, it was clean and pulled well, but going through the Casino Square he thought the carburettor engines had the edge. But it was a confusing situation, because going down the hill past the Tip Top, his brakes were far better than anyone else's.

The fourth UK Formula 1 race in the 1962 season was the *Daily Express* International at Silverstone, and Graham claimed pole position. Jimmy Clark took an immediate lead, while Hill sparred with Surtees's Lola Climax – nearly all the front runners had V8 engines by now. Then Hill began to lose his stack pipes, one by one, and this affected the engine's performance. The weather also took a hand, as it began to rain and, by the last lap, Hill was only three seconds behind Clark. The Scot was held up by Masten Gregory's UDT-Laystall Lotus 24 just long enough for Hill to make up that deficit, and both Lotus and BRM went through the old ultra-fast Woodcote corner side by side, jinxing right and left to out-fox one another. Hill took the win by a nosecone, in a thrilling finish. He came third in the GT race in Coombs's E-type and, for good measure, won the saloon car race in the same stable's Mk II Jaguar. Two wins

from three different race categories on the same programme suggests that he was at the peak of his form.

A pointer towards his maturity at the meeting came from Tony Rudd:

> One incident which should have provoked Graham, but didn't, was the International Trophy '62, when the stub exhausts fell off. He dropped right back, I think he was down to third and, going past the pits, Vaccarella had him off. Now, Vaccarella was his teammate in the Targa Florio Porsche, and I said to the people in the pits, 'now we'll see him go!' But he didn't. But then, they were not the sort of circumstances that he would have gone in, because it was raining like hell and he was driving to his limit in the wet anyway. You need it to be dry to drive a car right to its limits.

## First Grand Prix Win

The first round of the 1962 F1 World Championship was the Dutch Grand Prix at Zandvoort, an event notable for the launch of the new Lotus 25 with the first-ever aluminium 'bathtub' monocoque chassis. This endowed the car with greater torsional rigidity and provided an elegant solution to the problem of the stowage of fuel cells. At a stroke the Lotus 25's tub made the

For the 46th Targa Florio, Porsche teamed up with Scuderia Venezia, with Graham Hill sharing this red 2-litre twin-plug, flat-eight powered 718GTR coupé with local hero Nino Vaccarella and Jo Bonnier. The car was placed third after 7hrs 14mins. *(P)*

Serious discussion in the Porsche pits during the 1962 Targa Florio. From left to right: Edgar Barth, Jo Bonnier, Dan Gurney, Graham Hill, Herbert Linge. *(P)*

traditional multi-tubular chassis look outdated. Porsche too introduced its new V8-powered, torsion-bar suspension Type 80A F1 car, although that had a tube-frame chassis. In qualifying, Graham Hill was just pipped for pole by Surtees's Lola Climax, with Clark making up the front row in the new Lotus. Tony Rudd said:

> The introduction of the Lotus 25 obviously had an impact. Graham asked me what I thought about it. But it was early days, and I just didn't know. Then he told me that at Zandvoort it had more traction out of the hairpins, and of course it had much more torque, but he said on the faster corners he had the measure of it, although it was quicker down the straight. So he was very objective about some things.

It was Clark who made the best start, and he soon built up a three-second lead over Hill and Gurney. But the Lotus's clutch played up, and Hill was through to an unchallenged lead, which he held to the finish. He had won his first world

championship race after four years of trying, and for BRM it was only the second such event, the first since Bonnier won the 1959 Dutch Grand Prix. The team celebrated after the prize-giving later at the Hotel Bouwes, after which there was a mass skinny-dip in the North Sea.

Regarding the rapport between Graham and Tony Rudd, the BRM team boss had this to say:

> Graham and I had a good relationship, and he said he knew how I thought. We had a good rapport in all respects really. It wasn't like Chapman and Clark, but I never knew what that relationship was about, and still don't. As it developed, Clark didn't trust Chapman half as much as in the early days. Chapman had his own ideas and they used to fall out over money. Graham and I had no secrets at all. If I couldn't do something in time, I would tell him and tell him why. But you never knew what was going on between Clark and Chapman.
>
> My relationship with Graham changed

At last! The first Grand Prix victory came at Zandvoort in the 1962 Dutch Grand Prix, driving the BRM P57, fitted with the trademark stack-pipe exhausts. This was the meeting where the new Lotus 25 monocoque and eight-cylinder Porsche made their debuts, but once Clark had dropped out with his new car, the race was Graham's. *(FF)*

quite radically at Zandvoort in '62. When he first came to BRM in the winter of '59 and we were testing the new engine out, we didn't know what to make of each other. He didn't understand BRM, and it was an odd relationship to begin with, but he said he gradually realised that he knew what I was talking about on suspension systems. Then we had this fearful row at Zandvoort in practice in '62. Graham wanted to go out a second time in practice to see if he could beat his time, and we had got an oil leak from the gearbox that we were trying to fix, but the car could have run again. In fact, the mechanics were warming it up for him. Then somebody drove past in the paddock and showered the car with sand, and I wouldn't let him go out in it until we had stripped the throttle slides for fear that they would jam. And he was furious and we had quite a row, and I said it was my responsibility, and when the throttles are cleaned out, you can go. By the time we had got it cleaned it was nearly the end of practice and he changed his mind and he was simmering with rage, and he thought I was being unreasonable. He did come and apologise, and said he

was always a bit on edge on these occasions; 'winning means a lot to me,' he said, and I said, 'd'you think it doesn't mean a lot to me, Graham?' and he held me at arms length and said 'yes it does', and from then on, we got on very well together. He recognised that I wanted to win as much as he did. He could be quite generous, and say 'I'm sorry I gave you a hard time'. He was good from that point of view.

By the time of the Monaco Grand Prix on 3 June, the majority of cars were running Climax V8 engines and Colotti gearboxes. Exceptions were Ferrari, Porsche and BRM, who were self-sufficient in power train technology; Cooper whose Climax engines were mated to their own gearboxes; and Team Lotus who used ZF transmissions. Back then, the Monaco starting grid was on the sea side of the pits with a 200 yard sprint to the Gasworks hairpin. This was fraught with danger, and some teams, including BRM, curtailed the front of their cars almost to the radiator so there was nothing to block the airflow in the event of a crunch. Clark, Hill and McLaren were on the front row, and the race got under way with a jump start by mercurial Belgian Willy Mairesse, whose Ferrari bounced off the two British cars, only to slide wildly at the Gasworks hairpin. While the first three cars got through, the rest of the field was too bunched up and mayhem ensued. Mairesse repeated the mistake at the Station hairpin, but Hill was motoring serenely on, pursued by a recovering Clark. By lap 45, just one second separated them, until they came up to lap Surtees's Lola and Bandini's Ferrari, which were contesting sixth place. Hill nipped by them and Clark was caught up. But around half distance, Hill became aware that he was losing oil pressure in right-handers, which meant that he must be losing oil. Sensibly, he only accelerated when the oil pressure registered on the gauge, and backed off when it zeroed. But with just seven laps to go, a con rod snapped and went through the engine casing. The strange rules credited Hill with sixth place, even though he did not finish the race. The

After the first corner fracas in the 1962 Monaco Grand Prix, McLaren's Cooper had the lead until Hill in the BRM P57 overtook him. The situation was reversed on lap 93 when the BRM's V8 engine blew up. The car ran with part of the engine cover removed to aid cooling. *(FF)*

BRM mechanics deduced afterwards that there was just half a gallon of oil left in Graham's car, and it had digested 3.5 gallons of oil during the race. This was partly due to the low gear ratios necessary at Monaco and the incessant hard acceleration that sucked the oil down via the valve guides and up past the piston rings, thus consuming the vital lubricant.

For the Whitsun meeting at Mallory Park on 11 June, Graham was back in a single-seater Lotus, driving Rob Walker's four-cylinder hybrid 18/21. He was ranged against the works Lotus 25 of Clark, with Brabham's borrowed Lotus 24 and Surtees's Lola. When Clark dropped out, it was down to Surtees to win from Brabham and Hill, which was not bad for a car that was nearly obsolete. Hill also drove the Coombs E-type in the GT race and finished second in his heat and in the final.

The ultra-fast Spa-Francorchamps circuit, the home of the Belgian Grand Prix, has always been

one for the heroes, and Graham secured pole position, aided by the fact that Clark's car had a major engine failure in practice and the replacement unit failed to arrive in time for the final session. In fact, Clark's Lotus teammate Trevor Taylor had a better time of it, starting his Lotus 24 from the inside of the front row. Taylor traded places with Mairesse, but the Ferrari's shark-nose knocked the Lotus out of gear, and both crashed heavily at 100mph. Hill's BRM was plagued with a misfire as one of the exhaust pipes became disconnected, and Clark won as he pleased, giving the Lotus 25 its maiden victory. Hill was second, placing him back in the lead for the World Championship. Phil Hill finished third, making him runner-up in the championship race.

Next came the Le Mans 24 Hours, and Graham was entered by the David Brown Organisation to drive one of the fabulous 4-litre Aston Martin 212 prototypes. His co-driver was BRM teammate Ginther who, at 5ft 3in, was some nine inches

One of the richest prizes in British motor racing was the Mallory Park 2,000 Guineas, an F1 race held on Whit Monday 1962. Hill finished third in Rob Walker's Lotus 18/21. The supporting GT race was staged in three heats and a final, and Graham, seen here in the Coombs E-type BUY1, came second in his heat and second in the final, behind Parkes's Ferrari 250 GTO and ahead of Surtees's 250 GTO in both races. *(FF)*

shorter than Hill, requiring a seat-within-a-seat arrangement when the Californian drove. The Aston Martin had poor aerodynamics, and became light on the undulations of the Mulsanne straight. Ginther recommended fitting a rear spoiler or Gurney flap, like the Ferrari 250 GTO would have, but Aston Martin were unreceptive to the idea. Hill led comfortably on the first lap, and was second for several hours thereafter, duelling with Phil Hill and Olivier Gendebien in the 4-litre V12 Ferrari 330LM, but the Aston expired during the evening with a burst oil pipe, and the Ferrari went on to win.

The non-championship Reims Grand Prix found Hill in the middle of the front row of the grid on another high-speed circuit, and his BRM was fitted with low-level exhaust pipes. Hill nosed into the lead when the BRM engine outpaced the Climax V8 in Brabham's Lotus 24 on the long straights, only for the Australian to pull away under acceleration from the tight corners. McLaren had been holding back, and he came

through to take the win from Hill after Brabham's car faltered with fuel starvation. 'Graham never told me that the BRM engine was so much faster than the Lotus's,' said Tony Rudd, 'Jimmy told me.'

A week later came the official French Grand Prix at Rouen-les-Essarts, and Graham led from Surtees, Clark and Gurney, until lap 30 when he lapped Jack Lewis's Cooper going into the top hairpin. Lewis braked late as Hill came by, and shunted the BRM into a spin. Hill lost only one place, and a couple of laps later he regained the lead from Clark, setting fastest lap in the process. It was incidents such as this that really inspired him – he relished triumph over adversity. But after 42 laps, a fuel injector mixture control malfunction put him back to ninth place, 10 laps down, leaving Gurney the undisputed winner in his Porsche.

The venue for the 1962 British Grand Prix was Aintree, a flat circuit with five hairpins and three fast corners. It was not a track that suited the BRM, mainly because it was a relatively heavy car, which could not put its power down out of tight turns as well as the nimble Lotus 25. The race was a Jimmy Clark benefit, although Graham had a scrap with Brabham's Lotus 24 and McLaren's Cooper. Around half distance, Hill saw in his mirror that the outside rear tyre was virtually tread-less. The implication was clear – he would have to go harder round left-hand bends and very gently on right-handers, but since the majority were right-hand bends it was something of a tall order. Nevertheless, he managed to bring the BRM P57 home fourth. Clark's win brought him within a single point of Hill's championship-leading 19 points, and made BRM and Lotus equal in the Constructors' World Championship stakes.

## Camera Angle

Graham had a bizarre accident during practice for the German Grand Prix at a twisty downhill section of the Nürburgring called the Fuchsröhre, or Foxhole. Travelling at 130mph, he rounded a bend and was confronted by a black object right on the racing line, leaving him little option but to run over it. The errant item punctured the BRM's oil tank, which threw its viscous contents all over the back wheels, causing Hill to spin off into a ditch, tearing off wheels and suspension in the process. At that moment, Tony Maggs's Cooper arrived on the scene and he spun on Hill's oil, wrecking the car but, like Hill, escaping injury. The latter then ran back up the track, waving his arms, just in time to prevent Trintignant from doing the same thing. After the nearest marshals' post had been alerted, Graham went to investigate the foreign object, and discovered that it was a new-fangled on-board TV movie camera that had fallen off Carel de Beaufort's orange Porsche. Despite having strained his neck and sustained some bruising, Hill practised again the following day and was able to compete.

He wore the latest perspex visor attachment on his helmet rather than goggles, as it was pouring with rain, and the start was delayed while a mud-slide was cleared away. Both the BRM's front and rear anti-roll bars were removed to provide an advantage in the wet, and Hill went in for a bit of gamesmanship. He asked the mechanics to fit some brand new Dunlop SP tyres just for his warm-up lap; these had been made specially for the Porsche sports-racing cars and were not legal in Formula 1. So a lot of the drivers promptly protested to Dunlop that BRM were out of order, when in fact Hill had no intention of using them in the race. It was just a wind-up, masterminded by Hill, Rudd and chief mechanic Cyril Atkin, who knew perfectly well that the SPs reduced the BRM's ground clearance to an unacceptably low level. The proper wheels were refitted on the starting grid.

Hill's main opposition came from the two Porsches of Gurney and Bonnier, Clark's Lotus and Surtees's Lola. Clark put himself out of contention by omitting to switch on his fuel pumps at the start, and Gurney led initially, followed by Graham Hill, Phil Hill and Surtees. Graham passed Gurney on the pit straight and never lost the lead. The BRM mechanics cut a hole in the wire mesh fencing behind the pits so that, when Hill and Ginther came past, having gone around

the South curve, they could be given lap times that were just half a minute old in the calculation, instead of the full 10 minutes of a complete lap. The rain was interminable, as was the battle between Hill, Gurney and Surtees, and Hill excelled himself to keep them at bay. For Tony Rudd, it was a vindication of his appointment as team manager, and guaranteed another year's funding from the parent Rubery-Owen concern.

The day after the German Grand Prix was bank holiday Monday, and Graham was back in the UK racing the Coombs 3.8 Mk II Jaguar at Brands Hatch. Just as in Germany the previous day, it was raining, and water was getting into the stripped-down car. Hill's foot slipped off the rubber brake pedal and onto the accelerator, propelling the Jag into the bank at Druids hairpin. Tiredness from his recent exertions told. But he always wore seat belts in saloon cars, so was unhurt. Safety measures were in their infancy at the time. Seat belts were not worn in single-seaters, and although fire extinguishers were universal, they were diminutive hand-held affairs that could explode in excessive heat.

## Tourist Trophy

By mid-August, John Coombs had acquired a new Ferrari 250 GTO, and Graham was to drive it in the Tourist Trophy at Goodwood – sponsored by the *News of the World*. Hill described the GTO as a 'beautiful car to drive, especially at Goodwood with such long, drifting corners – a beautifully controllable car'. Hill's chief opponents from among a high-quality entry were Salvadori in an E-type, Clark in the Ogier Aston Martin Zagato and Surtees, Ireland and Mike Parkes in similar Ferrari 250 GTOs. In the event, Surtees and Clark made contact on lap 61 going into Madgwick and ended in a tangle against the bank, and Hill finished ahead of Parkes and less than four seconds behind Ireland, who had straight-lined the chicane when a brake locked up, but went unpenalised. Normally this would have incurred a minute's stop-go penalty. Neither Coombs nor Hill felt like protesting – people generally would not in those days as it was no way to gain a victory.

Graham came second in the Oulton Park Gold Cup, witnessed by his brother who lived in Canada and had never seen his sibling in action. BRM teammate Ginther had pole, but Clark and Hill made better starts, and eventually just the two Brits were on the same lap. Unusually, a third works BRM was entered for South African Bruce Johnstone, who finished fourth, four laps down. Tony Rudd commented:

> Although Graham was good at Monaco, he wasn't so good on the tight twisty circuits, they were Richie's circuits. Richie took to Oulton Park like a duck to water, and Graham knew it quite well, but it didn't appeal to him. He liked the people and the atmosphere of Watkins Glen though, and that was a lucky circuit for him.

Graham Hill and his mechanic check the brakes on his Coombs Ferrari 250 GTO during the 1962 Tourist Trophy at Goodwood. He had a steady drive to second place behind Ireland's UDT-Laystall team 250 GTO. The mandatory pitstop for about 15 gallons of fuel and tyres took Coombs's mechanics 36.8 seconds on Hill's car, bettered by the Parnell mechanics who turned Surtees's 250 GTO around in 33 seconds. However, due to a jacking problem, Coombs's pit crew took 76 seconds to administer to the Salvadori car, also in the picture. *(FF)*

In the supporting saloon car dice at Oulton Park, Graham emerged the winner in the Coombs 3.8 Mk II Jaguar, while his regular rival Roy Salvadori in a similar Jaguar lost control while braking for Cascades, rolling the car into the lake, where the cabin top was submerged. The normally dapper Salvadori was lucky to get out with nothing more than a soaking.

As the world championship rivals lined up at Monza for the Italian Grand Prix, Graham was still leading the points tally with 28, and Clark was on 21 points, with Surtees on 19, McLaren on 18, and Phil Hill on 14.

Clark and Hill shared the front row of the two-by-two grid, with Ginther and McLaren behind them. Almost immediately, the ZF transmission on Clark's Lotus 25 gave trouble, but Hill blasted on, lapping around 1min 43.0sec and over 200kph (124.5mph). In fact he led the entire race distance of 86 laps, and Ginther came second in a one-two finish for BRM. Hill's title hopes rose as his points total went up to 36 points while Clark's did not move, and his second slot in the championship chart was usurped by Bruce McLaren.

There followed an unusual three-week layoff before going to Watkins Glen, where Hill could have clinched the title by winning the American Grand Prix. BRM sent three cars and Graham was driving what the mechanics called 'Old Faithful', the car that had first run at Monza the previous year and with which Graham had just won the Italian Grand Prix. On account of the bumpy nature of the track surface and peculiar camber changes on some of the bends, several cars had spring and damper settings adjusted. Typically, Graham wanted these changes made and his rear camber was adjusted accordingly. On the second day of practice it rained, and Hill's BRM proved more stable than Clark's Lotus 25. As the track dried, the contest between the two became more intense than ever, both setting identical lap times. Eventually Hill was pipped by both Clark and Ginther, starting from the second row of the two-by-two grid alongside Gurney's Porsche. Tony Rudd remembers the tension leading up to the race:

> We had quite a row at Watkins Glen in '62. Graham wanted the engine changed the night before the race, because some engines were better than others, and we used to pick the best engine. If two engines had the same power, we would pick the one with the better history. When he went

to Oulton Park in '62 it was the first race with the new combustion chamber and he went a day early to see if he had got the gear ratios right. But they were wrong, so for the first day's official practice, Graham said to put the best engine in, the faster one. In effect he wanted the engine from the new car put into his old car. It was a big job, but I had it done because we had a whole practice session to put anything right. Graham won the race, and the engine he rejected was put in Richie's car and Richie said it was faster, so everyone was satisfied. When we got to Watkins Glen, we put the best engine in his old car and he said, 'the new car is faster, the engine is not as good, so can we switch the engine from my old car to the new car?' Of course, by then he was head to head with Jimmy for the championship, and I said 'no', and he said, 'why not, you did it at Monza,' and I said 'I'm not doing it here, it's the night before the race. We haven't got the mobile workshop, we haven't got all the facilities we had at Monza.'

At flag-fall, Clark was away first, followed closely by Hill, and when the Scot had problems overtaking a back marker on lap 12, Hill seized his chance and took the lead. The positions were reversed again on lap 19, and Hill had to settle for second place. The intensity of their battle can be gauged by the fact that they had lapped the entire field.

While he was in the States, Graham drove a couple of races in California at Riverside and Laguna Seca for Bill Sturgis, but the Cooper-Monaco T61 sports-racer developed gearbox trouble in both events. Back in the UK, Graham drove a single-cylinder, tiller-steered 1896 Lutzmann in the London-to-Brighton run. The ancient machine was virtually brakeless, unbeknown at the time to motorists in modern cars, and Hill and his companion hit and damaged two cars as well as wrecking a trailer en route to Brighton. So inadequate were the brakes in fact that the runaway vehicle had to be driven across the central reservation and up the wrong side of a dual carriageway in order not to plough into a queue of stationary traffic.

Prior to the South African Grand Prix at East London, staged immediately after Christmas, Graham raced in the Rand Grand Prix at the new Kyalami circuit, the BRM succumbing to ignition trouble. Then came the Natal Grand Prix at Westmead, Durban, and although he came second in his heat, the BRM again suffered problems with the new ignition system in the final.

## Down to the Wire

The 1962 championship had come down to the wire, then, and even Sir Alfred Owen was present for the big South African race, with TV coverage provided unusually by NBC and another US television company. In the World Championship stakes, Hill was nine points ahead of Clark and, quite simply, as far as Graham and BRM were concerned, Jimmy had to lose. If he gained nine points from a win, he would draw level with Hill, assuming that Graham failed to score. The driver with most wins would take the title, and Clark had four to Hill's three. There were yet more permutations, as in those days, drivers could only score the best five out of nine races. So if Hill came second to Clark, he would collect six points, but would be obliged to drop his next lowest result, which was also six points. On the other hand, if Clark won, he could count all nine points and thus win the championship.

Graham's car was a lightened version of the 1962-spec model, made of thinner gauge aluminium sheet, with bolt-on front wheels and wider front track with larger wishbones and bigger discs. As well as Richie Ginther's car and Graham's spare – Old Faithful – a fourth BRM was on hand for Bruce Johnstone. The first day's practice was on Boxing Day, in hot, bright sunshine beside the Indian Ocean. The wind off the ocean affected handling through some of the more exposed corners, as well as gearing on the straights. The ratios would be changed between sessions to compensate for below-par revs, only for the wind to blow back, and the cars would then be over-revving.

Prior to the start, Hill and Clark were being interviewed by NBC commentator Chris Economaki, a well-known and knowledgeable racing journalist. He said to Hill, 'Well, Graham, what is it that bothers you on a day like this?' Came the acid reply 'It's people like you coming up and asking me questions like that.' That abrupt put-down serves as an indication that, prior to a race, Hill could become quite withdrawn and wound up spring-tight, so it was a dangerous time to approach him without a very good reason. Rob Walker confirmed that Hill needed to psyche himself up before a race. 'He wouldn't have anybody speak to him for an hour and a half before the start. He used to sit in the transporter and go through his black book, rehearsing every gear change on every corner, going through everything there was. He was absolutely meticulous.'

Following the exchange between Hill and Economaki, the drivers were taken on a parade lap in MG sports cars and spectators invaded the track en masse to show their support. In *Colin Chapman: the Man and his Cars*, Jabby Crombac talks about the 'tremendous needling' that went on between BRM and Lotus. He records that Chapman went and stood by the weigh-bridge at the East London circuit to see for himself whether the rumour was true that BRM had built a lightweight car for Hill. He had gone to a great deal of trouble in paring weight off the 25 in order to match whatever had gone on at Bourne, and was furious when he found that the Hill car was only a scant 5lb lighter than before.

Tony Rudd remembers Hill's approach immediately before this critical race:

The South African Grand Prix at East London was a key race. Literally everything went wrong there beforehand, everything, and the Lotus was just faster on that circuit, and they had fuel injection. Lucas broke the agreement providing them with a fuel injection engine, which irritated us, even though Graham always said that carburettor engines were better than fuel injection. Oil pressure was bad, that was our principal problem. Sir Alfred came to the garage before the race and the engines were all in a circle, all with their front covers and oil pumps off and trying the best set-up. He asked whether Graham had been in, and said that he'd better be. In the morning, he said to Graham 'You didn't get to the garage the night before the race.' Graham said, 'No, they told me to go to bed and relax and get a good night's sleep, so that's what I do, it's what I'm told to do.' Sir Alfred said, 'Oh, I thought you would have gone to have a look.' Graham said, 'No, I trust them, they will give me the best they can, and I would only make matters worse.'

Clark was quickest in practice, with Graham just 0.3sec slower. While Clark made a perfect start with no wheel-spin, Hill took off in a cloud of tyre smoke. The Scot led for 63 laps, then a bolt fell out of the engine, which lost all its oil, and with it went Clark's title hopes. Hill, some 27 seconds behind and a similar distance ahead of McLaren, inherited the lead and took an extremely popular win, consolidating his place at the top of the World Championship tree. The fans poured onto the track while Hill completed his lap of honour, and a teenage boy was accidentally pushed under the BRM's rear wheel, breaking his leg. Graham was most upset about this and corresponded with him for some time afterwards.

The World Championship victory in 1962 was confirmation, if any were needed, that Hill was a superb racing driver and on top form. It was the fruition of four years climbing the Formula 1 ladder – a relatively short time to make it to the top in any era. Through perseverance and skill as well as mechanical good fortune he had bested the top drivers of the day – Clark, Brabham, Gurney, McLaren and Surtees in particular, with that other potential champion, Moss, effectively eliminated for good.

# Chapter 3
# Mixed Fortunes

NOT many world champions could claim to have been 'banged up' in jail having just won the title. But that's what happened to Graham Hill. After the South African Grand Prix, the newly-crowned champ spent New Year's Day 1963 in a Karachi jail, along with his mechanic Peter Bryant and Innes Ireland. They were bound for New Zealand, and had landed at Karachi to change planes. There it was discovered that they had not had yellow fever jabs, which was an important omission as they had stopped off in Nairobi en route, where there had been an outbreak of the illness. So they were, in effect, quarantined in a prison cell until the delayed aircraft arrived to carry them on to Australia.

The first round of the Tasman series was held at Pukekohe, Auckland, and Graham drove the front-engined Ferguson P99 four-wheel drive car for Rob Walker. In a long and gruelling race, he lay second until the last lap, but the gearbox broke within a mile of the finish line. He flew back to the UK immediately afterwards to have his tonsils out, then returned to Australia two weeks later for the Australian Grand Prix at Warwick Farm, Sydney. He was driving Rob Walker's four-wheel drive Ferguson again, sharing the car with Innes Ireland. Although the four-wheel drive traction was an enormous boon at the start and in corners, the car suffered from a carburation problem that caused the engine to cut out on right-hand bends. Misfire notwithstanding, Hill came sixth in the sweltering Australian Grand Prix. He complained that the car understeered at the tight Warwick Farm circuit when in fact oversteer would have been preferable. The torque split between front and rear wheels could be altered, but because of the traction at

both ends with the Ferguson system, the driver was unable to control the car by drifting it as he could with a rear-wheel drive car. The Ferguson came into its own at Lakeside, Brisbane, which was a wet race, and Hill finished second to Surtees.

On 22 March, Graham was driving at Sebring,

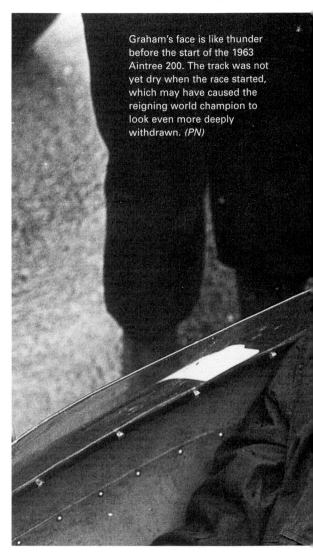

Graham's face is like thunder before the start of the 1963 Aintree 200. The track was not yet dry when the race started, which may have caused the reigning world champion to look even more deeply withdrawn. *(PN)*

and retired the Speedwell MG Midget from the 3 Hours. But in the following day's big-time 12 Hours race, he and Pedro Rodriguez brought the NART Ferrari 330LM/SP home in third place, despite an absence of lights during the night hours. Graham then put together a string of victories in assorted machinery, first at Snetterton in the Lombank Trophy in the P57-V8 BRM and in the GT event driving John Coombs's E-type. He won at Oulton Park in Coombs's Mk II Jaguar, and again, twice, at Goodwood in the same two Jaguars. At the non-championship Aintree 200, both Graham and Richie clocked identical times in practice, and the BRM pair held onto a tenuous lead from McLaren, Ireland and Trevor Taylor. At Silverstone for the *Daily Express* Graham was second fastest to Innes Ireland's BRM-powered Lotus 24, but the works BRM retired with electrical trouble. Ireland went on to set fastest lap, having spun almost the length of the pit straight. Graham made up for his retirement with a win in the Jaguar E-type over the similar cars of Salvadori and Dickie Protheroe.

Graham Hill applies opposite lock out of Tatt's Corner during the 1963 Aintree 200, coming up to lap Chris Amon's Reg Parnell Racing Lola Climax V8. *(PN)*

Graham had it pretty much his own way in the 1963 Aintree 200, the BRM P57 running faultlessly in first place with only Innes Ireland's Lotus 24 BRM presenting any real opposition. The picture is from early in the race when the BRMs of Hill and Ginther were running first and second. *(FF)*

## Richie Ginther Supports the First Monaco Win

Tony Rudd remembers that Hill and Ginther were a good driver pairing at BRM:

> Ginther had been an established Ferrari driver, and Graham remembered his drive at Monaco in '61 in the first of the 120-degree Ferraris when he was trying very hard to catch Moss. Graham would talk to Richie about the peculiarities of each circuit, but they were completely different people. As far as Graham was concerned, he understood the suspension, but the engine simply made a noise, got hot and drove a rev counter, whereas Richie would give you information on the engine in great detail.

> The first big clue Richie ever gave me was at Aintree in '62 when he said Graham was blowing smoke rings at him going down the straight. There were little tiny round puffs of grey smoke, he said, and the compression ratio was too high and we were detonating the corners off the sharp edges of the valve cut-out on the pistons, and that's what it was. We stripped Graham's engine first and looked and there was the little grey edge on the cutter. But Graham couldn't nurse a sick engine the way Jimmy could. He did notice in '62 when the chimney stack exhaust fell off, he had noticed that it was losing out on bottom-end power but picking up on top-end power. He sensed the effect of that. He latched onto the fact that the engine was designed and stressed to run to 12,000rpm, but there was no point in taking it there because it didn't give any more power. All it did was boil the oil, and he remembered that. He did hang onto the lower gears for better acceleration when most of the chimney stacks had fallen off.

Prospects for Hill and Ginther for the Monaco Grand Prix did not look especially brilliant, as their cars were virtually the same spec as they had been at the South African Grand Prix. It also looked as if they would remain that way for much of the season. Jimmy Clark was quickest in the Lotus 25 in practice, with Graham alongside him on the front row, and Surtees and Ginther behind on the grid. For the first time, the start-line was moved to its current location, instead of being on the seafront side of the pits. This was done mainly for safety reasons, so that the cars no longer rushed into the first hairpin after the start and collided, as had frequently been the case. They had to negotiate the 90mph Ste Devote corner instead, going through in single file. The BRM duo took an immediate lead, although Clark was soon into second, with McLaren and Surtees in pursuit. After trying on both sides, Clark passed Hill on lap seven for the lead and Ginther performed a supportive role, keeping the opposition at bay – apart from Surtees's Ferrari, which passed Hill at one point, before dropping back with low oil pressure. The combative Hill was handed the race on a plate when Clark's transmission failed on lap 70, and Ginther made it a BRM one-two. It was the first of Graham's string of Monaco successes and, in a way, justice had been done, since by rights the race had been his the previous year, but for a few litres of oil.

At Spa for the Belgian Grand Prix, Graham's pole time was almost a full second quicker than Dan Gurney's 3min 55sec in the Brabham Climax. But the initial leaders were Hill and the mercurial Clark, and these two were in a class of their own until Hill's new six-speed gearbox failed on lap 18. Shortly after his retirement, the Ardennes circuit was drenched by a heavy thunderstorm, and Chapman and Tony Rudd negotiated with the organisers to see about getting the race stopped, so dire were the conditions.

## Gas Burner

At the Le Mans 24 Hours, Graham and Richie were co-drivers in the Rover BRM gas-turbine car. This was a 1961 P48 Formula 1 car converted into a sports-racing chassis, effected by cutting the F1 chassis in half and inserting a two-seater tube-frame centre section. The Rover gas-turbine power

Graham acknowledges the plaudits after winning the Grovewood Trophy race at Mallory Park in July 1963, driving John Coombs's E-type Jaguar. *(FF)*

unit revved to 35–40,000rpm, developing some 150bhp using paraffin fuel, and drove through a BRM gearbox and torque converter. There were just two pedals, the accelerator 'button' – a sort of on-off switch – and a large brake pedal for left or right-foot braking. When started up, the engine sounded like a jet aircraft, but once on the move it was virtually silent. The engine characteristics meant that the brakes had to be kept on to prevent it rushing off at idle, and because of the two or three-second throttle lag, the accelerator had to be depressed long before it would normally have been in a conventional engine. Throttle power had thus to be balanced against the brakes. The Rover-BRM was clad in an open-top state-of-the-art aluminium bodyshell, and Graham tried it first at the MIRA test track, and then at the Le Mans test weekend in April, where the target set by the race organisers was an average speed of 150kph. Hill and Ginther averaged 179kph during the test weekend, which looked promising.

For the Le Mans race proper, the Rover BRM was permitted to start after the rest of the grid had departed because of the time it took for the gas-turbine engine to reach operating speed – some 11 seconds – and to avoid confusion it was allocated the number 00.

Hill and Ginther developed a technique which involved braking hard about 300 yards short of a corner such as Mulsanne using left-foot braking, and 100 yards before the corner they applied the accelerator again. When the power started to come in, the brake pedal was released, and by this time the apex of the corner was in sight. Mastery of this technique would stand Graham in good stead later in his career, as he would drive the Rover BRM gas-turbine car again in 1965, and the Lotus 56 turbine Indianapolis car in 1968. The Rover BRM's handling was excellent, and Hill was able to go through the White House bends quicker than in any other car he had driven at Le Mans. Because there were no hot water pipes in front of

Hill and Ginther drove the Rover-BRM gas turbine car at the 1963 Le Mans 24 Hours, finishing an excellent seventh on the road, but officially unclassified because it was seen as an experiment. Here the car, numbered 00, rounds Mulsanne corner ahead of the 12th-placed Hutcheson/Hopkirk MGB, which spent some time in the sandbank at this point. *(C)*

the drivers, they complained of cold feet during the night. But other than that, the car kept going and finished seventh 'on the road', although it was officially unclassified because of its uncategorised specification. It was eventually credited with a special prize, having covered 4172.9km at an average of 173.546kph. That compared with the winning Ferrari 250P V12 of Bandini/Scarfiotti logging 4561.7km at 190kph.

The 1963 season always looked like Jim Clark's year, but at Zandvoort Graham had the opportunity to race a brand new BRM. Designed by Tony Rudd, it was based on a Duralumin-sheet stressed-skin monocoque, with a tube-frame substructure located behind the rear bulkhead to carry the engine and rear suspension. According to *Motor Sport*'s Denis Jenkinson, compared with the old car, the new model could 'cope with a greater amount of acceleration through a given corner'. It was also very much lighter than its predecessor. However, Graham drove the old car at Zandvoort because of brake problems on the new one, and started from the centre of the front row. Clark led, while Hill battled with Brabham, all the while worried about the BRM's high water temperature. By half distance only Clark and Hill were on the same lap, everyone else having been lapped. But on lap 58, Hill was forced to pit to have the water situation checked and, sure enough, the engine failed on lap 70.

The new BRM, designated the P61, made its race debut at Reims for the French Grand Prix. The five-mile Reims circuit was roughly triangular, with a couple of tight hairpins and a fast right-hander over the brow of the straight beyond the pits. It was one of the fastest venues on the calendar. Graham had stayed on at Zandvoort to put in some testing and make adjustments to the suspension while Richie got acclimatised to the new car's handling characteristics. At Reims though, Hill's practice was compromised when the electrode of a KLG spark plug detached itself and ruined the cylinder head. Eventually the reigning world champion got down to within 0.7sec of Clark's pole time, but he incurred a one-minute penalty for a push-start. After the Scot had pulled

out a commanding lead, the battle for second place encompassed Ginther, Gurney, Brabham, Surtees, McLaren, Taylor, Hill and Maggs. In the end, Graham did well to bring the new car home in third place. At Silverstone for the British Grand Prix, however, Tony Rudd elected to run both Hill and Ginther in the old chassis, but with 1963-spec engines and six-speed gearboxes. Both cars had orange bands painted around their air intakes, ostensibly for recognition purposes. After a slow start, it became clear that no one would catch the flying Clark, but for the last third of the race it looked as though Graham had second place buttoned up. On the last lap though, his BRM began to run out of fuel, and he crossed the line with a dead engine, having been passed by Surtees's Ferrari. By the end of the race, only Surtees and Hill in third place remained unlapped.

Tyres wreathed in smoke, Clark's Lotus 25 beats Hill's BRM P61 off the line at Reims at the start of the 1963 French Grand Prix, while Gurney's Brabham gets away cleanly. Clark won from Tony Maggs's Cooper, with Hill third. *(JE)*

The P61 was back on the scene for the German Grand Prix, having had its lower front wishbones strengthened and the oil cooler and transistor ignition unit relocated. The engine cover now had air intakes on either side to feed the injection trumpets. BRM arrived early to get some pre-race testing in, but Graham was still not convinced by the new car's abilities, and elected to race the old model. Although on the front row with Bandini (Centro-Sud BRM), Surtees (Ferrari) and Clark (Lotus), he was still nearly 12 seconds slower than Clark's pole time. Some of the tail-enders at the back of the grid were over a minute slower. Hill's gearbox packed up on the third lap, while Surtees emerged the winner.

In the hot seat. Richie Ginther hitches a ride on Graham's engine cover, his BRM having broken a tappet halfway through Thursday afternoon's practice prior to the 1963 British Grand Prix. *(PN)*

A race-long battle raged between Hill's BRM P61 and Surtees's V6 Ferrari during the 1963 British Grand Prix at Silverstone. Just when Hill's second place (to Clark) seemed assured, he ran out of fuel, handing the place to Surtees and coasting over the line with a dead engine. No such worries for the canny Surtees, who had a three-gallon auxiliary tank fitted to the Ferrari the night before the race. *(PN)*

A mixed bag of non-championship race results followed. Graham retired the Maranello Concessionaires' Ferrari 250 GTO from the Guards Trophy race at Brands Hatch with a sheared throttle pedal, but won the Tourist Trophy a fortnight later at Goodwood in the same car. Over at Mosport Park in Canada, he came second overall and won his class driving the Ian Walker-entered Lotus 23B sports car in the so-called Canadian Grand Prix. The following day at Kent, Seattle, he placed second in heat one of the Northwest Grand Prix driving the 23B Climax under the Roy Winkelmann Racing banner.

Apart from a couple of brief periods when Parkes's Ferrari 250 GTO led the 1963 Tourist Trophy at Goodwood, Hill was dominant throughout. Here, on lap 46, his scarlet Maranello Concessionaires 250 GTO receives fuel and tyres, before motoring on to victory. *(FF)*

Driving the Maranello Concessionaires Ferrari 250 GTO, Hill was running fifth in the 1963 Guards Trophy at Brands Hatch when the throttle pedal sheared on lap 11. The overall winner was Roger Penske in the Cooper-Zerex Climax, while Hill's GT class was won by Sears's 250 GTO. *(FF)*

The Monza track-layout once again incorporated the normal road circuit and high-speed banked oval, and BRM were out testing early. Hill and Surtees turned in the fastest times on the banked section, and the former motorcycle world champion took pole in the new monocoque Ferrari, with Hill next up – over a second slower – and Clark and Ginther on row two. As so often during this period, Graham had to be identified by his christian name, since Phil Hill, the Miami-born 1961 world champion, was still present on the same grid. At flag-fall, Surtees bogged down with wheelspin and Graham took the lead, but soon came under pressure from Gurney. Clark joined them and took the lead in one of the great slipstreaming classics. But by lap 59 the BRM's clutch had cried enough. Clark took the win in his Lotus 25, ensuring himself of the 1963 World Championship, while Ginther came a stalwart (unlapped) second for BRM.

## Tin Tops

In British saloon car racing, the glory days of the six-cylinder Mk II Jaguar were numbered. The lithe Lotus Cortina was waiting in the wings to sweep all before it, and the rumbling big-engined American V8s were starting to flex their muscles. On former airfield circuits like Silverstone and Snetterton with long straights, such power could be used to good effect. Even at a curvy and undulating circuit like Oulton Park, Graham drove John Willment's 7-litre Ford Galaxie to second place behind Dan Gurney's similar car in the support race for the International Gold Cup on 21 September. The works Lotus Cortinas of Jack Sears and Trevor Taylor made their first international appearance in this event, beating all the Jaguars.

For the Gold Cup itself, the two BRMs were flanked on the front of the grid by the Team Lotus 25s of Clark and Taylor, with Hill and Clark tying for pole position. But Clark made no mistake about putting his stamp on the race, leading the BRMs by almost half a minute, while Graham and Richie swapped places a few times, with the American eventually leading home his English teammate.

Next came the US Grand Prix at Watkins Glen, and although it was almost the end of the 1963 season, BRM sent a couple of the previous year's P57 cars for Graham and Richie. After gear ratios were changed in practice, Graham went quicker still, and was credited with pole position ahead of Clark. As the flamboyant Tex Hopkins flagged the start with his traditional leap, Clark was stuck with a dud engine, and Hill whizzed off into the lead, challenged by Surtees's Ferrari. The Ferrari slipped by, followed soon afterwards by Gurney's Brabham, but after much slipstreaming, Hill retook the lead on lap 30. Then one of the rear anti-roll bar links became detached, sending the BRM's handling awry, and Surtees retook the lead. But when the Ferrari engine broke, Hill in the badly understeering BRM took the win ahead of teammate Ginther, who was running 40 seconds behind.

Having made the trip to the US, Graham went to California to drive the Ian Walker Lotus 23B Climax at Riverside, where he came 10th overall, and Laguna Seca where he placed 12th. A week later came the Mexican Grand Prix at Mexico City, the penultimate round of the F1 World Championship, and the victorious P57s from Watkins Glen were wheeled out again. Set in a 600-acre sports and leisure complex, the facilities at the 5km Autodrome were then rated the best in the world, although to the rear of the pits was a walled-off Indian graveyard. The high altitude of Mexico City (7,400ft above sea level) meant that the fuel injection metering cams had to be reshaped to weaken the mixture sufficiently. The engines were some 25 percent down on power, roughly translated as 100bhp, while the 12-cylinder engines were less adversely affected than the eight-cylinder engines. The physical effect was to render drivers breathless and raise their heart rate. Added to this, Graham was feeling unwell because his sinuses had been filled up with sea water while waterskiing at Acapulco. Starting from the second row, Hill's car jumped out of gear, immediately dropping him back to sixth. He spent much of the race dicing with Bandini's Ferrari, but spun on lap 59, which enabled Clark to lap him. Hill came home fourth behind Clark, Brabham and Ginther.

The final round of the 1963 season was the South African Grand Prix, staged on the Indian Ocean coast at East London. The P57s were in use again, while work progressed at Bourne on the new cars, and just three mechanics were on hand to service the drivers' requirements. Both BRMs were on the third row and Hill made a poor start, but this seemed to inspire him into pulling back lost ground and, in a race notable for his tail-sliding antics, he set about overtaking the cars in front. These included Brabham, Ginther and McLaren and, although lapped by Clark and Gurney, Hill managed to elevate himself to third place.

The reigning world champion had won just a single Grand Prix in 1963. His teammate scored more consistently through the season and they shared second place in the title stakes. Hill had more than his fair share of victories in other categories though, mostly in the Coombs Jaguars.

## The Full Monte

The American Ford Falcon was a tad incongruous as a rally car, being huge by European standards, and sporting a powerful 4.7-litre V8 engine. It came to be a firm favourite in circuit racing in the late 1960s in the hands of aces like Frank Gardner. No fewer than eight Falcons were entered for the 1964 Monte Carlo Rally, and Graham was among the race and rally stars of the day who were hired to drive them: Bo Ljungfeld, Peter Jopp, Peter Harper, Anne Hall, plus Jo Schlesser from the racing fraternity. Hill's co-driver was Ian Walker, and they took it very seriously, spending 10 days reconnoitring the special stages and making pace

Graham brought Ferrari its fourth successive victory in the three-hour RAC Tourist Trophy when he drove the Coombs/Maranello 250 GTO to victory at Goodwood on 24 August 1963.

notes. This was the first year of intercom systems planted inside the crew's crash helmets for use on special stages. Hill/Walker were among the runners opting to start from Paris, and their only major mishap was when the throttle stuck and in the ensuing crash the front of the car was crunched. They pulled it back into some sort of shape by attaching the front of it to a tree with a rope, then reversing. All eight Falcons finished, with Ljungfeld/Sager having led every stage, while outright victory went to Hopkirk/Liddon's Cooper S.

For the *Daily Mirror* Trophy at Snetterton, traditionally a curtain-raiser for the Grand Prix season, Hill sported a new type of visor mounted

Graham drove a couple of races at Goodwood on Easter Monday 1964. They were the F1 *News of the World* Trophy, in which he retired the new works monocoque BRM P261 with a broken rotor arm, and the Sussex Trophy, in which he came first, driving the Maranello Concessionaires 1964-bodied Ferrari 3-litre GTO from Jack Sears's AC Cobra. *(FF)*

on the sides of his crash helmet. It took the form of a circular plastic dish, with vanes on the front, and the idea was that it revolved at speed and threw off the raindrops. He was driving the new BRM P261 monocoque, with outboard springs and double wishbones, and a new anti-roll bar with rapid adjustment facility. In a notable design feature, the exhaust pipes from the BRM V8 engine passed through longitudinal channels in the rear of the monocoque – the pontoons either side of the engine bay were cut out, and a flanged steel sleeve inserted as a heat shield. Graham led the rain-soaked race until lap eight, when he came under pressure from Team Lotus debutant Peter Arundell. Nearing the Esses, Hill aquaplaned off into the bank, knocking a wheel off and running along the top of the bank and back onto the track. He had a lucky escape.

The works Ferrari 275Ps swept the board at the Sebring 12 Hours in late March, but Graham, co-driving the Maranello Concessionaires 4-litre Ferrari P330 with Jo Bonnier, retired with transmission failure. Back in the UK at Goodwood Graham had better luck, winning the Sussex Trophy in the Maranello Ferrari 3.0 GTO against opposition from Jack Sears in the Willment Cobra, although in the F1 *News of the World* Trophy the rotor arm failed on the BRM P261 when he was leading. The Formula 3 support race was won by a certain J.Y. Stewart.

The new 1-litre Formula 2 series opened with the annual race at Pau in south-western France, and Graham was invited to drive an Alpine, powered by a double overhead camshaft Renault-Gordini engine, alongside Mauro Bianchi and José Rosinski. However, Hill's designated car was patently not race-worthy, and he opted out after trying it in practice. While Clark won in the Lotus 32, the Alpines placed fourth and fifth.

Another non-championship F1 race followed, the Aintree 200, and Graham took pole in the P261. He led at first, but was overhauled by Brabham and Clark as the BRM began to give trouble when exiting corners. When Clark was baulked by back markers and crashed, Graham regained second place.

Hill had become something of a regular at the demanding Sicilian classic, the Targa Florio, and in this respect he was unusual among the Grand Prix fraternity. It says much about his appetite for road racing that he was enthusiastic about such an unstructured event. Other Grand Prix cavaliers who drove the Targa included Innes Ireland, and Americans Masten Gregory, Phil Hill and Dan Gurney. Clark, however, never did. For 1964 Graham was to co-drive Bonnier in the previous year's Porsche 718/8 sports prototype, part of a strong Porsche presence that included four of the new works 904 GTS coupés, which were challenged by Carroll Shelby's Cobras rather than

Having taken pole position for the 1964 Aintree 200 in the new BRM P261 V8, Graham was running second to Brabham when Clark appeared behind him on lap eight, bent on a meteoric rush through the field. When the Lotus crashed, Hill recouped second place. *(FF)*

works Ferraris. Although Bonnier led initially, a halfshaft broke on the second lap and Graham did not get his turn at the wheel. Hill, who had access to a plethora of cars in many different areas of the sport, was obviously an excellent and enthusiastic all-rounder. It was certainly apparent to his contemporaries. Mario Andretti, who has raced many different types of racing cars in a host of different disciplines, sees Hill as an all-rounder rather than an F1 driver:

You could tell he loved to drive, and he was one of those who would really apply himself. I don't think it came as natural as say Jackie Stewart or someone like that, except that he seemed to work so hard at it and practice so much. But he would get the job done. And he came to Indianapolis where it was totally foreign to him and before you knew it, he was up to speed, quick and real professional. When it came to sports cars it was the same, he was always a force to be reckoned with. He had that passion to drive and just loved to get into just about anything with wheels.

John Surtees thought that part of Graham's success was being in the right car at the right time:

> The important thing about Graham is that he was an enthusiast who actually liked what he was doing. In a way, a bit like me, he'd come up having started tinkering with things. I think that, either by being more astute than we give him credit for, or by the wheel of fortune, he managed to place himself in some of the best cars at the best times, which I think gave his career a greater level of success.

On 2 May for the 52-lap *Daily Express* International at Silverstone, an event promoted by the BRDC as the 'Festival of Speed', Graham looked set for another BRM victory. After early leaders Clark and Gurney had dropped out, Hill caught and passed Jack Brabham, who had been some 20 seconds in the lead. But the tenacious Australian hung on to the BRM's tail and slipstreamed past to retake the lead going through Abbey for the last time. Both Hill and Brabham were rated as excellent strategists at the time, and this was a fine example of both tacticians at work.

There was no gamesmanship here, just top-class motor racing. But Brabham was prone to drive a 'wide' car. Tony Rudd had this to say:

> Graham was old-fashioned. There was once a bit of a row with Brabham, when Jack wouldn't let him pass. That was the rules, and if anybody stopped you passing it was Jack. I've never heard of Graham's driving being criticised in Formula 1 racing, but it was slightly different in saloon cars like the Jaguars. I think Graham and Jimmy were much the most

Hill and Bonnier shared the second works Porsche 718/8 W-RS Spyder in the 1964 Targa Florio, and Bonnier led initially until a driveshaft broke and the car was stranded out on the course. Hill is pictured practising the car. *(P)*

The BRDC's 'Festival of Speed' on 2 May 1964 included the *Daily Express* International Trophy, which provided one of the closest races of the era, with Hill and Brabham the main protagonists. From lap 29 to the last (52nd) lap, the two strategists swapped places several times until it seemed that Hill, power sliding the P261 here, would win. But Brabham got a nose ahead coming out of Woodcote for the last time and won by a margin so tight that identical times were given. *(FF)*

gentlemen of drivers, and it was, 'After you,' 'No, after you'. I never heard of any suggestions of carving cars up. But Jimmy's tactics when the flag fell were that he was gone, he wasn't around any more. But I have a feeling that Graham was better at applying pressure than taking it. If somebody got on his tail and started to hassle him, he might not have held them off as well as a few other drivers. He was better at applying it. If you got Graham behind you, and saw his moustache in the mirror, better let him by, as he would be there forever. If he'd got something to chase, something to fix on, then he would go. That's why I was surprised at Brands

Hatch in '64 when he didn't try to get by Jimmy, because normally he would try.

However, Rudd confirms that Hill was adept at a mild form of gamesmanship:

Sometimes before the race you'd see him sitting on a pile of tyres in the pits. In Watkins Glen one year we had to go and fetch him. We'd got his car on the starting grid but he was reading a novel in the pits! Some of it was calculated, I'm sure.

He wouldn't go to the same lengths as Senna or Schumacher, say, and try to upset the other drivers. But he was good on race tactics generally. He would work out what he was going to do, and if he got it clear in his mind what was going to happen, he

Graham was always checking and changing suspension settings and tyre pressures – as he's doing here at Monaco in 1964 – searching for that little bit extra. Hill and Ginther had identical P261 V8s for the Monaco Grand Prix, running Lucas fuel injection and 13in wheels. *(PN)*

would tell me. I said to him at Watkins Glen with that novel reading business, 'if you were that bloody confident that you were going to win, why didn't you tell me?'

## New BRM

For the Monaco Grand Prix, Graham and Richie – recovered from a crash in practice at Aintree – had the new P261s at their disposal. The 1.5-litre BRM V8 engines were fed by Lucas fuel injection, while the stressed-skin monocoque chassis had simplified front suspension with inboard coil springs, compressed by rocker arm top wishbones. At the rear were single top transverse struts, twin radius arms and lower wishbones, and outboard coil-spring units.

Tony Rudd remembers the preparation for this race:

> We were very worried in '64 when we went to 13in wheels. They hurt us badly. We had Dunlop brakes, and to get a Dunlop calliper in a 13in wheel meant using a smaller disc, and smaller discs are bad things to have. They're not up to the job. So I hit on the idea of resurrecting the ventilated disc from the old 2.5-litre car, with single rear discs, and although they had to be cut down, they really worked. They won Monaco '64 for us. I was in the middle of a great big row with Dunlop, and at first they wouldn't let us race them, and I said 'I'm paid to win races, and here's my way of winning,' and they said they couldn't take responsibility for it. They finally handed over a letter stating that it was my responsibility. Then Graham got me on the morning of the race and said, 'you didn't tell me about this row about the brakes,' and I said, 'no, you've got enough to worry about! There aren't any risks.' The only risk we ran was that we had to make the pads thinner, but because they were running cooler, they wouldn't wear out as fast. He said, 'I know, I trust you, but you could have shared it with me, and told Dunlops that I knew about it and I was

happy to drive it. And if I was ready to drive it, then they should shut up!'

While Clark and Brabham shared the front row of Monaco's two-by-two grid, Graham and Surtees occupied the second row. Hill made a very good start and attempted to squeeze between Brabham and Clark, who closed in on him, trapping both the BRM's front wheels between their rear wheels, causing much tyre smoke. However, Hill's main opponent turned out to be Gurney, once Brabham had retired, although Gurney eventually pulled out with gearbox failure. But not before the calculating Hill had passed him under braking for Mirabeau at half distance. The flying Clark lost his rear anti-roll bar, and thus the lead, to Hill, and although he caught up again, the Lotus's Coventry Climax engine lost all oil pressure, and Graham was an untroubled winner, leading second-placed Richie home by over a lap. To get not just one, but both cars home at Monaco is a testament to reliability, and says much for the designer and team mechanics. But to win Monaco two years running indicates a driver on top form.

On lap 53, Hill took Gurney for the lead going down to the Station hairpin, then opening up a gap from Clark, who was soon past the American's ailing Brabham. Eight laps from home, Hill was on his own, and took the win for BRM with Ginther second. *(FF)*

A week later, Graham drove John Coombs's new Cooper T72 in the Formula 2 race at Crystal Palace, and in spite of serious problems with the car's dampers and loss of the rear anti-roll bar, he won his heat and came second in the final. This race was won by Jochen Rindt, demonstrating that he too was a force to be reckoned with.

Graham generally excelled in Formula 2, and in the London Trophy at Crystal Palace on Whit Monday 1964, he beat Clark to win the first heat, and was involved in a close fight with Alan Rees in the final. However the rear anti-roll bar of his Cooper T72 Cosworth came adrift, causing alarming understeer, and he was fortunate to finish second to the virtually unknown Jochen Rindt. *(FF)*

At Zandvoort for the Dutch Grand Prix, BRM fielded the P261 V8s as raced at Monaco. Hill joined Clark and Gurney on the front row, and the three raced each other off the grid to see who could claim the racing line though Tarzan hairpin. Clark grasped the inside line and took the advantage, pursued by the other two, and the rest of the field followed through. Clark was unstoppable, but Graham's engine began misfiring due to fuel vaporisation caused by the injection pump overheating. He came into the pits, where Tony Rudd threw cold water over the pump to cool it off, and the BRM rejoined the race, eventually finishing fourth.

Graham was back in the driving seat of one of Colonel Ronnie Hoare's Maranello Concession-aires Ferraris, this time a 3.3-litre 275LM/P, for the Nürburgring 1000km, with Innes Ireland as co-driver. This model surely ranks as a top contender in the 'best-looking racing car ever' stakes. Graham perceived events like this as good fun, where an efficient and enterprising privateer outfit was pitched against the works teams. With Ireland leading, Ferrari team manager Dragoni ventured to Col Ronnie Hoare that he should slow his boys down so as not to jeopardise a Ferrari result – the works cars were in the hands of Scar-fiotti/Vaccarella and Surtees/Bandini. Predictably, the Colonel invited the Italians to slow down themselves, or words to that effect. But on lap 29, Ireland ran out of fuel, and ran the mile or so back to the pit, exhausted. An official told Hill that he

Hill gives a thumbs-up to the Le Mans crowds (as Porsche's Huske von Hanstein makes for a handshake), having come second with Jo Bonnier in the 1964 24 Hours marathon. Their Maranello Concessionaires 4-litre Ferrari 330P completed 343 laps, five less than the winning works Ferrari 3.3-litre 275P of Guichet/Vaccarella, and seven more than the third-placed factory 330P of Surtees/Bandini. For the time being, Ford's challenge had been thwarted. *(LAT)*

could carry a can of fuel to the car – by hand – so that it could make it back to the pits, which he did, although in this case it was an unwieldy five-gallon drum.

Once the tanks had been properly replenished, he promptly rejoined the race. The official was in error though – refuelling outside the pits was not allowed – and the car was soon black-flagged. It was later discovered that a fuel tank had split, causing a substantial leak.

At Spa-Francorchamps for the Belgian Grand Prix, Hill had the choice of two BRMs, a brand new one with the old-type six-speed gearbox, and the Zandvoort car with a new gearbox. Gurney was on pole, with Hill and Brabham alongside on the front row. At flag-fall, Peter Arundell surged

through into the lead in the second Lotus 25, but was soon passed by Gurney, Clark, Hill and Surtees. As the race split up into several groups, inevitable on a high-speed slipstreaming circuit, a prominent feature was the dice for second place between Hill, Clark and McLaren. In this race, possibly more than any other, Gurney demonstrated his true potential and left everyone in his wake.

Although Clark could overtake Hill out of La Source hairpin, the BRM's greater power enabled Hill to retake the lead on several occasions. The Lotus began to overheat, forcing Clark to pit, dropping him back behind McLaren to fourth place. Then, with three laps to go, Gurney found he was running out of fuel. Unfortunately, the

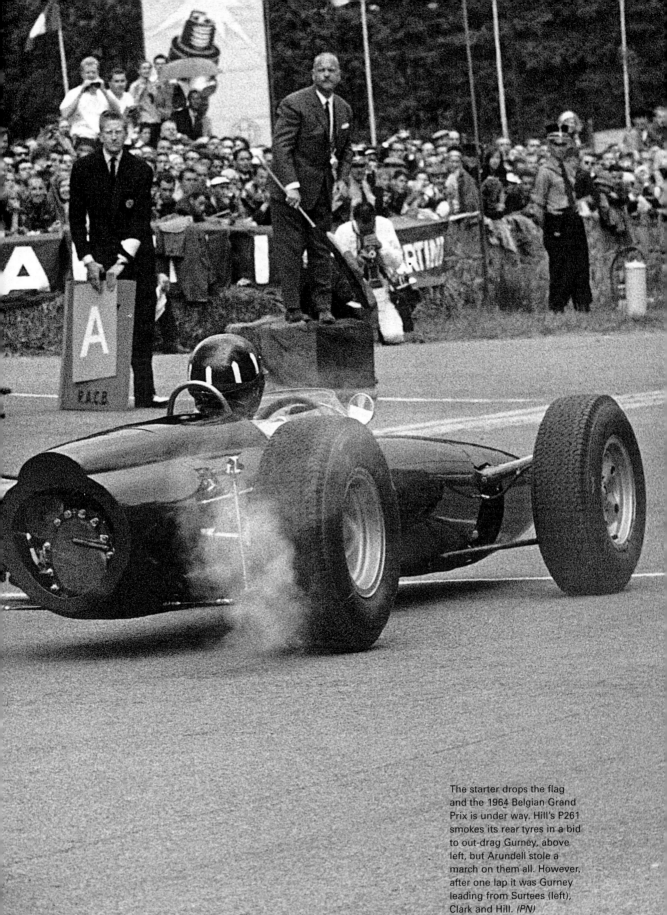

The starter drops the flag and the 1964 Belgian Grand Prix is under way. Hill's P261 smokes its rear tyres in a bid to out-drag Gurney, above left, but Arundell stole a march on them all. However, after one lap it was Gurney leading from Surtees (left), Clark and Hill. *(PN)*

Brabham pit had none to give him, so he rejoined the track, only to run dry on the far side of the circuit. This left Hill in the lead. But on the very last lap, he too ran out of fuel. As Hill stood fuming by the side of the track, McLaren went past with his Cooper's engine coughing and spluttering. He made it to the hairpin and the final run down to the line, freewheeling at some 10mph. And then came Clark, really motoring after his pit stop, and he pipped McLaren for the win by a car's length. Clark didn't realise what had happened – and in fact Ginther in the other BRM was mistakenly given the chequered flag first in the belief that he was actually Graham Hill, and then Clark too ran out of fuel at the same place as Gurney. As the pair were commiserating, the announcement came over the tannoy that Clark had won the race. Hill, meanwhile, had good reason to feel dejected. His car had an auxiliary fuel tank containing six gallons, which was not connected to the BRM's two main tanks, and at half distance he was given a signal from the pits saying 'fuel pump on.' Accordingly he flicked the switch to activate the pump that would then transfer the fuel into the main tanks at a rate of about a gallon a minute as the car sped round the circuit. However, it was discovered that the pump had failed after just two minutes. Frustratingly, one more minute's worth would have pumped another gallon over, and the race (and, theoretically, the 1964 World Championship) would have been in the bag.

## Le Mans Podium

The following weekend was the Le Mans 24 Hours, and Graham and Richie should have been driving an updated Rover-BRM gas-turbine car, but the engine suppliers were in difficulties over the heat exchanger, and it was a non-starter. However, Graham was brought into the Maranello Concessionaires' team to drive Col Ronnie Hoare's Ferrari 330P alongside his other regular partner Jo Bonnier, which gave him at least a realistic chance of victory. The car was dogged by a number of minor mechanical problems during the race, which meant replacing the throttle cable

and twice swapping the condenser, as well as overheating. All this contrived to drop them five laps behind the leading Ferrari of Guichet/Vaccarella as a result of their pit stops, but nevertheless they came second overall ahead of Surtees/Bandini in a similar P3. This was the first year of Ford's onslaught on the event, with a trio of Lola Ford 4.2-litre V8 GTs present, backed up by a pair of 4.7-litre Daytona Cobra coupés. While the Lola Fords retired – Phil Hill having set fastest lap – the fourth placed car was the Gurney/Bondurant Daytona Cobra.

The 50th French Grand Prix was staged at Rouen-les-Essarts, set in a wooded valley south-west of the Normandy city. The circuit consisted mainly of 6.54km of public roads, closed for the duration of the event, which wound down to La Source hairpin at the lowest point and up a series of fast open sweeps to La Scierie at the summit. The excuse for the change of venue was that it was the 70th anniversary of the first-ever motor race, from Paris to Rouen, in 1894. The engine of Hill's preferred 'old' car was over-revved before it even left the garage, so he took the new P261 that did not have the benefit of suspension set up for Rouen. All three BRM P261s – Ginther's included – used 1963-spec six-speed gearboxes, since the 1964 gearbox would not accommodate a low enough bottom gear for the Rouen hairpin. Graham was unhappy with the handling, especially on the fast downhill sweeps, and not prepared to commit as fully as his main rivals. He thus started the race from the third row, and at the end of the first lap lay sixth behind Phil Hill's Cooper. Graham then spun out of the hairpin and was down among the back markers, in a race dominated by Clark and Gurney. But amazingly, by lap 37 (out of 57), he had taken Brabham for second place, and with Peter Arundell in the works Lotus 25 in pursuit, made much use of kerbs to maintain momentum, showering the hapless Team Lotus driver with stones in the process. Graham thus finished second, just over a minute behind Gurney, in a drive of typical Hill resilience.

Just a week later, Hill and Bonnier were reunited to drive the Maranello Concessionaires

Ferrari 275LM in the Reims 12 Hours. The race started at midnight on the Saturday with a flood-lit Le Mans-type start, and finished at midday on the Sunday. Although the pit area was brilliantly lit, the majority of the circuit was in darkness. This meant that drivers had to go flat-out into the pitch-dark night from the illuminated pit area, with mirrors full of headlights. Hill's main opposition came from Surtees's works Ferrari 275LM and Ginther in the new Lola Ford GT. They were travelling at speeds of up to 180mph along the straight roads through the cornfields of the Champagne region. However, some of the slower cars were not even reaching a maximum speed that equalled the average 130mph being logged by the fastest works cars. Eventually the Lola Ford went out, leaving Hill/Bonnier to duel with Surtees/Bandini. The result turned on the final pit stops. With two hours to go, Hill's car was refuelled and got out again, with Bonnier at the wheel, in 1min 6.0seconds. Surtees had meanwhile gone by, but his pit stop took twice as long because the works car's brake pads needed changing as well. Surtees then preceded to shave some four seconds a lap off Bonnier's 100-second lead, only to burst a tyre, forcing another pit stop. Hill and Bonnier thus won a notable endurance race.

The supporting race at this event was a 37-lap Formula 2 race, with several of the top names like Brabham and Clark present, all 1-litre Cosworth SCA-powered. Having just finished the high-speed 12-hour thrash, Graham was down to drive John Coombs's Brabham BT10 in the F2 slipstreaming derby, but retired. *Motor Sport*'s Denis Jenkinson described the wheel-to-wheel dicing as 'bloody stupid', and a serious accident befell Team Lotus driver Peter Arundell that effectively ended his top-line racing career.

In the background, Graham's Speedwell tuning company continued to flourish. Better known for its comprehensive conversions for BMC models that could enable a Riley Elf to do 110mph, the most lucrative kit they sold was for the regular 850cc Mini. This included the Speedwell alloy cylinder head – for which patterns had to be made in Italy – twin SU, Amal or Weber carburettors,

and a twin-pipe exhaust system with Supertone silencer. Two stages of tune were available, GT or Clubman, the latter incorporating bigger valves, improved combustion chambers and a higher compression ratio. Thus equipped, a standard Mini was elevated above Cooper standards. The other thrust of Speedwell activities was the EMPI Camber Compensator for VW Beetles, which looked like a transverse leaf spring and was aimed at maintaining wheel contact with the road during cornering.

Another event to move from its traditional site was the British Grand Prix, staged at Brands Hatch instead of Silverstone, and sponsored by the *Daily Mirror*. The event was also billed as the European Grand Prix, and as such was organised by the RAC, and run for the first time on the 'long' circuit. This meant that hardly any of the star drivers had experienced the more dramatic sections that included Dingle Dell dip. BRM fielded three cars for Hill and Ginther, the Englishman preferring his earlier '64 car, and all three fitted with earlier type gearboxes. The four-wheel drive BRM that Richard Attwood was debuting had also arrived, hot from testing at Snetterton. This was a hybrid, constructed under Tony Rudd's direction from a P57 spaceframe and the Ferguson P99 driveline. The BRM engine and transmission were rotated by 360 degrees to suit, and the driving position canted over to accommodate the transmission shaft. Drivers were spurred on during Thursday morning's practice by the incentive of 100 bottles of champagne, finally won by Dan Gurney. Friday's gritty practice session established a grid order that placed Clark a mere 0.2sec ahead of Hill, with Gurney a tenth slower to make up the front row. It was clear that the battle would be between Hill, Clark, Brabham, Gurney and Surtees. But Ginther was back on row six and, with only limited practice time, Attwood had not managed to qualify the four-wheel drive car. At the start, Clark took the lead with Gurney and Hill behind, and when the Californian dropped out with ignition trouble, it developed into a two-horse race, with Hill harassing Clark for much of the race. By two-thirds distance,

Surtees's third-place Ferrari was the entire length of the Brands short circuit behind them, and the only driver not to be lapped. The margin between the Lotus and BRM was 2.8sec after two-and-a-quarter-hours' racing.

Team Lotus chief mechanic Jim Endruweit snapped Hill looking grim after he'd returned to the pits after the British Grand Prix, having failed to catch Clark by just three seconds. The picture has an illicit quality, because Chapman would not have been at all happy that his second-in-command was taking photographs. *(JE)*

The way we were. A typical scene in the Brands Hatch paddock, spectators (close enough to touch the cars) watch Graham take the P261 out of the assembly area at the 1964 British Grand Prix meeting. *(FF)*

In the early stages of the 1964 British Grand Prix, Clark and Hill circulated together at the front of the field, but after getting baulked as they lapped slower cars, Graham gradually fell back, and Jimmy went on to win. *(FF)*

Tony Rudd vividly remembers this classic Hill-Clark contest:

> At Brands Hatch in '64, they were fairly evenly matched in practice, and Jimmy realised he was going to have a job on with Graham. And Graham was pounding around in his fashion, getting closer and closer, and then the oil went down and the track became very slippery, and Graham was all over him, but wouldn't pass him. When the race was over, I said, 'What was wrong?' He said, 'Nothing. When the oil was down, I was all over him, but when the oil dried up, we were evenly matched. I might have had the edge on him in one or two places, and he had the edge on me in one or two places.' I asked him, 'Why the hell didn't you try and take him?' He said, 'I don't know'. But I knew it was because nothing had happened to provoke him. If something had happened to get his blood up, then he would have gone.

In his book *All But My Life*, written in 1963, Stirling Moss wrote tellingly:

> Graham is in my view the ultimate mechanic-driver. Perhaps he is the archetype of the driver of the future; precise, smooth, knowing. Given the equipment, he'll go

really quickly, he'll stay out of trouble and, if it's possible, he'll keep the machine out of trouble. But if your car is faster than Graham's, you'll have a fair chance of beating him. He is not the type to risk blowing up an engine or going off the road to catch you, 9 times out of 10.

## Crowded Calendar

In practice for the German Grand Prix, both Ginther's and Hill's cars over-revved because of missed gearshifts, possibly due to flexing in the chassis, which put the gearbox selectors out of synch with the gear lever. The unfortunate BRM mechanics were thus kept busy with the vain quest to change two engines between sessions. In the race, it was Surtees's turn to dominate, with a slender margin at first over Clark, Gurney and Hill. Then Clark's engine burned a valve, and Gurney's began to overheat, and although Hill's engine misfired throughout the second half of the race, he managed to finish a distant second to Surtees.

Between the German and Austrian Grands Prix, Graham suffered a slight neck injury due to whiplash sustained in a crash while testing at Snetterton. The team had been experimenting with softer damper settings. During this exercise Hill's BRM veered abruptly into the bank on the inside of the long Coram right-hander. It was then pitched back across the track into the bank on the outside of the circuit prior to Russell – in those days much more of a high-speed kink than the laboured affair that it is today. Graham was taken to the Norfolk & Norwich hospital where an X-ray revealed a small bone was chipped in his neck. Tony Rudd remembers that Hill had turned his mirrors so that he could watch the rear suspension working. 'He ended up in hospital because he was too busy watching the suspension going up and down. The surgeon said, "Mr Hill, when did you last break your neck," and he thought it was a hell of a joke.' He acquired an inflatable rubber collar that he wore for about six months when racing.

That the next event was the inaugural Austrian Grand Prix, staged at Zeltweg on the military airfield, was unfortunate, since the surface was in ageing corrugated concrete, making serious demands on Graham's reserves of tenacity, not to mention occasioning the consumption of copious amounts of painkillers. He had to drive the corners with one hand holding his head and the other gripping the steering wheel. Astonishingly, he set fastest lap in practice in spite of this, but was still obliged to dose himself with codeine for the race. After a poor start with excessive wheel-spin, Graham's car lasted only six laps before failing with the distributor drive broken. Many others retired, including Clark, with broken suspension or transmission, caused by the poor track surface. Despite this, Graham was still leading the championship, with 32 points to Clark's 30.

The 1964 Tourist Trophy was run at Goodwood for sports and sports prototypes in two classes, over 1600cc and over 2000cc, attracting entries as diverse as those seen at the recent Guards Trophy at Brands Hatch. These included Elva BMWs for Trevor Taylor, Tony Lanfranchi and Frank Gardner, Clark's Lotus 30, McLaren's Cooper Oldsmobile, plus five AC Cobras, three E-types, one Aston DB4GT, and four Ferrari 250 GTOs. Graham was in the Maranello 330P once again. McLaren led initially but was soon out, giving Clark the lead from Hulme's Brabham, Taylor and Hill. In a flurry of pit stop activity, the big Lotus was under-fuelled, and Clark lost the lead when he had to pit again for a splash-and-dash, much to Chapman's fury. Graham was now in the lead by a minute, and the small crowd was treated to the spectacle of Clark at his best, hurling the recalcitrant beast through Goodwood's high-speed curves. Suspension trouble ended the Scot's endeavours, and Hill cruised leisurely home, averaging 97.13mph, followed by David Piper's Ferrari 275LM and a trio of Shelby Daytona Cobras.

Both the BRM and Honda teams went to Monza early to test new cars, or in BRM's case, new engines, the V8 having been redesigned. Tony Rudd described the routine:

> We used to have a sandwich lunch, Richie, Graham and I, and we would have a

Graham drove the Maranello Concessionaires Ferrari 330P to fourth place in the 1964 Guards International Trophy at Brands Hatch, although the car was a handful around the corners. Opposition included Indy winner A.J. Foyt, Brabham and Hulme, while the outright winner was McLaren in the Cooper Oldsmobile. *(FF)*

The line up for the 29th Tourist Trophy at Goodwood on 29 August 1964 had McLaren on pole in his Cooper Oldsmobile, Clark in the Lotus 30, and Hill in the Ferrari 330P. Initially McLaren led from Clark and Hulme's Repco-Brabham BT8, but when the leader retired, Hill moved up and began to press Clark. The Lotus was under-fuelled at its pit-stop however, and Hill gained a lead he was not to lose. *(FF)*

Rubbernecking. Graham suffered a slight neck injury due to whiplash sustained in a testing accident at Snetterton, and he was obliged to wear an inflatable rubber collar for about six months when racing. *(PN)*

In 1964, Graham would have been more familiar with the cockpit of a BRM P261 or Ferrari 330P, so he regards the controls of the Ford GT40 prototype pensively. *(FMC)*

Best of friends. Formula 1 drivers were inclined to spend more time in each other's company in the 1960s. Here, Hill shares a joke with Jimmy Clark and Mike Spence. *(FMC)*

session and go on talking. I remember discussing the new exhaust system. Then we measured it and crossed the pipes over underneath the sump – which we could do on the test bed – and it did work. Richie said, 'why can't you turn the heads the other way round and cross the exhaust pipes over. You don't need to cross the inlet channels over, so have them on the outside,' and from then on, it was a crusade. The first time we ran them was at Monza in '64 and that was when it was getting tight for the '64 championship. There was a hell of a scramble to get two engines there; the second one went out in the boot of my car. When Graham saw the racing car, he was interested, but what I didn't tell him was that Weslake had said that downdraught ports were bad for turbulence and wouldn't give any power. I left him to find out for himself. He was wearing his neck brace after the Snetterton

Graham drove the Maranello Concessionaires Ferrari 330P to victory in the 1964 TT at Goodwood, ahead of David Piper's Ferrari 275LM and Dan Gurney's AC Cobra. A regular feature of Hill's cars was now the improvised fresh air ducting visible by the windscreen. *(C)*

Brabhams were the cars to beat in Formula 2, and in the Oulton Park Gold Cup, run for F2 cars in 1964, Jack Brabham was fastest in practice with Hill second quickest in John Coombs's Brabham BT10 Cosworth. Clark's Lotus 32 led initially from Hulme, Hill and Brabham, but on lap seven, Hill's car chewed up a driveshaft doughnut. It was changed in the pits, but he later retired with engine failure. *(PN)*

accident, and he was very worried because a high-revving engine like ours was at a loss at altitude, compared with thumpers like the Climax. Graham was pretty tense about that race, but we were quite relaxed.

The Italian Grand Prix was a debacle for Hill, because although he qualified third fastest, and was thus on the front row, the clutch burned out on the grid. He raised his arm aloft, and fortunately all the other cars missed him. Amid official mayhem the BRM was pushed to the pits, and then to make matters worse, Surtees's win made him a third contender for the world title with 28 points.

Graham posted a further two retirements, one in the Oulton Park Gold Cup with engine failure in the F2 Brabham BT10, and then at Snetterton in the Autosport 3 Hours because of falling oil pressure in the Ferrari 275LM. He drove Coombs's Brabham again at Montlhéry, placing ninth in the F2 Grand Prix de l'Ile de France. Prior to the US Grand Prix, BRM signed Jackie Stewart for the following season, while Richie Ginther was snapped up by the nascent Honda team.

At Watkins Glen, a third BRM was available for US superstar A.J. Foyt, but he declined to race it. With a win and a second place at the last two US Grands Prix, Graham was becoming an expert at

Watkins Glen. His practice times placed him on the second row with Gurney, with Clark and Surtees on the front row. Clark led until lap 44, when his engine began misfiring, and Graham took the lead, with Surtees and Gurney battling it out behind him. The Ferrari spun off at one point, and then Gurney's engine packed up, leaving Graham the clear winner, with just Surtees on the same lap.

In order to win the championship, Graham had to win the last race – the Mexican Grand Prix. Taking into account his best six results, he had 39 points, with Surtees on 34 and Clark stuck on 30. So the outcome of the title race hung on the results in Mexico, which meant that there was a huge amount of pressure on the three main protagonists. According to Tony Rudd:

> Sir Alfred used to have a monthly meeting with Graham and me, and at the meeting before we went to Mexico, Sir Alfred said, 'what do you think the chances are? I think you ought to make a superhuman effort, and I am going to make sure you do. I am going to give you a £5,000 bonus to win the championship,' and in those days my salary wasn't £5,000, so it certainly made me interested. Graham heard it and sensed the mood, and he said to Sir Alfred, 'I am sure he will', which was very nice. He said something which implied he would do the same, so we all went to Mexico pretty gung-ho on that.

Graham had two cars to choose from – a new chassis with altered front suspension geometry and powered by the Watkins Glen engine – plus the old car as a standby. Richie's car was his regular chassis. Practice was punctuated by the failure of the electric timing system, and the appearance on the track of a large dog. Meanwhile, Graham was finding it difficult to match the times of Clark and Gurney and the two Ferraris of Surtees and Bandini. He tried altering tyre pressures, and had to settle for sixth fastest, placing him on the third row alongside Mike Spence in the second works Lotus. He was 2.5sec slower than Clark and 1.1sec slower than Surtees. It didn't look too good, although a brand new engine had arrived from England and this was fitted after practice. Any realistic chance that Graham had seemed to evaporate on the starting grid, as Tony Rudd recalled:

> The strap of his goggles broke, and he was re-adjusting his spare goggles when the flag fell. He made a very bad start, that's why he was so far back, and all Sir Alfred's minions could say was, 'we surely pay him enough to have a spare pair of goggles.'

Surtees had also made a bad getaway, but Clark meanwhile was extending his lead with each successive lap. It was the kind of challenge that Hill responded to, and by lap eight he had tigered his way up to third. All was looking hopeful until lap 28, when Bandini began to challenge him on successive laps at the hairpin, in spite of Graham's waved fist. On lap 30 the Italian's front wheel caught the BRM's exhaust and spun both cars, allowing Surtees through to third. And while Bandini was able to continue, Hill had to pit to get the ends of the exhaust pipes cut off to free the apertures that had got burred over against the barrier. He was obliged to pit again to have a throttle return spring replaced, which had been knocked awry in the collision, and he was thus demoted to 11th place, two laps down. While this was going on, Clark was noticing a trail of oil around the hairpin, and by altering his line he was able to deduce over two or three laps that it was actually coming from his own Climax engine. An oil line had split, and as he backed off, Gurney took the lead. But if Clark could still limp home ahead of Surtees, there was still a mathematical possibility of Hill taking the title. It was not to be, as the Lotus's engine seized solid on the last lap. Team orders then came into play at Ferrari, and Bandini was told to drop back to let Surtees through to second place, and the ex-motorcycle world champion duly added the drivers' crown to his achievements. Graham was not aware of any of these dramas, except that Clark had retired. Only as he returned to the pits after the slowing-down lap could he tell from the BRM team's expressions that he had not won the title. Tony Rudd recalled the disappointment:

Bandini hit Graham's exhaust pipes which projected behind the tail, and folded them flat. The mechanics put a jack handle in them and bent them out, but in the process they hit the throttle which lay over the top of the engine in that area, and he couldn't carry on. He probably would have finished third, ahead of Surtees, so he was pretty disappointed. I am sure we had valid grounds for protest. It was really dirty driving and we should have known Bandini could do that. But he didn't do it on purpose, because he said afterwards – he was very nearly in tears – that BRM had always been very good to him. Graham took that very philosophically. We were asked if we were going to make a protest, but I said no, because it wouldn't make any difference to the championship. All we could have done was eliminate Bandini, not Surtees. As we went back to the hotel Graham said 'you're quite right, it's not the way to go'. And at the prize-giving party he was the life and soul of the party.

Hill appeared philosophical, and we can gauge his humour – pragmatic, light-hearted, but suitably barbed – by the fact that he later sent Bandini a book on driving techniques. The World Championship was not quite the be-all and end-all back then that it became in the commercially governed 1990s and, in any case, drivers were busy in other avenues of the sport.

# Chapter 4
# Young Cub, Old Lion

THOSE who could, travelled to the southern hemisphere during the winter lay-off, with the Springbok series of races held in South Africa, the Tasman series in Australasia and, some years later, the Temporada and Torneio in South America. Graham ended the 1964 season with a win in the first heat – and first on aggregate – in the non-championship Rand Grand Prix at Kyalami on 12 December, driving the Willment Brabham BT11 powered by a BRM V8 engine. This event marked Jackie Stewart's Formula 1 debut, driving a Team Lotus type 33 to victory in the second heat, reaching 17th overall. It wouldn't be long before he represented a real threat to the likes of Hill and Clark, who would effectively become the 'old guard'.

Still in South Africa, the first round of the 1965 F1 World Championship was held at East London on 1 January. BRM sent three cars, Graham's being the same one he used at Mexico, while new recruit Jackie Stewart had a brand new one, and the spare was an old chassis. Graham tried Goodyear tyres first, then swapped to Dunlop R6 yellow spots, which proved to be good for a second-a-lap over a 90-second lap. This was the first time a back-to-back evaluation had been carried out. But a camshaft sheared in the brand new engine and curtailed Hill's first practice session. Eventually, Graham was on the second row alongside Spence's Lotus, with Clark, Surtees and Brabham ahead. Stewart was just under two seconds slower, back on row five. But the result turned out to bear a strong resemblance to the balance of power that had held sway at the end of the preceding season. Clark drove an exemplary race and was the clear winner, with Graham third

In the South African Grand Prix staged at East London on New Year's Day 1965, Hill came third in the BRM P261. He tried hard in the early stages of the race to keep pace with Brabham, but they couldn't catch the Lotuses of Clark and Spence, nor Surtees's Ferrari V8. *(FF)*

behind Surtees, while Stewart was an excellent sixth.

Jackie Stewart revealed:

I learned a great deal from Graham. As a young driver, I had chosen to drive for BRM, although I had been offered a drive by Colin Chapman in the Lotus team, which was a very good and tempting offer, because the Lotus 33 was unquestionably the best and fastest car. But I didn't want to drive in the same team as Jim Clark. First of all, I saw how good he was, and secondly, his teammates had historically enjoyed little or no success, and little or no growth in their career curves. And they were good racing drivers, whether you're speaking of Peter Arundell or Trevor Taylor for example, or Mike Spence later on.

Pupil and master. Jackie Stewart joined BRM rather than Lotus in 1965, mainly because he thought he could learn more from Hill than Jim Clark, who he saw as a natural driver, whereas Hill's attitude to racing was deeply analytical and methodical. *(LAT)*

They were just never in the same class as Jimmy, because Colin and Jim Clark worked hand-in-glove, just beautifully together. When Jimmy was testing he would go faster or slower depending on what Colin did to the car. Jimmy had this unique relationship with Colin, and Colin will go down in history as the greatest designer of racing cars ever, he was so innovative. Jimmy, I think, was also the best racing driver of his time and the two together were unbeatable.

I had driven the latest Lotus 33 at the Rand Grand Prix when Jimmy had slipped a disc throwing snowballs in Cortina at the launch of the Ford Cortina. So I knew how good the car was. It was absolutely incredible, I mean I had got pole position in my first ever Formula 1 race. Graham Hill, Jack Brabham and Frank Gardner and all the other top drivers were in the race, but the doughnut in the Lotus driveshaft broke. Typically, Colin had made something that was not strong enough, and there was metal fatigue in the driveshaft, which was chromium plated, which didn't help. But the race was in two heats, and I started on the back row in last position for the second one, and I won the race, because the car was so good it was unbelievable. But by that race I had decided not to drive for Team Lotus but to go to BRM. And that was because it was a strong, reliable team that did a lot of testing, and it had Graham Hill on board. He seemed to me a journeyman racing driver who I could learn from. Jimmy and I had already become friends; we shared an apartment in London, and I had learned to understand Jimmy and his idiosyncrasies in the way he went about his business. I don't think there was a lot to learn from Jimmy, in the sense that he was such a natural driver that it was just second nature for him to drive a racing car. He didn't have to psychoanalyse himself as to why he did

something in a particular way, whereas Graham did, and therefore it was educational to work with somebody who was that bothered and committed.

Surtees's view was:

I don't think Graham was exceptional at anything, but he was a damn good performer across the line. He'd pedal his way along pretty well in the wet, but he wouldn't be the one to have the biggest go and show the most aggression, like Brabham and perhaps Gurney. But on the other hand, Jim Clark didn't either, so he wasn't a racer as such. He was a very solid performer who could be relied upon.

It wasn't his natural tendency to be an aggressive, forceful driver. He was very competent, and by the time I came in, he was very experienced and one of the establishment. One of the good things about Graham, he wasn't one of those establishment people who took a dislike to this new boy coming in and actually being able to compete.

Hill, the inveterate mechanical meddler, didn't always obtain Tony Rudd's approval for his tinkering, especially after Stewart came on board. Tony said:

There were one or two things Graham didn't tell me about. When Stewart came on the scene, he would ask his mechanics to change the suspension without talking to me about it. And I complained and said, 'if you stop telling me your reasons for making changes, I will stop learning,' and he said, 'No, no, they're just routine things.' But it was quite noticeable, and after the Tasman series in '65 he realised that Stewart was as good as he was. Of course he wasn't getting any younger either.

Graham's racing during the first three months of 1965 was all confined to New Zealand, Tasmania and Australia, driving the Scuderia Veloce 2.5-litre Climax-powered Brabham BT3. He won the New Zealand Grand Prix at Pukekohe

Having won the 1965 New Zealand Grand Prix at Pukekohe on 9 January in the 2.5-litre Scuderia Veloce Brabham BT3 Climax, Hill went on to win the *Launceston Examiner* race at Longford and place fourth in the Australian GP at Longford, Tasmania. He takes a tight line here at Sandown Park during the International Cup race. *(PN)*

and the *Launceston Examiner* Race at Longford, Tasmania. In Australia he was fifth with the Brabham at Warwick Farm, in a race won by Clark's similarly-powered F2 Lotus 32B. Hill had looked set to win until steering problems caused him to ease off. Back at Longford for the Australian Grand Prix on 1 March, Graham was fourth, ahead of Clark but behind McLaren, Brabham and Phil Hill in a Cooper.

The first European race for Formula 1 cars was the *Daily Mail* sponsored event that became known as the Race of Champions. Held on the Brands Hatch long circuit, a 20-strong grid of F1 cars was assembled. There were two 40-lap heats, with the finishing order of heat one determining the grid order for heat two. BRM sent three P261s for Hill and Stewart, and Hill separated the works Lotuses of Clark and Spence on the front row for the first heat. There was not a lot that the BRMs could do against the works Lotuses and Brabhams, and Hill came fifth and Stewart seventh in the earlier heat. In the second heat a water pipe split inside Hill's BRM tub and he retired with consequent overheating, while Stewart came fourth. Clark wrote off his Lotus 33 on the earth bank behind the pits while dicing with Gurney, but Spence took the honours overall, with Stewart second, in only his second meeting with the BRM team.

Graham tried John Coombs's formidable Group 7 McLaren Elva Oldsmobile at a washed out Silverstone meeting, and then drove John Mecom's Ferrari 330P in the Sebring 12 Hours, partnered by Pedro Rodriguez, but was sidelined with clutch failure. The race was won by the Chaparral of Hall/Sharp, followed by the new Ford GT, precursor of the GT40, driven by McLaren/Miles.

The 25th Pau Grand Prix was staged for Formula 2 cars, and Graham drove the Brabham BT16 with its BRM-built 1-litre engine. BRM were in full production mode with the F2 engine, although they were initially dogged by failures of their OPUS ignition systems, and six other cars including Stewart's Tyrrell Cooper were using them. Race day was wet, and Clark just drove off into the distance in the Lotus 35, while Graham among others was involved in Frank Gardner's spin at the first corner. Although he recovered enough to regain third place behind Stewart, the Brabham's final drive seized suddenly, ending his race.

He was at the wheel of a Porsche again for the 49th Targa Florio, teamed with Bonnier in a flat-eight powered, fibreglass-bodied 904 coupé. Bonnier was delayed by the throttle cable sticking, so Hill had his work cut out to catch up on the tortuous mountain roads, but this he did, and they finished fourth, just nine minutes behind the winning Ferrari 275P of Vaccarella/Bandini after seven hours of racing. Porsches filled the results sheet from second to fifth place.

Porsche had three 904 coupés running in the 1965 Targa Florio, and Hill and Bonnier renewed their partnership in this flat-eight powered model. It had been intended that they would handle the experimental 904/8 Kanguruh Spyder, (visible to the right), but they rejected it after a trial run, and it was driven to second place by Davis/Mitter instead. Hill/Bonnier finished fourth overall in their 904 coupé. *(P)*

Tyre choice was the main issue at Silverstone for the International Trophy meeting on 15 May, and both BRMs were fastest in practice, shod with Dunlop R6 rubber. Thus, all but Lotus (on R7s) followed suit, and Hill and Stewart diced with Brabham and Surtees until valve gear problems struck Graham's car. Stewart took the lead from Surtees's V8 Ferrari, and held it till the end, notching up his first F1 victory. The BRMs were running new, smaller combustion chambers that allowed them to rev to 11,500rpm.

# Monaco Hat-trick

The 1965 Monaco Grand Prix was the zenith of Graham Hill's racing career. Having won at Monaco the previous two seasons, he was the favourite. As usual, three cars were available for Hill and Stewart, all of the latest type with central exhaust systems. Conditions were good, and lap times were well down on the previous year. After two practice sessions when Hill and Brabham traded fastest laps, Stewart astonished everyone with a potential pole time. But in Saturday's final qualifying, Hill knocked a couple of seconds off this time, with Brabham equally quick. It was obvious that Hill and Brabham had their cars set up absolutely right for the circuit, better traction allowing them full commitment in corners. With scarcely any Armco, the unyielding urban obstacles presented a daunting threat to anyone going off-line.

Hill preferred his cars to be set up with a firm ride on a dry track, and not too much roll. He liked them to be capable of being provoked into a wild tail slide, or oversteer whenever he felt like it. This explained why he took bends like the Gasworks hairpin in a full-opposite lock slide. The variables that allowed the car to be set up in this way included damper (shock-absorber) settings, tyre pressures, spring characteristics, anti-roll bar thicknesses, camber angles and toe-in settings. Dan Gurney liked his cars set up in a similar manner. On a wet track, such a set-up counted for naught, however, since the violent application of the throttle broke the back end away, causing loss of adhesion and drastically increased lap times. The contrast in approach with Clark was marked, as Jackie Stewart describes:

> Graham liked his cars set up very firm, very hard. He wasn't a driver that liked compliance in a car, and everything was rock solid, the shock absorbers and the springs were much stiffer than most drivers would ever have used. I don't think Colin Chapman would ever have allowed a car to be that tight. And yet, when he drove for Colin, many times he was every bit as fast, if not faster than Jim. He

bullied the car, whereas Jimmy felt a car and went with the car. And I always went the same way – I wanted to allow the car to have its head and to breathe a little bit. Graham was much more under control, batten-it-down type of thing. And that was the way he drove the car, any car – any dynamic movement, he avoided it. The stiffer it was, the better it was. And that was true of any car that he drove that I was involved with.

So it was that the two-by-two grid for Monaco had Hill and Brabham at the front, with Stewart and Bandini on the second row and, right at the back, the two Honda V12s of Bucknum and Ginther. No Jim Clark though, because he and Colin Chapman were over in the States in their successful bid to conquer the Brickyard and win the Indy 500. Although race day in Monte Carlo was dull and overcast, atmospheric conditions were good for racing. Straight away the BRM duo dominated proceedings, Stewart slipstreaming Hill, with the Ferraris of Bandini (V12) and Surtees (V8) in pursuit. Then on lap 20 it all went awry. Graham exited the tunnel at full bore and, approaching the chicane at 120mph, found Bob Anderson's stricken Brabham in his way, and was obliged to take to the escape road. He came to a standstill, accompanied by lavish skid marks, leapt out and pushed the BRM back to the circuit before rejoining the race, losing about 35 seconds. Stewart, meanwhile, spun out of the lead he had inherited, and rejoined ahead of Hill, the irate BRM drivers now lying fourth and fifth. Hill was sufficiently wound up for there to be no mistaking his purpose, and Stewart quickly moved aside. By lap 53, Surtees too was unable to withstand the pressure, and Hill was up to second. It was now Bandini's turn to feel the heat, and Hill sized him up at the Gasworks hairpin, a potential passing place under braking. He overtook Bandini at the same place as he did Surtees, on the short straight after Casino Square going down the hill towards Mirabeau, one of his favourite passing places. The Ferrari tried in vain to keep up with him, but it was to be Graham's day, and he pulled away

It took an incident like this to really get Hill fired up. He was forced to take the escape road at Monaco's harbour chicane when the line was blocked by Anderson's ailing Brabham – note the skid marks – and he had to push his BRM back onto the circuit. He drove the rest of the race at a furious pace, licking the two Ferraris on his way to victory and shattering the lap record in the process. (PN)

remorselessly from the red cars, breaking the lap record several times in the process. He was even close to lapping his teammate, who took third place as Surtees ran out of fuel on the last lap. Hill was the star, having completed a magnificent hat-trick, with three wins at Monte Carlo in three consecutive years. The 100-lap race had lasted 2hrs 37min 39.6sec, and the BRMs had functioned perfectly, despite being driven to their limits. Post-race celebrations for Graham included the prize-giving dinner at the Hotel de Paris, and afterwards at the Tip-Top bar, which was a popular watering hole with the British contingent.

Tony Rudd thought that this was one of Hill's most characteristic performances:

> Graham would have to be provoked to do really well, and the form that he showed in Monte Carlo in 1965, Jimmy could not have lived with that. When Graham's blood was up, he could produce more than you thought he could, and the next lap he would do it again even better, he was quite remarkable. And at other times he would be quite stupid.

But Rudd recalls that it took an exceptional incident to get Graham fired up:

> At Silverstone 1960, he stalled on the line, for instance. And Monaco '65, he really drove! People say you can't pass at Monte Carlo, but Graham passed Surtees, and afterwards they were so polite to each other! There was a bit of needle between Graham and Surtees, and I think Graham felt obligated to confront Surtees, come what may. It was temperament; they were opposites.

Surtees himself said:

> We didn't have a big social relationship at all. I often sat at GPDA meetings with him, and he'd doze off and wake up when it came to a vote, and Jackie Stewart would tell him what he should vote for. I don't think anyone had any animosity for Graham. They thought perhaps he was a little wavy in things he did off the track, but generally on the track he was at his steadiest.

Looking pleased after finishing second on aggregate behind Clark's Lotus, Graham shows off John Coombs's F2 Brabham BT16 BRM after the London Trophy race at Crystal Palace in 1965. *(FMC)*

According to Rudd, Graham was unlikely to react if deliberately provoked:

That wouldn't work, circumstances had to happen. So if you fed him the information and he was cross with something he would get fired up. I warned the [BRM] drivers to keep clear of each other, because the last thing I wanted was one of them running into the other. And of course one time Stewart sat on his tail when they'd got a clear run and had got away. And he just sat on his tail, and once or twice when he went by the pit Graham signalled to me, because he thought Stewart was too close. But Stewart wouldn't fall back, and of course the inevitable happened because he hadn't developed his own braking point and shut off points. So when Graham got clear of him, he was in trouble, and he hit the kerb and broke a chunk out of the wheel rim. But the tyre didn't deflate so he kept going.

There was no way you could provoke Graham. If that were possible, I would have done. But circumstances had to happen. If it was a clear cut race he thought he could win, he went out to win it. It was the way he was made.

Back in the UK, Graham participated in the London Trophy, an F2 race at Crystal Palace, placing second in both heats and thus second on aggregate, driving the now familiar Brabham BT16 BRM. A week later came the Belgian Grand Prix at Spa, and in practice Graham was some two seconds faster than Jim Clark, lapping at a shade under 140mph in a car whose maximum speed was 165mph; the bottom-gear hairpin at La Source was taken at 40mph, so the curves out on the circuit were extremely fast and daunting places. Graham had given the newcomer Stewart a conducted tour of the circuit in a VW Beetle, so Stewart caused a few raised eyebrows by lapping in under four minutes, ending up on the front row of the grid with Clark and pole-man Hill. Already he was being described as a 'natural high-speed driver'. As rain started to fall just prior to the race, Graham elected to go in the spare BRM. The plan to shut the door on Clark did not come off, although Graham held the lead through the spray until they reached the Masta straight. Clark got by, and built up a substantial lead; neither Stewart nor Hill could hold him on the slippery surface. Hill's superb set-up that enabled him to dominate practice let him down completely, since the conditions dictated a much softer set-up – 'like driving on ice' was how he described it. Jim Clark liked the much softer set-up that typified the Lotus 25 and 33, and this helped him to romp away with the race, lapping the struggling Hill on lap 18. An incredible drive by Stewart placed him second, half-a-minute behind his fellow Scot, and the only other driver not to be lapped.

Jim Clark's victory in the French Grand Prix at Clermont-Ferrand put him firmly in the lead for the World Championship, while Jackie's second and Graham's fifth meant that the BRM duo tied for second in the title race. During practice, Graham's chances were compromised by an accident on a tight series of bends where there was no run off or any chance of applying the brakes or ignition cut-off. He strained his neck once again, but the car was repaired for the race. Tony Rudd remembered:

> He was quite good at Clermont-Ferrand. But he went off when stones got in the throttle and jammed it. He damaged the front of the car and, as a consequence, he didn't make a very good start. He was well down the back of the grid, and he was saying it was a change being back down there, 'you meet a nicer class of person here,' he said. He was making light of it, but it was slightly forced humour, one might say.

Hill completed the whole race without the use of his clutch, due to a total loss of fluid.

Hill and Stewart were teamed up again for another crack at the 1965 Le Mans 24 Hours in the Rover-BRM gas-turbine, entered by the Owen Racing Organisation. This was the year that the giants Ford and Ferrari clashed head to head, with no fewer than 11 varying models from each camp ranged against one another. Just five Ferraris survived and one Ford – and that a Shelby Cobra (Sears/Thompson), while the Rover-BRM soldiered on with a degree of overheating, due to damaged compressor vanes, to finish 10th overall, to a tremendous ovation from the spectating crowds. It was the highest-placed British car, having covered 2,370 miles averaging 13.52mpg. Apart from the damaged compressor, it was found to be in virtually perfect condition.

Jackie Stewart recalled:

> In the early laps Graham had gone wide at Mulsanne corner, and it swallowed some sand which affected the blades of the turbine. So from that point on we had to keep the temperatures and the revs down, and that lasted for the whole race unfortunately! We were passed something like every three laps by Masten Gregory and Jochen Rindt, who were driving the winning LM Ferrari. They lapped us many times, which was very annoying as we were old pals.

Jim Clark was fastest in practice for the British Grand Prix at Silverstone, with Graham second fastest and Stewart and Ginther in his Honda V12 tying for the remaining front-row grid positions. A third BRM was built to replace the one Hill crashed in France, basically built up around his 1964 Monaco-winning chassis with the latest running gear. Race day was dull and overcast, and Ginther had the lead for half the first lap, but he was soon passed by the determined Clark, with Hill and Surtees following through a lap later. With 50 laps gone, Clark's Lotus began to misfire due to an oil leak, and Hill, half a lap behind, started to close up on him. Frantic pit signals to both drivers told them of their rival's performance. The Lotus was seriously short of oil, and Jim was coasting around corners and using the power just on the straight so as not to seize the engine. On the last lap, Hill had Clark in his sights, but the Scot had matters in hand and they finished just 3.2 seconds apart, Hill having set a new lap record on the final tour. He had been handicapped by coping with a faulty brake master cylinder from the third lap, so that he had to pump the brake pedal for the duration of the race, using his right foot, since left-foot braking was not possible, probably because the steering column was in the way. While Clark had just posted his fourth British Grand Prix victory, Graham never won at home, although he was twice runner-up. And he did win the *Daily Express* International Trophy there twice, in 1962 and 1971.

The British Grand Prix was on the Saturday and on the Sunday, Graham had flown over to France to drive John Coombs's F2 Brabham BRM in the Rouen Grand Prix. Again, he finished second to Jimmy Clark and set fastest lap. Then the following weekend came the Dutch Grand Prix at Zandvoort. Clark romped away with the race and Graham had to settle for fourth place. The fact that his rev-counter packed up did not help matters and, having set pole time, it was something of a disappointment. Hill and Clark pressured the early leader Ginther, but after relegating the Honda driver, Hill was overtaken first by Clark and then by Stewart and Gurney. This victory consolidated Clark's hold on the championship, although Hill could still win it if he won the four remaining championship races while Clark failed to score.

By this time, Jackie Stewart was well established in the BRM team. Hill played an important role,

but things were run on very different lines to Team Lotus. Stewart said:

At Team Lotus, any alteration came as a directive from Colin Chapman. He led the operation, whereas Graham led BRM much more. Although Tony Rudd was a very skilled engineer, there was no doubt that Graham made the team what it was. Graham and I were forever pressuring Tony Rudd to improve the cars. For example, you would be driving along behind a Lotus or another car. And you knew which cars had good driveability, the ones that had immense adhesion leaving a corner, or the cornering forces, or just that little bit extra. You were up close and personal. The variables were much smaller then than they are today. If the BMW engine today is producing 875bhp and someone else with a very good engine may be producing 830bhp, that's a lot of cookies, whereas in those days the differences were very small. So although you saw considerable mechanical grip, there was no aerodynamic grip. The cars were all the same shape, like cigar tubes, although the BRM was never as good as the Lotus in terms of grip – strength and

Hill leads Gurney in the 1965 Dutch Grand Prix at Zandvoort. But the number one BRM driver lost second place to the number two Brabham when Stewart started to pressure them. Gurney went round the outside of Hill at Tarzan and made it stick by the next corner, Hunze Rug. Before long, the number two BRM driver had taken them both. *(PN)*

Richie Ginther started the 1965 Dutch Grand Prix from the front row in the Honda V12, and led until the third lap when his former teammate took him on the inside at Tarzan hairpin. While Hill came fourth, Ginther finished sixth after a couple of spins. *(PN)*

The BRSCC's August bank holiday meeting at Brands Hatch in 1965 included the Guards Trophy for big bangers in which Graham had a miserable time in a McLaren-Elva Oldsmobile. He fared better in the 20-lap F2 British Eagle Trophy however, and is pictured on his way to fourth place driving John Coombs's 1-litre Lotus 35 BRM. *(FF)*

reliability were its real forte. So if we saw another car with some good mechanical grip, we would go into the pits and complain to Tony.

It was Stewart's turn to amaze by achieving the quickest times at the Nürburgring Nordschleife in preparation for the German Grand Prix, going nine seconds under the existing lap record. Jim Clark went quicker still, taking pole, with Stewart, Hill and Surtees occupying the rest of the front row. Clark typically made the best start, and Chapman made use of the TV in the Brabham pit to monitor the gap between his driver and Hill in second place. The battle at the front raged as both broke the lap record. Eventually, Clark pulled away, leaving Graham under pressure from Gurney, Stewart having gone off and bent the

BRM's suspension. Clark had now clinched the championship with 54 points, while Hill was runner-up with 36.

Formula 2 was just as prominent as F1 in the mid-1960s, and top-flight racing drivers like Hill had a busy international schedule. Graham was present at the Gelleråsen circuit at Karlskoga in Sweden to drive the Brabham BT16 BRM in the Formula 2 Kanonlopet race. The following weekend, the British Eagle Trophy combined F2 and F3 race played the support role to the Guards Trophy event for Group 7 sports-racers, and Graham came fourth in John Coombs's new Lotus 35 BRM. Graham retired early on in the Guards Trophy when his McLaren Elva Oldsmobile had an electrical glitch. The race was won by Surtees's Lola T70, with Stewart third in another Lola.

For the Italian Grand Prix at Monza, BRM sent the usual three P261s, with a spare for Hill. He drove chassis 2516 and Stewart had 2517. Clark had the pole, with Surtees and Stewart beside him, and Hill and Bandini were on row two. For lap after lap, Clark and Stewart shared the lead, with Hill snatching it on a couple of occasions, and Surtees hanging on in there as well. Then, on lap 64, Clark's engine blew, leaving the BRM duo to fight it out. Tony Rudd had told Hill and Stewart to increase the pressure on Clark to force his Climax engine to over-rev in the slipstreaming contest. The Lotus was geared for 10,250rpm, but on the back straight the rev counter was showing 10,600rpm, and shortly afterwards Hill saw the tell-tale puffs of grey smoke that soon became a cloud. Team Lotus's official explanation was that Clark's fuel pump had packed up. But the outcome was far from clear. Approaching the Parabolica on the penultimate lap, Stewart came up on the inside of Hill, who deferred gracefully, expecting to slipstream him out onto the pit straight, no doubt, and grab the win. But Hill got onto the marbles on the dirty part of the track and momentarily lost control. It was enough for Stewart to race on to his maiden Grand Prix victory. The race was pivotal in different ways for both Hill and Stewart, as Rudd recognised:

> It all came out after Monza '65. Graham said that Jackie should have given way to him in the last corner, but Jackie assumed that Graham would slipstream him out of the last corner. But he was just too far back and he got on the loose stuff on the outside of the corner. Basically, Graham made a mistake. All through the season we had assumed that Graham was the number one driver, but they were so evenly matched in that race.
>
> I knew we had the edge on everybody with the exception of Ferrari. The power curve of the cars went on up quite steeply to about 10,500rpm and it gradually turned over and flattened out at 11,750rpm. Graham started pounding around and I said, 'Graham, take the spare car,' and he said 'No, I want to check this and check that,' but I said, 'in the spare car.' He was quite cross about that. I said, 'you're not having the spare engine, it's the night before the race.' He grumbled a bit about it but he was pretty confident.
>
> The pit signallers who came out to give the signals had to wear an orange tabard. The deal was that, towards the end of the race, I said, 'if you see me come out wearing the orange waistcoat, you can let it fly.' It was well into the race, and there was only Clark left. He was in a sandwich. Jackie led most of the time and Graham was behind him, all close together. All three came round together and saw me hold the board up, and Jackie knew what it meant as well. Clark looked very curious and Graham just nodded. Clark told me afterwards that he was wondering all the way down the pit straight 'what the hell does that mean.' Going down the back straight, he was in Jackie's slipstream and looked at the Lotus rev counter and it was 10,600rpm. Then he knew what the signal meant. Graham said he saw a puff of grey smoke come out of Jimmy's exhaust, and he pulled out of the slipstream so he didn't run over the wreckage of the engine, and that was Clark fixed. Instead of backing off, Graham and Jackie raced each other. The lap times were coming down, and they were going faster and faster, when there was no need, with no one within miles of them. I really was mad with them. It was no disgrace that Jackie had led more laps than Graham. Jackie could have just slowed down and let Graham by. I did show them the race order – they had symbols, Jackie had the St Andrew's cross, Graham had the BRM green and white cross – but they wouldn't have it.

But Rudd recalls that the friction didn't last long:

> As far as Jackie was concerned, it was all over, but Graham was pretty off about it.

Graham shared the 2.5-litre Climax-powered Lotus 15 at Le Mans 1959 with Australian Derek Jolly. Chapman's plan was to go for outright victory with this car, while Ireland and Stacey would drive the works 2-litre 15 in support. Here, at a roadside referral near Mayet, Hill ponders his chances while Chapman has a laugh with Costin *(right)*, as the local rockers gaze on. Hill was running a strong seventh in the race, but Jolly over-revved the engine when it jumped out of gear. *(DJ)*

Monaco 1964, and Hill was never lower than fourth, taking the lead from Gurney at half distance and setting a new lap record on his way to victory. *(PN)*

Having set pole at Spa in the BRM P261 V8 in 1965, Hill was hampered by a wet and greasy surface in the race, coming third, a lap behind the invincible Clark and teammate Stewart. *(PN)*

Graham with P261 minus engine cover, studying form prior to the 1965 Monaco Grand Prix, a race he would go on to win after out-driving both works Ferraris. *(PN)*

The BRM mechanics apply the race numbers to Hill's P261 before the 1965 Italian Grand Prix. He would finish second to teammate Stewart, the winner on his first visit to Monza. *(PN)*

Embracing his P261 as it rolls out of the BRM transporter, Graham discusses testing plans with Tony Rudd and his mechanic in the Brands Hatch paddock, 1964. *(FMC)*

Hill's Red Ball Lola is surrounded by Lola engineers, Firestone technicians and members of the John Mecom team, including George Bignotti's pit crew, for the 1966 Indianapolis 500. Hill was recommended for the drive by John Surtees, who was a confidant of Lola's Eric Broadley. *(Indianapolis Motor Speedway)*

Graham rummages for his kit in the Brands Hatch paddock during a test session with the new monocoque BRM P261 early in 1964. In the background, Jack Brabham transfers from Sunbeam Tiger to race car. *(FMC)*

Above: The 1966 Good Friday meeting at Snetterton featured the Archie Scott Brown Trophy, with Hill in the Team Surtees Lola T70 Chevrolet getting away first from Bruce McLaren in his McLaren Elva Oldsmobile and Denny Hulme in the Sid Taylor Lola T70. While Hulme emerged the winner from Amon in a McLaren and Attwood in a GT40, Hill retired with a seized transmission. He would finish third in the same car in the Guards Trophy at Brands Hatch later in the year. *(IC)*

Left: Testing a rather battered looking Ford GT40 prototype at Goodwood in 1964. Two years later, Graham drove an Alan Mann GT40 at Sebring and a Mk II Ford at Le Mans, but did not finish either race. *(FMC)*

Pit-lane conference between Graham and Tony Rudd during the British Grand Prix at Brands Hatch. Note the additional perspex on the P261 windshield. Around the halfway mark a tussle developed between Hill and Clark for fourth place, although they were both passed by Hulme who had the advantage of 3-litre Repco power. *(LAT)*

The Team Lotus pits are a hive of activity before the 1967 British Grand Prix, as Clark's car undergoes a last-minute check and Hill dons his driving gloves. The 49s occupied the front of the grid (note BRMs, Eagle and Brabham in shot), Hill's car having been built up back at Hethel overnight following a practice breakage. It broke again while he was leading, handing victory to his teammate. *(FMC)*

The 1968 South African Grand Prix was the last time the works Lotuses raced in their green and yellow colour scheme, and even here, advertising is more prominent than before. As Hill prepares for the race in 49/R3, a purposeful Chapman (wearing shorts and driving gloves) can be seen to the right, with mechanics Bob Dance and Dougie Bridge behind the car. Hill came second, 25 seconds behind Clark, in what was to be his final Grand Prix victory. *(FMC)*

Calm before the storm: Clark and Hill in contemplative mood during one of the rounds of the 1968 Tasman series, the first time the cars appeared in Gold Leaf livery (note the sailor's head logo blanked out). Although Chapman was generally thought to favour Clark, there was never a hint of acrimony between the two drivers. *(PN)*

Hill and his mechanic Bob Sparshott get ready for practice in the Brands Hatch paddock before the 1968 Race of Champions. The car (49/R5) proved difficult to handle around the undulating circuit, and Hill retired out in the country with a broken driveshaft. *(IC)*

In the wake of Jim Clark's death, Graham's win at Jarama in the Spanish Grand Prix was a real morale booster for Gold Leaf Team Lotus. Graham spent much of the race in combat with Hulme's McLaren, taking the lead in 49/R1 when Amon's leading Ferrari expired. *(PN)*

On his way to victory on the tight, twisty Jarama circuit, where there was little to choose between the Cosworth-powered cars, Hill's 49/R1 was challenged hard by Denny Hulme, who backed off when it was clear that Graham would not allow him past. *(FMC)*

But the Stanleys had a big dinner in Milan to celebrate, and I think Graham's wife Bette needled him a bit over it. But the next time we met it was all over. It wasn't bad blood or anything.

Stewart got on well with Hill professionally and developed an intimacy with the Hill family away from the circuits:

> I became close to Graham, of course. We travelled together, our families were close, and we holidayed together. Things like that don't happen very often today among racing drivers or the teams. Graham was a good and charming man. He was a good solid individual, and he was old enough for me to be able to look up to him, and of course he'd already won the World Championship. He was hot property, so to speak, and to understudy Graham was a very important part of my career. And, by the way, he dealt with that very well. Because here was a young upstart, if you like, coming into the team, bright-eyed and bushy tailed, and it was a great surprise to me that I was as fast as some of these big stars that I had worshipped. Now, Graham could have crushed me, or manifested enough things within the team to make it very uncomfortable for me. And he did none of that. He dealt with my perform-ance and, indeed, my subsequent World Championships, with no malice at all. We always stayed friends. He was the president of Springfield Boys Club that I was vice-president of, so he was very into the Boys Club and a stalwart fundraiser and so forth. We shot together a lot – I started him shooting actually – and we always stayed close. It was a good relationship. But Graham and Jimmy were good friends as well.

For the Oulton Park Gold Cup, Graham was driving the Lotus 35 BRM and was on the front row along with Clark and Jochen Rindt. The first five cars were closely bunched for the first few laps – Rindt, Rees, Hulme, Surtees and Hill. As the race progressed, the first two fell by the wayside due to mechanical mishap, and the eventual finishing order was Surtees (Lola), Hulme (Brabham) and Hill.

## Watkins Glen Hat-Trick

The same three BRMs as raced at Monza were sent to Watkins Glen for the autumnal US Grand Prix, and Graham was only marginally slower in the spare car, vying with Clark for the pole. They lined up in two-by-two formation, with Graham on pole and Clark alongside, followed by Spence in the second Team Lotus 33 and Ginther's Honda V12. Stewart's BRM and Bandini's Ferrari V12 were on row three. The two leaders raced off side-by-side, with Hill just ahead. Clark forged by on lap two and Hill re-passed him three laps later. Clark retook him for just a single lap before the Lotus burned a piston, leaving Hill with a fairly secure lead. Gusts of wind were affecting the cars' handling. A sudden localised squall on lap 37 caused him a fright as he arrived at a right-hander round the back of the circuit to find the track surface like glass, and he took an involuntary trip onto the grass for some 200 yards. This allowed Gurney to catch him up, but he too overdid things, and then it was Brabham's turn to overhaul Hill. The Australian made an error, and Hill was once more in the lead, followed by Gurney, and that was how it finished. Graham had notched up a hat-trick of victories at Watkins Glen, setting fastest lap in the process.

The World Championship season concluded with the Mexican Grand Prix on 24 October, and most people were looking ahead to the new season, which would usher in the new 3-litre formula. Hill had never been especially keen on the 1.5-litre Formula 1, even though it did yield him his first world title. He felt that F1 should be the pinnacle of the sport, and thus the province of the quickest cars around a race circuit. That was not necessarily the case any more, since the best sports prototypes could lap faster, running far more powerful engines. Honda concentrated more than most on this, the last race of the 1.5-litre F1, and it paid off for them, as the Mexican race was won by Richie Ginther who led from start to finish. It was Ginther's first Grand Prix win, and opened the score sheet for Honda. Here was a company on a mission, for the 1-litre Honda engine would be virtually unbeatable in Formula 2 the following year. The BRMs were off the pace in Mexico however – Jackie's clutch failed on lap 35 and Graham's engine blew up on lap 56. So Clark won the championship and Hill was second for the third time, on 40 points. Stewart was third on 33 points.

## Little Black Book

Jackie Stewart has his own views on the allegation that, whereas drivers such as Clark were natural practitioners of the racing drivers' art, Hill had to really work hard for the results:

> I would have called Graham a really skilled genuine driver, with very compart-mentalised skills, which he took to a far higher level than a lesser man would ever have achieved. But he didn't have the flair in his driving. It was more of a mechanical exercise. I don't think there was any driver that was more thoroughly diligent about setting a car up. He had a little black book, which was probably 6 or 7 inches by 3 inches. And every time he stepped into a car he would record every roll bar diameter and how it was set up, every spring rate, every shock absorber adjust-ment, and he would register it all very meticulously by hand in that book. He would date it, with the location of the track, whether it was a Grand Prix or a test session at Snetterton for example. He would have everything written down, condition of the circuit, the weather and everything else. That notebook was his Bible, in a way. He was very methodical in that respect, and an incredibly serious man in the way he went about his business. It was like he was two different people, contradictory to one another.

It was obvious by now that Stewart was an enormous natural talent and was potential World Championship material. It was probably only a matter of time before Stewart would eclipse his team leader. Tony Rudd cited a test session at Snetterton in 1965:

> We had the beginnings of an on-board data recovery system. We recorded it on light-sensitive paper tape. When the car stopped, we could take the tape out and we could read what the car was doing. We had one of the corners marked out with light readings so we could analyse the cornering. Graham would go into the corner slightly faster than Jackie, leave his breaking later, then stand on the brakes, and his speed would drop lower than Jackie's. But Jackie would be on the throttle first but not so much, whereas Graham would come bursting out of the corner, and the net result was that Jackie was maybe half a second quicker around the corners because of smoother acceleration. So I showed this to Graham and he wouldn't have anything of it. He said, 'let the bloody box drive it, then.'
>
> I was surprised by that, because normally he was interested in any data he had when we were testing. I used get on a bend and take photos, which I would later show to Graham, and we used to analyse and learn things from them. He was intrigued when I showed him a book by Monkhouse about Dick Seaman, and how Seaman learned from photographs. He just found it interesting. But in 1965/66 he wasn't so interested, he gave me the impression that he thought he wasn't learning at the same rate, and I was a bit disillusioned at this session at Snetterton, where previously he would have spent hours latched onto the data.

At BRM, Stewart could soon match Hill, though he was still learning from him:

> I don't think I ever thought I was better than anybody else, I always thought I had to try harder than them and find ways of doing things differently in order to get an

edge. But in the first half of '65, although I had pole position and I finished sixth in the first Grand Prix of the year, Graham was ahead of me. And I was kind of disappointed, and wanted to be equal with him because of testing and so forth, but I had to try harder. There was so much I had to learn, that much was obvious. I had some good results, like the Race of Champions, and I was in pole position on Easter Monday 1965. I didn't win the race, I broke down, but I'd still made pole position. And Graham was second fastest. Jim Clark and I hold the Formula 1 lap record at Goodwood to this day. I think I finished second to Jimmy in three consecutive Grands Prix – the French, Belgian and Dutch. And that put me ahead of Graham in the World Championship, but since he actually finished second in the championship, it wasn't a question of feeling I had the better of him. And of course, he was the number one driver. But there were no team orders as such.

What was undeniable was the difference in the two BRM drivers' physiques. Graham was taller than Jackie, and therefore needed a taller windshield, and when Graham's windscreen extension was fitted to Jackie's car, the 1000rpm advantage that Stewart had previously enjoyed disappeared. 'Graham was bigger than Jackie,' confirmed Rudd. 'We found that the windscreen Graham needed was quite a bit bigger than Jackie needed. We put Graham's windscreen on Jackie's car and Jackie told us that it wasn't as much as 2000rpm, but it was more than 1000rpm, which made us realise that Stewart's assessments were honest and realistic.'

## Going Down Under

Instead of contesting the non-championship South African Grand Prix on New Year's Day 1966, run to the new regulations, BRM dispatched cars to New Zealand for the 2.5-litre Tasman Formula Grand Prix at Pukekohe. Sir Alfred Owen was keen for the team to go to New Zealand because

he aimed to establish a spares-manufacturing plant in the country to service the forthcoming Austin-Morris factory there. The BRMs would therefore race in New Zealand in a bid to attract business partners for Rubery-Owen. The BRM V8s were bored out to 1,918cc, increasing their weight by some 200lb (90.72kg). Stewart and Hill's P261T BRMs were powered by these 2-litre V8s, running on Shell pump fuel, thanks to bonuses from the petrol company, as opposed to Avgas, which was within the regulations. The team was managed by Tim Parnell with Alan Challis as chief mechanic, and Graham and Jackie proceeded to lap all other finishers twice in this local derby, after Jimmy Clark's 2.5-litre Climax FPF-powered Lotus 33 R12 retired. The following three races in New Zealand were won by the BRMs of Richard Attwood (Levin) and Jackie (Christchurch and Invercargill). At Warwick Farm, Hill came second to Clark in the International 100 and he won the Australian Grand Prix at Lakeside, Brisbane. Stewart won the final two rounds at Melbourne's Sandown Park and Longford, Tasmania, with Graham third and second at these events. BRM had thus won seven out of eight rounds and Stewart was the runaway Tasman Champion.

The rest of the year was destined not to be so successful for BRM.

The 1966 Tasman series gave Graham a couple of wins, three second places and a third, and he is pictured here at Lakeside, Queensland, on the way to winning the Australian Grand Prix. He checks the mirror of the BRM P261T to view Clark's progress in the 2.5-litre Climax-engined Lotus 33 R12, which came third. *(PN)*

What, no beauty queen? Hill still looks reasonably pleased at having won the 1966 Australian GP at Lakeside but, as laurel wreaths go, this one's on the modest side – and where's the bubbly? *(PN)*

## Dawn of the 3-litre Formula 1

On 26 March 1966, Graham and Jackie were down to drive one of the two Alan Mann Ford GT40s in the Sebring 12 Hours. This was part of Ford's plan to wrest the Constructors' World Championship for GT and prototype sports cars from Ferrari, who had claimed it for the previous six years. Hill led initially, but Stewart later spun on some oil and the back of the car caught fire. Although it was extinguished, the car subsequently retired. Graham drove another big-engined car, the open-top Team Surtees Lola T70, in the Archie Scott Brown Trophy on Good Friday at Snetterton, having been on pole, but the transmission seized on lap 18 as he was dicing with Amon's McLaren.

Hill flicks the rumbling Lola T70 through the old Russell corner at Snetterton during the Archie Scott Brown Trophy race on Good Friday 1966. He'd set pole in the Team Surtees Lola T70, but the transmission seized on lap 18 when he was being pursued by Amon's McLaren. *(IC)*

Graham had always excelled in Formula 2, and in April he had three fairly good outings in F2 races in John Coombs's Brabham BT16 BRM. The Honda-powered cars of Brabham and Hulme were superior, but Graham fought for fifth in the *Daily Mail* Trophy at Goodwood, third in the Pau Grand Prix, and sixth at Barcelona.

During the winter lay-off, the BRM staff had been labouring to get the new 3-litre engine up and running. This was the H-16 unit, in effect two flat eights lying on top of one another, each with its own crankshaft. It was a bold move, since precedents for successful 16-cylinder engines were few and far between – the Auto-Union from the mid-1930s being an exception. The H-16 was relatively heavy, weighing 555lb (252kg) with clutch and gearbox adding a further 118lb (53.5kg). Its problems included harmonic vibrations passing between the two crankshafts that could lead to broken valve springs and damage the valves and crankshafts. The firing order was important and required different crankshafts, and for some time it suffered from oil feed problems. To complicate matters at BRM, Colin Chapman had made a deal to buy 3-litre H-16 units, although clearly this would not do for long, as Lotus was BRM's greatest rival at the time. Chapman had also convinced BRM chief Sir Alfred Owen to make a 4.2-litre version for Indianapolis, much against the better judgement of senior BRM staff.

Monaco was the first world championship event to be run under the new 3-litre Formula 1 rules, and BRM fielded the 2-litre Tasman cars, with just one H-16 unit present for Hill to evaluate. Of the top teams, only Ferrari, Cooper and Brabham had 3-litre cars in evidence, while Bruce McLaren's new enterprise had a down-sized 3-litre Ford V8 (reduced from 4.2-litres by shorter stroke and sleeved-down bores) installed. Clark's Lotus was fitted with a big-bore, short-stroke version of the Climax FMWV V8 engine, and he took pole position in this final version of the type 33 with Surtees alongside him in the new Ferrari V12. The BRM duo made up the second row, Graham having tried Goodyear tyres in practice as a comparison with BRM's regular Dunlops. The cars worked quite as well as they had done in the Tasman series. Stewart harried early leader Surtees until lap 13 when the Ferrari faltered, letting the Scot through to lead. Hill, meanwhile, was locked in a battle with Jochen Rindt's Cooper Maserati and Bandini's 2.4-litre V6 Ferrari. He had to contend with a slipping clutch for the whole race, and only managed to finish third behind Bandini. Jackie won, setting a new record average speed, giving BRM their fourth consecutive win at

With the new 3-litre regulations coming into play for 1966, the BRM 261s ran 2-litre V8s, and Stewart proved they worked by winning Monaco. Here is Hill at the harbour front chicane on the first day of practice after a rain shower. *(PN)*

Monaco. There had been just four finishers, with Bob Bondurant's ex-works BRM V8 bringing up the rear.

This was the event where John Frankenheimer filmed MGM's wide-screen movie *Grand Prix*. The film crew largely took over proceedings in Monte Carlo (as at Spa and subsequent Grands Prix that year), much to the annoyance of hard-pressed mechanics. As well as the real-life action footage, special scenes were run using F3 cars made-over by the Jim Russell Racing Drivers' School, then at Snetterton, fitted with dummy exhausts – including the BRM's H-16 system – and authentic-looking works paint schemes. Graham appears in the film from time to time, acting as racing driver 'Bob Turner', and speaks to camera on one occasion with the cheesy tongue-in-cheek quip: 'It couldn't be worse than last year!'

A second film company was on hand to make a movie starring Steve McQueen, and the racing world was divided into two camps about which company would get the nod to proceed. Graham backed the Frankenheimer film, as did Bonnier, Ginther, Spence and Phil Hill, and the McQueen project was favoured by Moss, Clark, Stewart, Surtees and Sir John Whitmore. After a certain amount of legal wrangling, the McQueen faction withdrew due to the film-star's ill health – he would of course return to the racing scene later to make the flawed Le Mans epic.

Tony Rudd recalled:

Graham's favourite circuit certainly was Monaco. We'd got it worked out between us, because at Monte Carlo we used to run the gearbox with first and second gear very close together, and the two top gears were close together. We used to use two lower gears at the beginning of the race, when the car was full of fuel, because in the old days, Monte Carlo was 200 miles and you carried a lot of petrol. The 1.5-litre car, poor little thing, was lugging about 30 gallons of petrol. So we used to use the lower of the two gears at the beginning of the race when the car was heavy, and from halfway through, we would use the higher of the two, so there were fewer gear changes. There were one or two things like that. We used to set the car up for the chicane and not for the hairpin, because the two hairpins are that slow that it doesn't matter what you've done for it, you could be in a taxi. But you could set it up for the chicane and that would make up time. We had a superstition that came about after the first time he won. After the prize-giving, the Prince used to give a dinner in the Hotel de Paris with a big table, and you have to had a dinner jacket and black tie. But the first and second year he won, we hadn't got smoking jackets, but in '64, he said, 'what do you think about the smoking jacket?' I said, 'I don't know, I don't think I dare take mine, it would be asking too much,' and we never did take them. After the dinner he used to go down to the Tip Top, which was a club on the way down the hill from the casino, and he would have plate of spaghetti and he would be singing rowing and football songs. It used to be quite a rowdy evening, which went on till dawn. All his old friends from his earlier days would be there. Graham would stay for a long while, but I think Bette used to drag him away. Of course in the early days he hadn't got a lot of money, but in the days when he had more money he could afford to stay at the Hotel de Paris in great style. In the old days he used to stay in the Metropole.

An odd string of coincidences attaches Hill to Monaco. He drove his first and last Grands Prix there – although he failed narrowly to qualify for the latter. He overhauled Fangio's long-standing record points tally at Monaco in 1970; his 150th Grand Prix start took place there in 1973; and he scored five victories there, eclipsed by Ayrton Senna on the road, although not in the hearts of the Monegasque population.

## The Indianapolis Victory

The 1966 Indianapolis 500 was run on 30 May, and Graham and Jackie were hired by John Mecom to drive a couple of 4.2-litre Lola Ford T90 V8s alongside his star driver Roger Ward. The cars were prepared by Mecom's eminent mechanic George Bignotti, who had already engineered two Indy victories for A.J. Foyt. Bignotti had tried to buy Lotus 34s or 38s for the occasion but, through an association with Eric Broadley, was able to use the Lola T90 monocoque chassis. Graham's entry came late in the day, as he was standing in for Walt Hansgen, who had been fatally injured in Le Mans qualifying in a works Ford Mk II. Originally, John Surtees had been in the frame for the Mecom drive, but because he was injured, he suggested

Hill would be a good contender in his place. He explained:

I was in hospital in Canada with rather serious injuries and, having worked with George Bignotti and Eric Broadley on the Indy programme, when they asked me who should take my place, I recommended Graham. Here was a new car and with a very experienced team manager and chief engineer, Bignotti, and I thought that Graham was a good journeyman driver with a touch of speed, and this fitted the requirement at that stage.

It was not Graham's first visit to Indy: in 1963 he had tried to qualify a mid-engined Mickey Thompson special that possessed a body shape similar to a flattened rugby ball. He lost a wheel, and had come away most unimpressed. Now, due to commitments in Europe, Graham was obliged to qualify for Indianapolis during the first weekend of qualification, as well as pass his 'rookie' test, being essentially a first-timer at the Brickyard. Each car was allowed three attempts, with four consecutive laps each, and the grid position was established at the end of that day's qualifications. No further improvement was then allowed for that car. Hill's Lola was bedecked in the predominantly white livery of the American Red Ball transit company – along with copious decals from other backers, and he qualified 15th out of 33, which placed him on the fifth row of the three-by-three grid. Not all cars had asymmetric suspension layouts in 1966 (the left-hand side of the Lotus 34 being 2.38in shorter than the right, ostensibly to aid turn-in on the all-left-hand layout of super-speedways), and Mario Andretti's pole-winning Brabham Ford and the All-American Racers' Eagle Fords had symmetrical set-ups.

Just after the start came one of the biggest pile-ups in Indianapolis history. It was occasioned by the fact that many of the hot-shoes were at the back due to the idiosyncratic qualifying system, the slow progress of the pace car, and the vast differences in specification between turbo and non-turbo engines, automatic transmission and multi-speed gearboxes, all of which led to a chaotic getaway. Foyt, escaping the carnage via the safety fence, tried to pin the blame on Graham. There had to be a scapegoat, but it was not to be Hill.

An hour later there was a restart. Andretti led briefly from Jim Clark and, when he broke down, the Scot led until he spun on lap 65 for no apparent reason, and without losing the lead. He spun again on lap 85 due to the oil-smeared track, and thus relinquished the lead to Stewart in the second Mecom Lola. As Jackie prepared to lap his Mecom teammate Hill, a race developed between them, despite pit signals from Bignotti for Stewart to ease up. Hill had raised his game, triggered by the prospect of being lapped by his BRM partner, and the pace was too much for Stewart's four-cam Ford engine. When Jackie's oil scavenge pump failed on lap 191, Hill took the lead and went on to victory.

Controversy lurked in the lap charts though. The lap score on the Indy tower suggested that it was Clark who was in the lead. This was supported by lap charts in the STP-Team Lotus pits, who were busy telling Clark that he was leading. But the tower scoreboard was discredited, and Hill was declared the winner. Having received the chequered flag, Graham motored to Victory Alley and was in the throes of receiving the adulation of the assembled officials, dignitaries and beauty queens. When Clark turned up there, believing that he had won, it was immediately clear that Graham had already 'drunk the milk' traditionally given to the winner. Clark accepted the situation without hesitation, offering Hill his congratulations. Although there continued to be doubt about the lap scorers' records, promoted principally by the STP faction who adhered to the view that they had mistaken Clark's car for Al Unser's and thus missed one of his laps, there was never any question officially that Hill was the victor. The official verdict was not delivered until the morning after the race, but the dependable lap chart of Jabby Crombac, a noted Lotus aficionado and close friend of Clark, also had Hill down as the winner. It was only the second time that a rookie driver had won at Indianapolis, and it made Graham richer by $156,297. At the post-race victory banquet, Graham declared himself surprised to have won, yet impressed by the size of the cheque. With typical dry humour, he joked that he had brought along two Scottish accountants – presumably Clark and Stewart – to handle it.

Apart from his rookie win, Graham made a contribution of an entirely different nature to the chequered history of the Indy 500, and that was the transformation of the male lavatories from communal mediaeval latrines to something approaching modern privacy. Fêted as Britain's ambassador by all and sundry, including circuit owner Tony Hulman, Graham was asked for his opinion of the Brickyard. Andrew Ferguson tells us in *Team Lotus – the Indianapolis Years* that:

> ... Graham recited the usual platitudes, then dived in with a comment about the uncivilised planks (that all males were obliged to sit upon to perform their natural bodily functions). That night the carpenters and workers were brought in to rectify the matter, and from then on we could all relax within the newly built cubicles.

Mario Andretti first met Hill at Indianapolis in 1966. During their careers, their paths crossed several times – at Indianapolis, Le Mans and at Team Lotus. He recalled:

> I remember the drivers' meeting at Indianapolis in '66, where of course there was Jackie Stewart and Graham and Jim Clark – there were an incredible amount of Grand Prix drivers that year. It was fabulous to see them there. It just raised a bar at Indianapolis. It increased the popularity of Indianapolis and also made it that much more meaningful to be able to win when you had that sort of talent in the field, no question about it. I always characterise the races that I've won by who finished second behind me, and again, the better the talent, the more prestigious and meaningful the win would be. But just to be in those races, like me as a rookie at Indianapolis, and having finished third behind Jim Clark and Parnelli Jones, was to

me probably the best thing that could have happened, career-wise. Again, I recall also the fact that the influx of Grand Prix drivers during that period meant they were setting attendance records everywhere whenever they appeared. Not only Indianapolis, but the following race was in Milwaukee, and there was the biggest crowd that they had ever had.

Andretti had great respect for Hill as a driver, and enjoyed his company.

Obviously we were both worlds apart in some ways, but at the same time, Graham Hill was someone that you could warm to instantly. Socially he was such a pleasure. He always had something to say, and it was always something funny, appropriate to the occasion, hilarious at times. I just so thoroughly enjoyed whatever time I was able to spend with him and Bette. He was such a special breed. Whatever time I spent with him was all too brief, but because it was so special, he was a delightful, delightful individual to be around – no question.

## Film Stars

After the cut and thrust of Monaco's street circuit, the F1 circus moved to an equally exacting venue, but this time of the high-speed kind. The 1966 Belgian Grand Prix at Spa continued to hold the title of the world's fastest road race, and the MGM brigade was on hand to weave the event into the movie. Phil Hill was drafted in to drive a McLaren (and a Lotus 25 at Monaco) as a camera car that could keep up with the pukka F1 cars. It was still early days for the new 3-litre formula, but both BRM and its Team Lotus customer had their H-16 engined cars on hand to test, along with their regular cars, now running 2-litre V8s. Stewart set the pace initially in the 2-litre BRM, and he ended up on the front row with the Cooper Maserati of Rindt and Surtees's V12 Ferrari, four seconds quicker than Hill and Clark, who occupied row four. Surtees got down to 3min 38.2sec – a shade under a 145mph average and some 11 seconds

under Gurney's old lap record with a 1.5-litre Brabham Climax. The start was characterised by Surtees and Rindt taking charge of the race, with Stewart in hot pursuit. Then the fickle Ardennes weather played its trump card. The heavens opened and the far side of the circuit was engulfed in a rain storm. Accidents were inevitable. Bonnier and Spence were first to go off, and then Stewart, Hill and Bondurant all went off at the notorious kink on the high-speed 150mph Masta straight. Hill's BRM was unscathed, spinning into straw bales, but Stewart had gone right off the road. As he was trying to get the BRM started and into gear, Graham noticed Jackie's wrecked BRM down below the circuit in a farmyard. He clambered down and turned off the car's fuel pump, which was still pumping out petrol and drenching Stewart. Hill quickly realised he would have to take the steering wheel off before Stewart could be released, so he had to run off to find a marshal and borrow a spanner. Bondurant then appeared, having extricated himself from his upturned BRM, and he and Hill managed to get Stewart out, taking him to a nearby farm building. Hill removed the Scotsman's petrol-sodden overalls, then ran back to the marshal's post to telephone for an ambulance. When they arrived on the scene, the first thing the nurses did was to cover Jackie up again with his wet overalls. Hill then drove back to the pits but, having lost a lot of time, there was no point in continuing with the race. Louis Stanley ensured that Jackie was taken to hospital and then flown back to the UK.

Stewart recalls the event vividly, and there is no question that it consolidated the bond between him and Hill:

Graham could have continued. His car was undamaged, but he saw me down in a 'lower-basement' type area by a farmhouse – the road was higher – where there was a cavity with the road supported by a brick wall. And I ended up down the bottom of that, luckily the right way up. And Graham did the same manoeuvre as I did, which was aquaplane on a river of water and gyrate down the road. Fortunately there was nothing for him to hit. In spite of stalling his car, he could have restarted. In fact, the way the race turned out, he would have finished in the top three. But he saw my predicament, and I must have been looking very secondhand! He came down with Bob Bondurant, who was ironically driving another BRM, and spent a lot of time getting me out of the car, more than 20 minutes, including borrowing spectators' tools and spanners. There were no marshals or rescue people there, only spectators, and then no ambulance. I was trapped in the car, and the car was very badly damaged. A lot of other people would have got on with the race. But he was a teammate, he was a friend, and absolutely always a gentleman.

Tony Rudd said of the incident:

> After he pulled Jackie out of the ditch at Spa he came into the pits and he said, 'I stopped for Jackie, he's alright, and they've got him in the ambulance. But he's been sitting in petrol for a long while and of course its burning his skin. I couldn't leave him.' He was very apologetic because, in effect, he'd thrown the race away to help Jackie. I said, 'You know, I didn't expect you to, forget it.' Sir Alfred's minions would have said 'he's paid to race', but Sir Alfred wouldn't have.

## Dearborn Giant

Graham was meant to have shared one of the mighty 7-litre Mk II Fords at Le Mans with Jackie the following weekend, but the American Dr Dick Thompson was appointed substitute driver. Thompson was alleged to have punted another GT40 off at White House during practice, and was disqualified by the organisers. So Ford's racing director Leo Beebe arranged for Brian 'Yogi' Muir to partner Hill in the silver-coloured Alan Mann-entered car. Graham liked the Mk II and its under-stressed pushrod engine, feeling it could 'go on for ever'. The big Ford V8s were capable of over 200mph along the Mulsanne straight. Graham led the race in its opening stages. But a front wheel casting let the car down around midnight, and the front nearside suspension collapsed

Driving one of the eight Mk II Fords in Dearborn's assault on the 1966 Le Mans 24 Hours, Graham led initially in one of the Alan Mann-prepared cars, followed by Gurney in a Shelby American-run car. Hill's planned pit stop for fuel was foiled because there were too many other Fords trying to pit at the same time and he had to go round again. Co-driven by Brian Muir, Hill's car broke its suspension just before midnight. *(FMC)*

Graham Hill practised both BRM's 3-litre H-16 engined P83s at Reims for the 1966 French Grand Prix but, as he had to hold the gear lever in place with one hand much of the time, he elected to race an old 2-litre P261. The potential was there, though – he clocked 188mph along the Thillois straight. *(PN)*

Graham Hill's victory in the 1966 Indy 500. While Mecom teammate Stewart's four-cam Ford engine failed, Hill's kept going, and when Clark's Lotus spun, Hill never faltered. When Stewart threatened to lap him, Hill picked up his pace by 3mph per lap, and to the chagrin of team manager Bignotti and the Mecom pits, Stewart went after him. The fact that they were also teammates at BRM meant that egos were high, and Hill won out as Stewart's engine let go with just 10 laps to go. Hill commented dryly afterwards 'I'm a bit surprised to have won.' *(PN)*

as Hill was negotiating Arnage at 100mph, forcing immediate retirement from what was Hill's ninth attempt at Le Mans. It was nonetheless a triumph for Ford, with three of its Mk IIs filling the first three places. Porsche Carrera 6s occupied the next four places on the results sheet, while the highest-placed Ferrari was eighth, a Maranello Concessionaires car (Pike/Courage's 275 GTB) at that.

The real potential of the BRM H-16 engine became apparent at another high-speed circuit, Reims. It was clearly much faster than anything else in a straight line, witnessed by those in the pits as Hill came past at full bore. Stewart was still unfit, so Graham had two H-16 cars and his regular 2-litre BRM at his disposal. It was early days for the H-16s, and they were having gearbox

A cockpit consultation in the Brands Hatch pits between a less than impressed Hill and BRM team boss Tony Rudd. The P261s were still in service while the transmission for the H-16 engines was being sorted out back at Bourne. *(FF)*

problems (as were Lotus), so he raced the V8, despite going fourth quickest in practice in one of the H-16 cars. Hill latched onto Mike Parkes's Ferrari slipstream only for the BRM engine to over-rev and brake a camshaft on lap 13.

A Formula 2 race supported the Grand Prix, and Graham was driving John Coombs's new Matra MS5-BRM. The engine blew up in practice, spewing its hot oil all around the hapless driver's backside. Hill stopped, and entertained spectators as he danced around – in agony – removing his race suit and underwear to ease the pain. He came 11th in the race, but the burns became infected, and at Rouen the following weekend for another F2 race he experienced serious discomfort. Not as much as poor John Coombs though, who almost had a heart attack while trying to dissuade Graham from meddling with the Matra's set-up.

## Brabham Revival

There followed three Grands Prix on the trot, with Brands Hatch taking its turn to host the British event. Having won in France, Jack Brabham looked to be favourite. He was enjoying a renaissance, having shrewdly picked Repco V8 engines to power his cars for the 3-litre regulations, albeit sticking with tubular space-frame chassis. Hill and the recovered Stewart used the V8 BRMs again, being fourth and eighth quickest in practice, respectively. In the race, both Hill and Clark were at a disadvantage to the new 3-litre machines, which were improving at every outing. The pair of them battled it out for the first half of the race, until Jimmy had to pit to have a brake cylinder replenished, while Graham finished third behind Brabham and Hulme. These three were

Just after the start of the 1966 British Grand Prix, Hill and Surtees collided inadvertently and the BRM P261 sustained a bent wishbone. A duel developed between Hill and Clark for fourth place – both were using 2-litre engines against the 3-litre Repco V8s powering the Brabhams – and when the Lotus's brakes faded, Hill was through to third place. *(FF)*

shod with Goodyear tyres, which was a novel situation in Formula 1.

During practice for the Dutch Grand Prix at Zandvoort, the BRM drivers jousted with each other, being separated by just a tenth of a second on the third row of the grid. As the race started, the two Brabham drivers used their speed advantage to baulk Clark, so Hill was able to catch them up too. Clark amazingly pulled out a short lead, but was obliged to pit for water replenishment, eventually coming third behind Brabham and Hill, with Stewart fourth.

The tyre war was well under way as teams assembled at the Nürburgring for the German Grand Prix. At BRM, Hill was on Goodyears and Stewart on Dunlops. Allegiance to one tyre manufacturer or another was fickle as teams like Lotus swapped from brand to brand between

While the Brabham duo of Brabham and Hulme played a tactical game running in close formation at Zandvoort in 1966, Clark and Hill kept station behind them. The BRM V8 was not in top form, and Hill gradually fell back, and was eventually lapped by Clark and Brabham, although he inherited second place when Clark retired. *(PN)*

The first practice session for the 1966 German Grand Prix was run in bright sunshine, and here Hill is negotiating the Karussell banking in the P261 V8. He was 10th fastest in practice. *(PN)*

practice and the race, bearing in mind the intermittent rain. A reflection of this was that Stewart was on the front row of the four-by-three grid and Hill was on the third rank. Due to patching and resurfacing over the years, the Nürburgring was something of a patchwork of surfaces, and some sections were more slippery than others in the wet. Brabham won after a battle with Surtees's overweight Cooper Maserati, which had an advantage in the wet. In so doing, the Australian clinched the world title for the third time, in a car bearing his own name. Hill finished fourth after duelling with Clark, Gurney, Hulme and Stewart. To get the better of such opposition on such a circuit – in the wet – was testimony that Hill was still very much on top of his game.

Tony Rudd had been told not to take the P261 2-litre BRMs to Monza for the Italian Grand Prix and was obliged to run the T83 3-litre H-16 cars. There were still developmental issues to be ironed out with these engines. Hill's was fitted with a new eight-throw crankshaft, which had a different firing order to the original double-eight layout, intended to reduce torsional vibrations inherent in the original flat-plane crank unit. It then sounded like a 16-cylinder engine ought to, rather than a regular eight-cylinder job. Although seemingly smoother running, the original double-eight engines were susceptible to broken cams and crankshafts. Balance weights and damper discs were applied to cranks and cams and the vibrations were reduced to some extent. When Hill's car proved troublesome, a race-worthy P261

Hill and Brabham were both great tacticians, but the Australian's choice of Repco engines for 1966 proved a masterstroke.
(*PN*)

The speed potential of the H-16 engined BRM T83 was evident at Oulton Park during the 1966 Gold Cup, where Hill and Brabham traded fastest top speeds along the straight from the Esso hairpin – Hill being quicker with a 156.5mph blast. *(FF)*

2-litre BRM was conveniently extracted from an exhibition at the local motor museum at Monza, but this was equally unreliable, so Hill was forced to run with the H-16 car. Although Clark had placed the H-16 powered Lotus 43 on the front row, the works BRM T83s languished on rows four (Stewart) and five (Hill). It was all over for Hill by the first corner on the first lap as the H-16 engine blew; Stewart's car succumbed to a fuel leak six laps later. The cars performed slightly better at the non-championship Oulton Park Gold Cup, taking the fight to the Brabhams of Brabham and Hulme. Hill was actually leading when his engine blew up.

Between the F1 races, Graham had three outings at F2 races in France with the John Coombs Matra MS5 BRM, placing eighth at Montlhéry and 10th at Albi. Variety was always a

hallmark of Hill's driving career, and after yet another abortive outing in the T83 H-16 BRM, this time at Watkins Glen for the US Grand Prix, where Jimmy Clark demonstrated that it could actually hold together and win (in the Lotus 43), Graham went to the Fuji speedway in Japan for a round of the USAC Championship. Here, in the shadow of Mount Fuji, he and Jackie drove John Mecom's Lola T90 Indy cars – powered by 4.2-litre Ford V8s – in a field of 20 USAC contenders shipped over from the States. Graham was fifth in the first heat and retired late on in the second after battling with his Scottish teammate, who went on to win.

The last race on the F1 calendar was the Mexican Grand Prix, and despite having rebuilt engines – the latest version for Hill and a pair of 'double-eights' for Stewart – there were still niggling electrical problems. Clark, on the other hand, was able to place the H-16 powered Lotus 43 on the front row again. Hill gave up when his misfiring engine began making metallic clunking noises on lap 18.

Hill had had a poor F1 World Championship season, and was now looking at alternatives to BRM. Tony Rudd gives a fascinating insight into the financial arrangements and the other issues that Hill had to consider:

I don't know when various other teams made overtures to him and, of course, BRM would not pay more than £10,000 per year. Sir Alfred Owen as the chairman of the company paid himself £10,000 per year so he wasn't going to pay anyone else the same. Graham had had quite a few offers in the '63 era which were more than £10,000, and the only way we could get round that was to pay him a fee on top of his salary for testing. He was aware that he could command more money if he went elsewhere. Rob Walker had always said there was a job there whenever he wanted it, but Rob wasn't the sort of person who was persistent, and of course the ultimate was from Fords. They offered him £40,000.

Perhaps Hill could also see that Jackie Stewart was going to usurp him, though Rudd feels that Hill may have overestimated the danger.

I don't think he would have done quite then, at the time of the 1967 season, because, although I could relate well to Jackie, we couldn't communicate properly. I think Graham probably recognised that Jackie had more skill, but Jackie couldn't have exploited that skill to the full at BRM at that time. For instance, he would describe to me what the car was doing in the corner after the pits at Snetterton, but I hadn't got a clue what he meant. I would go and watch him in the corner, and he despaired of telling me, until he finally pulled his crash helmet off his head and

said 'You go and do it'. So I drove it round the corner and I couldn't recognise that there was anything wrong with it. Looking at the photographs of it, I think it was beautifully balanced and neutral. So Graham's apprehensions about Jackie weren't real.

But I know that during the Tasman series, Jackie was Graham's only taboo. Jackie had become tremendously popular down there and had got the hang of the car. And when Graham got out there, he realised that Jackie had moved up a notch in the team. But Graham was quite fond of Jackie, and there was no ill-feeling at all. There were still a lot of good drives left in Graham, don't forget. In the early days, Graham was very good-natured, he would talk about where he changed down, where he braked and so on, but you noticed he didn't do so much of that later on.

Rudd recalls how Stewart's and Hill's earnings reflected their standings in the team:

Jackie was on £4,000 a year initially, and Graham was on £10,000. There was what was called the Frankfurt scale, there was so much money according to the driver's previous season's world championship points score. You got start-money for the car, appearance money for your driver, and of course Jackie hadn't got any world championship points, so he got nothing, whereas Graham had got about 40 world championship points in '64 so he got quite a bit. Surtees won the championship but Graham had more points. That was what the driver kept. I told Jackie when we did the deal that I would pay him so much as a retainer, and I paid him the points money he earned there and then, so much in lieu of points to start with. So the first race in '65, I paid him the points money that he earned, and he was soon into it. He went up to £10,000 in '66, but Graham got the testing fee.

# Chapter 5
# Joint Number Ones

TOWARDS the end of 1966, Ford's competitions manager Henry Taylor approached Graham to see if he would consider returning to Team Lotus. Ford had committed to funding the new 3-litre Cosworth DFV Formula 1 engine to the tune of £100,000 (a huge sum back then), and wished to safeguard its investment by having two top-class drivers at Team Lotus, who would have exclusive use of the engine for at least its first full F1 season. For his part, Graham could not see a quick solution to the ongoing reliability problems with the H-16 engine and its slow gear change. Aside from his Indy conquest, there had been little success during 1966, and Hill was concerned that BRM was taking on too many commercial contracts, which distracted the operation from its Formula 1 effort. These included work on the Matra V8 and V12 and the Ministry of Defence 2-litre V8s, as well as Chrysler hemi-head V8s and turbines.

The reverse side of the coin as far as Tony Rudd was concerned was that Graham had spent less and less time at Bourne telling him what he felt needed to be done to the cars, preferring instead to relay the changes he wanted via his mechanic Alan Challis. As much as anything this was a reflection on Hill's busy schedule, which had been less pressing in his earlier days at BRM. Hill's own book *Life at the Limit* implies that he felt he was being taken for granted at BRM. Perhaps Hill also saw that aspects of life at Bourne were becoming chaotic, with internal pressures distracting Sir Alfred Owen from Formula 1. Sir Louis Stanley took more and more of a controlling interest in the F1 racing team. Stanley's own comments on

Graham's career, published in his book *Strictly off the Record* are interesting. Big Lou thought that, during his seven-year stay with BRM, Graham changed to a marked degree. 'In the early days,' wrote Stanley, 'he used to get ulcerously edgy before a race, especially if it rained. In time his style matured and grew more relaxed, almost aloof.'

According to Jackie Stewart, Hill had decided that the writing was on the wall as far as he and BRM were concerned:

> When he was made an offer by Ford which he couldn't really refuse, he went to Lotus. I think he was becoming dissatisfied with BRM. The H-16 engine was not going to be a success, and in '67 Ford had this new Formula 1 engine, which was lighter, better and less complicated than anyone else's, and Graham came to the conclusion that that was the future. Ford – under the direction of Walter Hayes – looked back at the halcyon years of Moss and Fangio with Mercedes, and the pre-war era with Mercedes and Auto Union, who employed all the great drivers of the time, and they decided it was better to have two drivers on their team who could win. And at Lotus – who got the Ford engines – those drivers were Jim Clark and Graham Hill, and that was one very good stable. So for Graham, that was a great opportunity, and it won the first Grand Prix it was entered in. Graham could just as easily have won that race as Jimmy.
>
> The best years for BRM were behind us,

although at the time I didn't see any logic in me going anywhere else. But by the time '67 came round I had other ideas. I left BRM because I saw them waning. It was a question of leadership. Who was owning it – Sir Alfred Owen was no longer interested – and the Stanleys were very much involved of course and, in a way, it was Tony that had to carry the whole business side of it, everything, and I think it was beginning to lose its momentum. And in fact he didn't even stay that much longer.

For Hill, there was a handsome transfer fee from Ford and the prospect of a £40,000 salary to cushion the move. At a stroke, a new super-team was created, with the two top British racing drivers on its strength. Hill's move from number one driver at BRM to a joint number one situation at Team Lotus was quite a gamble. Although Chapman had sued Hill for quitting Lotus for BRM back in 1960, there had been a swift rapprochement between them and, on the face of it at least, all was well.

Clark remained Chapman's favourite: the rapport and success they shared was inestimable. Bette Hill, quoted in *Lotus 49: the Story of a Legend* by Michael Oliver said that: 'Graham had come into an established relationship. It was like being a lover on the outside… In many cases, both Graham and I felt that Graham was not getting fair do's.'

Jim Endruweit, Team Lotus racing manager at the time, said:

When he came back in '67, it was a different kettle of fish. I suppose I was the only one who'd known him before, in the early days. But the years at BRM had spoiled him completely as far as I was concerned, because he'd been top dog there, and he was used to getting his own way. I guess BRM probably had more facilities than Lotus. So if Graham wanted something, he generally got it. He was used to getting his own way on anything and everything. We, on the other hand, had always looked to the Old Man [Colin

Chapman]. The Old Man was the source of everything. What you did to the car, how you tweaked it, that arrangement stemmed from the deal between Jimmy and Colin and, well, Colin was Colin. He designed the car and was the fount of all knowledge. But he worked unbelievably well with Jimmy. Jimmy would come in and tell him what the car was doing, and Colin could translate it into what needed to be done mechanically. We always felt that if we provided Jimmy with a car that held together, he would win with it, and that's what made him so rewarding to work with. If he needed an engine change, for instance, the lads would do it willingly, even if it meant an all-nighter. Graham, on the other hand, had grown used to making his own decisions.

Tony Rudd was a very good engineer, but I imagine that Graham used to work through endless possibilities and logged it all in his brain and his notebook, and we weren't too used to working like that. So the mechanics always felt he was giving them a hard time. He'd come in a bit pissed off, and say, 'right, I want this, I want that', and expect it to be done, and we weren't used to that way of working. It was the Old Man who said if we had to do something different with Jimmy. The instruction came from Colin. Jimmy didn't want to make decisions; he trusted Colin to sort that out for him. Suddenly, there's this driver saying 'I want this'. So we might say, 'Why do you want this?' And he'd say, 'I want to try it'. And we'd go to a circuit, and he'd have all the notes from the last time he was there, damper settings, gear ratios, the lot. It would drive the lads mad. But OK, he did a good job, so that was fine. Meanwhile, Jimmy just went on as he always went on, and Colin and Graham remained separate in a way. Colin would try and influence Graham, but not very successfully. So there was a little friction between Colin and

Wearing his ubiquitous driving gloves, Colin Chapman has a word in Graham's ear before the 1967 British Grand Prix at Silverstone. By the time he returned to Team Lotus, Graham had become used to getting his own way at BRM and, although the Lotus boss tried to influence him, Hill carried on pretty much as if nothing had changed. *(FMC)*

Graham. They both had their own opinions, and they'd hold on to those opinions.

Jimmy Clark was sometimes known as 'Gentleman Jim' because of his polite and rather deferential manner. Jackie Stewart saw a clear contrast between the characters of the new Lotus teammates:

Jim Clark was a modest border farmer, and was just a gentle man. Graham was, by comparison, city slick. He always dressed very trendily and I think he won some 'best-dressed man' award, while Jimmy would wear flannels and a sports jacket. He was a farmer and wore the sort of clothes a farmer would. His public speaking skills were limited, while Graham's were expansive, and Graham also won 'after dinner speaker of the year' award or something. For me, he was a fantastic study for what I wanted to become, and I saw him as a total racing driver. He gave a firm opinion to me that, if I was to be successful at the business, I had to have all the best people around me, not to imitate, but to learn from.

As Sir Louis Stanley so eloquently put it: Externally, Graham was emphatically the professional, as smooth and hard as perspex. He analysed himself as lethally as he analysed his opponents. Extremely self-assured, he had an intimate grasp of the English art of one-upmanship. He needed his public as much as any other man who goes surf-riding on enthusiasm. Emotion of any kind he expressed by thrusting out his chin and knitting his eyebrows. He was one of those curious Englishmen who are almost concretely English in appearance. His features, personal mannerisms like a brush at his moustache, reticent clothes, handkerchief surreptitiously tucked away

Looking mighty pleased with his new toy, Hill had his first outing in the sparkling Lotus 49 on the Hethel test track on 23 May 1967. He described it as 'a piece of modern sculpture'. Powered by the 3-litre Cosworth-Ford DFV V8 engine, which was a stressed chassis member, the 49 was a quantum leap in racing car design. Nevertheless, there was an 84-point job-list to attend to after this trial. *(FMC)*

in his pocket, well-scrubbed face, suggested an Army officer on leave or a school master fresh from morning roll-call. He attempted to be with it by growing his hair exceptionally long. It did not work. Away from the track he looked like a militant plain-clothes friar in need of a tonsure.

We notice again the reference to Hill's military bearing, which was an important aspect of his personality and how he projected himself.

Said Jim Endruweit:

Graham wasn't given to tantrums and tirades. More like a good sneer, I'd say. If you cocked something up, if you'd made a mistake, you'd get the rough end of his tongue. If the car broke, I mean, like the chassis broke because of a design fault, that was one thing. But if the mechanic cocked up, like, failed to do a nut up, then the mechanic would get hauled up, and he'd say, 'I don't want him working on my car'. Graham didn't suffer fools gladly. If I said it had been done, then he trusted that, but other people's work he'd check. I never had a problem with him.

## Enter the 49

Jimmy Clark had recently become a tax exile based in Bermuda and living part time during the European season in Jabby Crombac's Paris flat. So Graham took the limelight when the new Lotus 49 chassis and its DFV motor were announced to the press on 23 May 1967, since Clark was unavailable. It allowed Hill to do some of the initial testing prior to its race debut at Zandvoort.

The genesis of the Lotus 49 that would eventually bring Hill his second world crown went back to Chapman's overtures to Ford's Walter Hayes in 1965 when Clark and the Lotus 33 were dominant. As Hayes states in Michael Oliver's *Lotus 49: the Story of a Legend*, the project was under way by mid-1965, and the first official drawing of the type 49 is dated 14 July 1966. Michael Oliver reveals an interesting coincidence in the background to the DFV engine, in that its designer Keith Duckworth had been Graham's understudy in Lotus's Tottenham Lane gearbox department back in 1957 trying to sort the idiosyncratic Lotus 'queerbox'.

The presence of the two acknowledged 'superstars' of British motorsport in the same team allowed much more direct and intimate comparison between their styles and temperaments. Jim Endruweit said:

> Whether Graham would have been Colin's first choice as co-driver for Jimmy, I've no idea. But the Old Man was quite happy about it. I don't think Jimmy and Graham ever fought. I think they got on quite well. They respected each other as drivers. Graham was no mean driver, he just had a different way of operating. He wasn't a natural talent like Jimmy was. He was a worker. In a way you had to give him credit for that, he'd push and try and work at it.

The differences in their driving technique were manifest in particular ways. Jimmy's one-time mechanic Alan McCall observed that Clark could carry more speed into and through a corner, without really using his brakes. According to Jim Endruweit, Clark could do virtually a whole season without changing brake pads, while Hill could scarcely manage a single race weekend.

Team Lotus mechanic Bob Dance looked after the Team Lotus F2 operation as well as the Lotus Cortinas at various times during the 1960s, and he was chief mechanic in 1968 and 1969. He said:

Graham had a pretty good feel for the mechanical side of the car. He spent ages consulting his notebooks and getting us to make endless adjustments to the suspension and roll bars. More often than not he'd end up with the settings he started off with. He was quite a big bloke for a racing driver, and one of the incongruous things about him in the original 49 was how upright he seemed to sit in it, with his helmet miles above the roll-over hoop.

There was a blow-up once between Chapman and Hill over his meddling with the cars. At an Oulton Park race, Graham pitted and asked his mechanic Bob Sparshott to cut off the bump-stop rubbers. Chapman overheard the exchange, and called Hill and Bob Dance into the transporter to explain in no uncertain terms that it was his car and as the designer he would decide what was done to it. Hill should seek his permission first. When Chapman was drawing up the basic features for the type 72, one of them was the rising-rate rear suspension, which could be flexible without bottoming. Denis Jenkinson remarked in *Motor Sport* magazine that one of the advantages for Chapman was that it enabled Lotus to 'do away with the over fastidious practice sessions in which Graham Hill played with bump stops!'

## Engine Irony

Graham's first race for Team Lotus was the South African Grand Prix on 2 January 1967 at Kyalami, ironically in a car powered by a BRM engine. The hapless H-16 was installed in the Lotus 43 chassis, and it was the same car and power unit that Clark had used to win the US Grand Prix. Both Hill and Clark were beset by problems during practice, including leaking fuel tanks, a broken diaphragm in the injection unit and a throttle sticking open. During the whole three days of practice, Hill managed just 13 laps. In the race he put a wheel on a kerb, bending a front wishbone and causing an oil pipe to rupture, spinning him off on his own oil.

Graham's next race for Team Lotus was at Warwick Farm, Sydney, a round of the Tasman series, and he persuaded Chapman to dispatch the

The brand new Lotus 48 Cosworth FVA Formula 2 car was shipped out for Graham to drive in the Australian Grand Prix at Warwick Farm on 19 February 1967, but after running a promising third behind Clark and Stewart, the crown wheel and pinion broke. In hot pursuit is Jack Brabham in the 2.5-litre Brabham-Repco V8. *(PN)*

Jackie Stewart and Jimmy Clark, one with a 2.2-litre BRM V8 and the other a 2-litre V8 Climax-powered 33, but the crown wheel and pinion failed.

Graham had better luck racing one of the works Lotus Cortinas at Brands Hatch in the Lombank Trophy race on 12 March, finishing second to Frank Gardner's Falcon and winning the up-to-2-litre class. This was the supporting event to the Race of Champions, in which no works Lotuses were entered. Graham made another appearance in a Lotus Cortina at

new Lotus 48 F2 car, powered by the latest Cosworth 1.6-litre FVA engine, for its race debut. He was running an excellent third place behind Snetterton on Good Friday, dicing with Vic Elford's Porsche 911 and ending up fourth behind the big bangers.

Although Team Lotus did not enter an F1 car in the 1967 *Daily Mail* Race of Champions, they did run a works Group 5 Lotus Cortina for Graham Hill in the two-heat Lombank Trophy. He came second to Frank Gardner's Alan Mann Falcon and beat Vic Elford's Porsche 911. Here, he drives up the Brands Hatch paddock. *(FF)*

A succession of outings followed for Graham in the Lotus 48 F2 car. These included the Good Friday meeting at Snetterton in which he finished a very close second to Rindt in the 40-lap final of the Guards 100. Graham was able to lead on occasion thanks partly to big Firestones that gripped well on corners – and a revised roll-bar setting – but Rindt was quicker down the straights. It was exciting stuff, as either driver could have won, and they equalled Stewart's lap record (set in the first heat) on the way. Rindt got the lead at the Esses on the last lap, and there was nothing Hill could do about it.

Next came the Wills Trophy at Silverstone on Easter Monday, almost a reprise of the Snetterton event, with all the stars present. Hill challenged Rindt during the final, having worked his way up from the back of the grid. But, having retired from the first heat, his second place in the second race was not enough to place him on the podium, although he achieved another lap record

nevertheless. He fared less well at the Pau Grand Prix on 2 April and a week later at Montjuich Park, Barcelona, retiring both times with gearbox and metering unit failures, although Clark beat Rindt in the Spanish race in the second Lotus 48.

At the International Trophy at Silverstone on 29 April, Graham drove the old type 33, chassis R11, with its 2-litre BRM V8 engine and Hewland gearbox. Despite a misfire on the warm-up lap, he set fastest lap in the race and, while he was out of contention for a win because of the presence of the 3-litre Ferrari, Cooper Maserati and Brabham Repcos that could draw away down Hanger straight, he managed to finish fourth.

Monaco was the first European Grand Prix in 1967, and it was the last outing for the long-serving Team Lotus 33s. Clark had his victorious R14 back from Australia, and Hill was in R11. The 33s were nimbler than the 3-litre cars around the narrow streets of the principality, but they did well to get them onto rows three and four of the grid.

Damon Hill tries the cockpit of his father's Lotus 48 for size while sister Samantha looks on. The occasion was the W.D. & H.O. Wills Formula 2 race at Silverstone on Easter Monday 1967, where Hill provided the only real challenge to Rindt, until the rear wishbone mountings pulled out of the Lotus tub. The Team Lotus mechanics bronze-welded the wishbone pivots back in place with strengthening gussets and, starting from the back of the grid in the final, Hill carved his way determinedly through the top-class field to finish second. *(PN)*

Hill and Chapman were fortunate to borrow a spare gear from Bob Anderson to replace a faulty Hewland component. In the race, on lap 38, Clark was running fourth, but his right-hand rear upright failed as he hurtled into Tabac in pursuit of McLaren, and he was instantly in the barriers. Hill had been running third, but clutch-slip obliged him to allow Amon's Ferrari by. Then Bandini, running second and pressing Hulme for the lead, suffered his sickening and ultimately fatal accident at the harbour chicane, and Amon picked up debris that meant a tyre change. The upshot was that Graham inherited second place and, with slipping clutch, broken chassis and suspension hanging off on one side, he finished the race, merely a lap down on Hulme. The fact that he was once again able to nurse an ailing car home at stop-start Monte Carlo probably says a great deal about Hill's mechanical sympathy, bettered at the time only by Jack Brabham.

Perhaps surprisingly, Graham did not have that many outings in the Lotus Cortinas, but in this instance he drives a works car on his way to fourth place behind the Falcons in the Group 5 saloon car bash that supported the F2 race at Snetterton on Good Friday 1967. His main opposition came from Vic Elford in a Porsche 911. *(IC)*

## Indy Debacle

As far as Graham and Team Lotus were concerned, the 1967 Indy venture was a disaster. To begin with, the plan to run 625bhp alcohol-fuelled BRM H-16 engines was sidelined late in the day due to doubts about its reliability. Working 24-hour shifts, the type 42 was converted to accept the longer (by 10in) Ford V8 that had been used in the previous year's type 38s. The full story is chronicled in Andrew Ferguson's *Team Lotus: the Indianapolis Years.* Having won the race in 1966 in a car with the same engine, Hill now struggled to qualify on the last weekend. On the Saturday morning of final qualification, the engine blew up, then on the Sunday morning while waiting to qualify, a water leak was discovered. He managed to qualify by the end of the afternoon at 163.317mph which, according to qualifying rules at the Brickyard, meant he was number 31 out of 33 even though he was by no means the slowest car. The debacle of a failed starter and duff engine as the race got underway was undone by rain, causing proceedings to be halted until the following day. The cars were impounded, so there was no real chance to investigate the running problem and, despite a change of plugs, Graham's race was run by lap 31. Jimmy's race in the type 38 was even shorter, terminated by a broken piston. Graham's speech at the post-race prize-giving ceremony lasted 20 minutes longer than his race.

Back in England, Hill began testing the new Lotus 49 at Snetterton ready for its debut at Zandvoort. He described it as a piece of modern sculpture, and was impressed by its 400bhp, a quantum leap from the F1 machinery he had driven previously. The first time Clark drove the sister car was actually at Zandvoort, while Hill took pole position with a time 4.2 seconds faster than the existing lap record, vying with Gurney's Eagle Weslake. At flag-fall, Hill shot into the lead and led the race for the first 10 laps. But the DFV engine faltered coming onto the pit straight, having broken one of the gears in the gear train to the camshaft. Clark saved the day, moving up through the field to win, first time out with a new car and a new engine.

At Spa for the Belgian Grand Prix, Jimmy and Graham were on the front row of the grid in their 49s, sandwiching Dan Gurney's Eagle. While Clark rushed off into the lead, Hill's starter would not operate due to a battery problem, and he joined the race half a lap in arrears. He was forced to retire on lap three when the gearbox failed, while Clark's DFV was let down by spark-plug failure, leaving the win to Gurney's Eagle.

Team Lotus mechanics Dougie Bridge *(left)*, and Dale Porteous *(right)*, get a hand from the Lucas technician to push Graham's 49/R1 prior to the 1967 Belgian Grand Prix. Hill suffered engine problems during Saturday practice, possibly under discussion here by Keith Duckworth and Ford of Britain's vice-president of engineering, Harley Copp, *(centre, in sunglasses)*. Despite this, the two Lotus 49s and Gurney's Eagle V12 were easily the quickest cars there. *(FMC)*

A pair of Formula 2 races straddled the French Grand Prix, staged on the 'Mickey Mouse' Bugatti circuit at Le Mans. These were the Reims and Rouen Grands Prix, and Graham came second and fourth respectively in the Team Lotus type 48. The new Le Mans Bugatti circuit incorporated the pits and Dunlop Bridge corner of the respected 24 Hours' circuit, and a made-up twisty section in the car park. It was originally built as a racing school circuit, and was inappropriate for Formula 1 cars. The entry was reduced due to apathy, and the Team Lotus transporter was detained at Dieppe. Having had to endure most of what remained of practice with a misfiring engine, Clark pipped Hill for pole in the dying minutes. But although the Lotus couple pulled out a good lead initially, both cars failed with stripped teeth on their crown wheels and pinions. After the race, steel side plate castings were made up by ZF for the housings,

The Formula 2 race that supported the 1967 Reims 12 Hours endurance event was a 37-lap slipstreamer (307km), dominated by Jochen Rindt's Winkelmann Racing Brabham Cosworth FVA, although Hulme, Hill and Surtees all took turns to lead, with Clark awarded fastest lap. Rindt just pipped Hill to the chequered flag by two-tenths of a second, and the first five cars were within a second of the winner. Here, Hill's Lotus 48 leads Hulme (Brabham), Surtees (Lola) and Clark (Lotus). *(FF)*

with bolts running right through, and the problem never resurfaced.

The 1967 British Grand Prix was staged at Silverstone, and as practice drew to a close, an awkward situation suddenly developed for Hill. Just as he was entering the pit road, a bracket retaining the bottom left rear radius rod pulled out of the monocoque, due to a faulty weld, causing the rear wheel to become detached. Despite the relatively low speed, the car was wrecked against the barriers. Making a split-second decision, Chapman flew Hill and his mechanics back to Potash Lane, Hethel, while the usable components from the damaged chassis were taken back to base by transporter. Using the only spare type 49 monocoque (49/3), a fresh car was built up overnight, with many new bits fabricated to suit. The only odd thing about it was the old type 33 nosecone. The car arrived at Silverstone just before the race. Chapman said at the time 'Sixteen of us did three weeks' work overnight!' Thanks to Graham's meticulous note-keeping regarding settings, the car could be set up fairly accurately for him. He and Jimmy were both on the front row of the grid, Hill's car having completed not a single lap of practice. Clark took an immediate lead, while Hill duelled with the Brabham pair as he felt his way with the new chassis. By lap 26, he took the lead. But on lap 55 as he entered Beckett's, one of the large Allen screws retaining the inner end of the upper transverse link in the rear suspension dropped out. Driving slowly back to the pits with the wheel leaning drunkenly inwards, another bolt was fitted and he rejoined, albeit two laps down. Then the engine blew up, and that was the end of a valiant attempt by all concerned. At least Jimmy Clark won, confirming the potential of the 49 and its new power plant.

A couple of Formula 2 races followed, with Graham coming sixth in the Lotus 48 at Tüln-Langenlebarn in Austria and posting a retirement at Madrid. His next outing was at Brands Hatch in the BOAC 500 enduro for prototypes and sports cars contesting the World Championship for makes. In 1967 the fabulous 36-car entry ranged from the winged Chaparral of Spence/Phil Hill (which won) to works Ferraris and Porsches, privateer Ford GT40s, Lola T70s (Brabham/Hulme had pole), a Gulf Mirage, Chevron B8s, Lotus 47s, Elans and the strangely anachronistic MGB and big Healey. Graham shared a

Hill watches as Dougie Bridge checks the plugs of the 49's Cosworth-Ford DFV engine during practice for the 1967 British Grand Prix at Silverstone. Keeping a note of things is *The Guardian*'s motor-racing correspondent Eric Dymock. *(JE)*

Co-inventor of the Cosworth-Ford DFV engine Keith Duckworth is on hand to assist as mechanics Dougie Bridge and Dale Porteous push Graham's Lotus 49 onto the Silverstone grid for the 1967 British Grand Prix. It was a brand new car, having been built up overnight back at Hethel after Hill's practice crash, and was fitted with an old type-33 nosecone. To the right is Siffert's Cooper Maserati. *(FMC)*

Hill was of relatively big build for a racing driver, and he sat rather upright in the Lotus 49, the car that would eventually bring his second world crown, with helmet somewhat higher than the roll-over hoop. *(FMC)*

2.2-litre flat-eight engined Porsche 910 with Jochen Rindt, starting from the middle of the third row, having logged identical times with the similar car of Siffert/McLaren and the Amon/Stewart Ferrari P4. Unfortunately for Graham, the 910 jumped out of gear when he was running sixth, early on in the race, and the engine over-revved, bouncing a valve, and that was that.

Graham's 49/1 had been repaired after its Silverstone shunt for the German Grand Prix at the Nürburgring, and it took some time to sort the settings out to his liking once more. He was down

in an uncharacteristic 13th place on row four of the four-three-four grid formation, almost 27 seconds slower than Clark on pole. He spun in the middle of the pack going down to turn one on the first lap, as someone banged wheels with him, then had a fright when one of the front wheels came loose as he was taking the fast downhill left-hander after the Flugplatz. After a pitstop to tighten it up, the rear suspension collapsed on the eighth lap.

Hill practised 49/R1 and 49/R3 for the 1967 German Grand Prix, crashing the newer chassis and using the original one for the race. Here on the Nürburgring pits apron, Chapman and Hill confer. *(FF)*

Back on the F2 trail, Jimmy and Graham went to Scandinavia in mid-August, placing third and fifth respectively at Karlskoga after a scrap with Stewart and Rindt. The Team Lotus drivers stayed with Jochen and his Finnish wife Nina in September while racing at Keimola and Hameenlinna near Helsinki – Hill came third and fifth. The Oulton Park Gold Cup, staged on 17 September, attracted a handful of F1 cars and the leading F2 protagonists, and Graham did well to bring the Lotus 48 F2 car home in third place. Lap records were set by Brabham's F1 Brabham at 1min 31.6sec (108.51mph) and Stewart's F2 Matra MS7 at 1min 32.8sec (107.11mph), showing that there was not much to choose between F1 and F2 in terms of outright pace, on a circuit like Oulton at least. There were no fewer than 25 Formula 2 events during 1967, most of which featured the top-line drivers. Some pundits felt that they should have kept away so that up-

The BOAÇ 500 six-hour race staged at Brands Hatch on 30 July 1967 was packed with exciting Group 6 prototypes and Group 4 sports cars, and Graham was paired with Jochen Rindt in a 2.2-litre flat-eight Porsche 910. They were not to know, of course, that they would be teammates again two years later. Early in the race Hill was leading the Porsche brigade when the car jumped out of gear, over-revved and burned a valve. *(P)*

and-coming drivers like Jackie Oliver and Piers Courage could shine. But there were not enough F1 races on the calendar to keep the likes of Graham Hill in full-time employment. Late in the season came the Albi Grand Prix, when Graham's 48 blew its engine, and the Rome Grand Prix at Vallelunga, where he came eighth. In races where both Team Lotus F2 cars were running, Clark usually finished the higher of the two, highlighting Hill's worse reliability record that year. Possibly he was overdriving his machinery in a bid to remain competitive with his teammate.

Graham's mechanic helps him buckle up on the grid at Vallelunga, 30km north of Rome, for the 1967 Rome Grand Prix, the final round of the European Formula 2 series. The aggregate result was based on two heats, from which Jacky Ickx emerged the winner and F2 champion, while Graham came eighth. *(FF)*

The support race at the 1967 Oulton Park Gold Cup meeting was the penultimate round of the BRSCC saloon car championship, won by Frank Gardner in the Alan Mann Falcon. Elford's Porsche 911 took the 1300–2000cc class after both works Lotus Cortinas crashed out. Here, Hill gets his Mk 2 version sliding nicely, while Ickx's older model can be seen in the ditch behind it. *(PN)*

At Mosport Park for the inaugural Canadian Grand Prix, Clark and Hill occupied the front row of the grid, along with champion elect Denny Hulme. However, the race was run in appalling conditions, and the electrics on Clark's 49 got saturated in the rain. The same thing happened to local driver Eppie Weitzes in the third works 49. Despite a spin, which required him to jump out to push-start the car, jump in while it was rolling and bump start it, Hill managed to recover and bring a 49 to the finish for the first time, coming in fourth.

Sometimes it can seem that everything at Monza teeters on the brink of chaos, as enthusiasm conflicts with officialdom. During practice for the Italian Grand Prix, the electronic timer went on the blink and issued optimistic readings, placing Hill on the third row of the grid. The regular drivers' briefing prior to the start had not taken place, so it was unclear whether there was to have been a dummy grid or just a straightforward 'off'. Thus when the flag fell (not the Italian one, it has to be said), most drivers, Hill included, set off at a cracking pace. Hill took second place as the pack tore into the first corner, the Curva Grande. Soon the leading bunch consisted of two Brabhams and two Lotuses. Brabham courteously indicated to Clark that he had a puncture, and the Scot pitted for a fresh wheel. Although the Cosworth DFV had the legs of the Repco V8 in a straight line, it lacked the reliability of the Australian unit, and Hill's crankshaft broke on lap 59 when he was a lap ahead. That was another example of Hill's bad luck, since by rights he had the race sewn up. Clark came home third (with a dead engine) behind Surtees's Honda and Jack Brabham.

## Winning the Toss

At Watkins Glen for the United States Grand Prix, Jimmy and Graham were both on the front row of the grid and, at last, Hill had pole position, set in the closing seconds of the final session. He netted a cool $1,000 for his efforts. For the first time since they'd been teammates, team tactics were discussed. In order that Ford's US hierarchy might witness a victory on its home turf, the Lotus drivers had express instructions from Walter Hayes not to clash with each other during the race. In the event of a close-run thing, the outcome would rest on the toss of a coin. The driver who won the toss (and therefore the race) would have to defer to his teammate if the same situation developed during the Mexican Grand Prix. In the event, Hill won the toss, and was in line to take the win at Watkins Glen, provided that he was ahead.

Graham made the best start and took the lead, with Gurney second and Clark third. Soon enough, the Lotuses were running first and second. But on lap 44, Hill's luck faltered as the 49's clutch began to baulk and gear-shifts became difficult. This gave Clark the opportunity to go by, and Hill now had to stave off Amon's works Ferrari. With two laps to go, Clark's upper transverse link snapped, causing the rear wheel to lean inwards, and allowing Hill to catch up. Thus, Team Lotus scored the much desired one-two result, with Hill finishing just six seconds behind Clark.

There was confusion at the start of the Mexican Grand Prix, as Clark was caught unawares by the starter's unexpected double-wave of his flag, and Gurney on the second row ploughed into the back of the Lotus, splitting his radiator. Hill had the

Ford's Walter Hayes is about to be baptised by Jimmy Clark's fizz after the Team Lotus duo scored a magnificent one-two at Watkins Glen in 1967. From left: Gordon Huckle, Chapman, Hill, Hayes, Clark, Keith Duckworth and Alan McCall. *(FMC)*

lead on the first lap, pursued by Amon and a recovered Clark. As the Scot took the lead, his clutch gave up and he drove the entire race without it. Hill's race lasted until lap 18, when a halfshaft broke, damaging the rear suspension in the process, while Clark went on to a comfortable victory.

From references to second-string drivers in his autobiography *Life at the Limit* it is clear that Graham had become rather elitist by this time in his career, and maybe even a touch xenophobic. For instance, he refers to Canadian Eppie Weitzes, who drove the third Team Lotus 49, not by name (although it is not an easy one to spell) but simply as a 'local driver' at the Canadian Grand Prix. Moises Solana gets the same treatment in Mexico. And of the inaugural race at Jarama in 1967, Graham wrote dismissively: 'We had run in a Formula 1 race there in the previous November – just Lotus and a few locals. We came first and second, but there wasn't much opposition; most of the other cars were Formula 2 anyway.'

The first race of the 1968 season was the South African Grand Prix at Kyalami, held on 1 January. Here, Graham found himself briefly back at the wheel of a BRM, giving spectators a demonstration run in a 1950 P15 supercharged V16 model, creating quantities of wheel-spin and tyre smoke that would not have disgraced a dragster.

Meanwhile, in the serious business of Formula 1, the action was running true to form, as Clark set pole, with Hill alongside him but slower by a full second. Stewart in the new, pale-green Matra MS9 Cosworth DFV completed the front row, a tenth slower than Hill. Graham's 49/3 was the same car he had used on occasion the previous season, although Jimmy's 49/4 was a new chassis. Stewart made the best getaway, followed by Clark, normally the start-line maestro, while Graham made a poor start. Clark was soon ahead of his fellow Scot, pulling away at a second a lap. Eventually on lap 27 Hill managed to claw his way past the understeering Matra. That was the way it finished, with Clark taking what was to be his final Grand Prix win, some 25 seconds ahead of his teammate. Hill had not had such an easy time of it, coming under pressure from Rindt, who was now driving for Brabham.

From South Africa, some of the Team Lotus outfit travelled to New Zealand for four races starting with the Grand Prix at Pukekohe on 6 January. Clark's 49/2 was fitted with a DFV engine with bore and stroke reduced to 2.5 litres to comply with Tasman regulations. This unit broke while Clark was in the lead, giving the win to Amon's Ferrari 2.4-litre V6. By the third New Zealand race at Christchurch, the news had broken that Team Lotus was to be sponsored by the tobacco company John Player, and the 49 was presented in the red, gold and white livery of the Gold Leaf cigarette brand. Jimmy gave the commercial partnership an excellent initiation with a start-to-finish victory in the Lady Wigram Trophy.

Graham arrived at Brisbane for the Rothmans International 100 race at Surfers' Paradise on 11 February, along with a similar 2.5-litre DFV powered 49/1. It was a Lotus one-two, with Clark winning, and the result was repeated at Warwick Farm a week later. Here the Scot enjoyed a more comfortable win, with Piers Courage third on both occasions. The Australian Grand Prix was staged at Sandown Park, Melbourne, and Clark, in fine form, won again, while Graham was third behind Amon. The final round of the series was held at Longford, Tasmania, but heavy rain compromised the F1-based cars' traction, allowing Courage in his F2 Cosworth FVA-powered McLaren M4A to run away with it. Clark was fifth and Graham sixth. Nevertheless, Jimmy had done enough to become 1968 Tasman champion.

The first race in Europe in 1968 was the Race of Champions, another regular event in the calendar. Just one 49 was entered for Graham, and it would not handle around the dips and sweeps of the Brands Hatch circuit. He eventually retired with a broken driveshaft.

## Tragedy

On 31 March came an F2 race, the Barcelona Grand Prix. The type 48s, which Hill described as 'very nice cars', were liveried in the same Gold Leaf colour scheme as their F1 counterparts, and Clark was second quickest to Stewart in practice. In the race he was punted off when Ickx misjudged his braking, while Graham's FVA engine broke. And so to Hockenheim, the first round of the European F2 Championship for non-graded drivers – which of course Hill and Clark were not, being F1 stars and thus not eligible for F2 points. It was an important race as far as Formula 2 was concerned, and a top-class field was present. The Team Lotus drivers were originally booked to drive one of the sleek Alan Mann 3-litre Ford P3 prototypes at Brands Hatch in the BOAC 500 race, which clashed with the Hockenheim event. But word of this assignment apparently reached Clark too late for him to feel comfortable about cancelling his F2 commitment. The weather at Hockenheim was dismal, and neither works Lotus was on the pace. Hill's car had the wrong gear ratios and was not handling properly.

Clark's fatal accident happened on the fifth lap when he was in eighth place. Poignantly, Hill wrote in *Life at the Limit*:

The murky weather at the Hockenheim stadium provided the setting for the tragedy that was about to unfold on 7 April 1968. Hill's mechanic Dave 'Beaky' Simms makes last-minute adjustments to the Lotus 48 Cosworth FVA as Graham prepares to climb aboard. *(JE)*

No one knew for sure that Clark had been killed until after the first heat of the Deutschland Trophy at Hockenheim was over, and Graham completed the full 20 laps, coming 12th. Naturally, the shocked Lotus team withdrew. *(JE)*

I realised straight away that whoever had gone off there was in serious trouble, but it never occurred to me that it might have been Jimmy. When I came into the pits at the end of the race, one of the mechanics told me that it was Jimmy who had crashed. All the mechanics were in a pretty shocked state, but I knew at once that he must have been killed – he would have gone straight into the trees at near maximum speed. My reactions at the time were a bit odd – I don't think I really took in what had happened. It took a while to register that that was the last time we were going to see Jimmy.

Graham goes on to provide a fitting tribute to his friend and teammate:

We were completely different. I was more relaxed than he was, or he was more nervous than I am – it's difficult to know which way to put it. He had the will to win, this tremendous urge to win, which you've just got to have. Some people have it more than others and he had it more than most. He was a fighter whom you could never shake off and whom you never dared underestimate. He invariably shot off in the lead and just killed the opposition, set up a lead and just sat there, dictating the race.

Jackie Stewart put Clark's death, and the enormous risks run by drivers of the period, into perspective:

I think we all dealt with it quite well in those days. We were all businesslike about it, and it was happening so much at that time. We were losing drivers ten a penny, in '68 we lost a driver every month. It got to a point where the first question I asked when I got out of the car was, 'Is everyone okay?' in case somebody had been killed. And these people had to be helped at home, the wives and families. There was nobody out there who would deal with that sort of thing, dealing with the bereaved families and friends. A modern Grand Prix driver wouldn't understand that. It was your own friends that did it, it was just a time when everybody had to deal with it.

# Chapter 6
# Team Leader

COLIN Chapman was devastated by Clark's death. He became reclusive, contemplating whether to disband Team Lotus and quit racing completely. When Mike Spence was killed at Indianapolis exactly a month later, in what should have been Clark's 56 turbine, the decision about whether to go on hung in the balance. The person who probably tipped it in favour of continuing was Graham Hill. A fortnight after Hockenheim, he drove the 49 at Silverstone in the *Daily Express* International Trophy. Sixth fastest in practice, Hill was running third in the race when a fuel line split on lap 14 and he parked it.

A week later, Graham was back in the thick of it in the Formula 2 Madrid Grand Prix at Jarama, working his way up to sixth place from a poor start, but retiring when a wheel hub peg broke. His new Gold Leaf Team Lotus teammate Jackie Oliver did not start, the mechanics having been unable to cure a practice fault.

The real morale booster for Team Lotus came at the Spanish Grand Prix, also at Jarama, on 12 May 1968. Graham started from the third row – shared with Surtees's Honda V12 and Ickx's Ferrari V12, and spent much of it battling with Hulme's McLaren. Amon's leading Ferrari expired, so Hill had the lead, and on the tight, twisty circuit there was little to choose between the Cosworth-powered cars. When it became clear to Denny that Graham

could not be passed, he backed off and Graham took his first Grand Prix victory since the 1965 American Grand Prix. Although Chapman was not present to see the win, for Team Lotus personnel it was just the lift that was needed. Jim Endruweit remembered:

The last meeting I attended as racing manager at Team Lotus was the Spanish Grand Prix in '68, a month or so after Jimmy died. And it was just Graham racing. We had the choice of Firestone or Goodyear tyres – it was a bit of a thing to have two different tyres from two different contacts. And he was saying, 'Can we try this, and can we try that', and there was all

In spite of the loss of Clark two weeks earlier, Graham was at Silverstone to race in the *Daily Express* International Trophy. Here he signs a young fan's dollar bill, having just opened the new paddock bar. Behind Hill is BRDC Chairman Sir Gerald Lascelles, and on the left is press officer Roger Palmer. *(RP)*

this routine stuff we were trying to do. Changing the tyres and the roll bars. Graham was just interminable. At one point he said that he'd do six laps practising just one corner of the circuit, trying to refine his line and throttle control through it. He knew exactly what he'd done on the last lap, and he'd try it differently on the next one. That was his approach, he was very methodical.

It was that very determination that helped pull Team Lotus out of its anguish.

Happy trio on the podium at Jarama – Denny Hulme (left) came second to Graham, with Brian Redman third in his works Cooper T86B BRM V12. *(FMC)*

Graham's win in the 1968 Spanish Grand Prix – the first world championship round after Clark's death – was a real morale booster for Team Lotus. Hill, in 49/R1, spent much of the race locked in combat with Hulme's McLaren M7A, and when it was obvious that there was no way past on the twisty Jarama circuit, Hulme backed off for Hill to win. *(PN)*

Prior to the Spanish Grand Prix, some members of the GPDA tried to get the Jarama race cancelled on safety grounds, but the matter was put to rights by the Royal Automobile Club of Spain and ODACISA, the circuit owners. The objections centred on cones marking some corners, loose gravel on the edges, and the varying height of guardrails. The official is explaining to Graham that last-minute work will have solved the problems. *(FMC)*

## Morale Raiser

Not that team members had been brooding inactively at Hethel. On the contrary, the revamped type 49, the 49B, was being readied for its debut at the Monaco Grand Prix on 26 May. This was 49/5, which Hill would drive, while the second 49B chassis R6 would be ready for Spa. The main differences were a slightly longer wheelbase, aerofoils either side of the nose-cone, and an engine cover that straddled the intake trumpets and ended in a wedge-shaped rear. In this, there were echoes of the type 56 Indianapolis gas-turbine shape, which was more of a pure wedge shape. These were the first serious ventures into F1 aerodynamics since the streamlined Mercedes-Benz, Connaught and Vanwalls of the 1950s. The 49's gearbox was brand new. The original ZF gearbox may have been as sophisticated and precise as a Swiss watch, but it was replaced by the tougher Hewland unit that was used in F2. This also had the advantages of being smaller and lighter than the ZF. The Hewland gearbox suited Graham better, as he preferred to do block shifts, going straight from fifth to second gear, say, whereas the ZF required shifting in sequence right through the gearbox. Driveshafts were also new. The entire rear end of the 49B – the rear suspension and wheels, gearbox, oil tank and cooler – could be detached for ease of engine changes. Hill, the master of Monaco, set fastest practice lap, but it was Johnny Servoz-Gavin who eclipsed him at the start, the Frenchman's Matra MS10 leading for three laps. Oliver, meanwhile, had crashed his 49/1 on the first lap – much to Chapman's fury – having been unable to avoid McLaren's own crash in the confines of the tunnel. The race developed into a battle between Hill and Richard Attwood's BRM, which set fastest lap right at the end in a bid to close down Hill, and it turned out to be a very close finish. Just five of the 16 starters went the distance – 11 had retired as early as lap 17 – and there was considerable surprise in the Lotus pits

that Hill's new car held together. So far so good: two wins, and a second place back in South Africa, meant that Hill was well placed in the world title stakes. And at this point, Graham was awarded the OBE in the Queen's Birthday Honours List for services to motor racing, acknowledging his success on the track as well as his role as elder statesman and the sport's ambassador.

There was certainly no drop in the variety of events Hill took part in. The demanding schedule involved the Indy 500 once again, and Team Lotus was present with the STP-sponsored type 56. Competitions manager Andrew Ferguson recalls in his *Team Lotus: The Indianapolis Years* that 'Graham was doing an incredible job bringing us all out of the stupor caused by Hockenheim. I really

Graham made it two Grand Prix wins in a row, leading from the fourth lap to the finish at Monaco on 26 May. Driving 49/R5, he turns into the chicane at the start of the harbour-front section, with Jo Siffert in Rob Walker Lotus 49/R2 behind, and Surtees's Honda RA301 V12 and Rindt's Brabham BT24-Repco in pursuit. *(PN)*

Hill and Chapman discuss the Lotus 56/3 four-wheel drive turbine during qualifying for Indianapolis in 1968. Graham was second fastest in practice, and a poll of the racing press prior to the event put him favourite to win at 5–3. But after 110 laps, a bush securing an upper rocking arm pivot bearing failed due to over-machining, and the car lost a wheel, pitching Hill into the wall at turn two, happily without injury. *(Indianapolis Motor Speedway)*

cannot praise him enough for his spirit and the enormous effort to keep us all in top pitch; after all, in Jimmy he had also lost a very close friend, but his character in blotting the affair from both his and our minds was extraordinary.' Ferguson goes on to relate how Graham took Chapman, Maurice Phillipe (Team Lotus's chief designer), Stewart and himself out for dinner one Sunday evening, when alcohol consumption was prohibited, and they drank wine out of coffee cups – fine until a novice waitress added coffee to the wine.

Another tragedy, however, was imminent. Mike Spence was asked to take out 56/2 to ascertain why STP's rookie Greg Weld had not gone very quickly in it. The unfortunate Lotus driver hit the wall at 163mph, and a front wheel was torn off and struck him on the head. He died in hospital that night. Chapman immediately relinquished all interest in the event, leaving Andrew Ferguson to mastermind affairs. The relationship with STP appears to have been turbulent, to say the least. Graham in 56/3 started from the front row alongside teammate and pole-winner Joe Leonard in 56/1, with Art Pollard behind them in 56/4. All three circulated comfortably in the top nine. But on lap 110 Hill's front suspension broke, the result of a fault in production. A front wheel came off, and Hill had nowhere to go but into the wall. Miraculously unhurt, he returned to England for the Whit Monday F2 race at Crystal Palace, where his 48 ground to a halt – yet again he had lost a wheel.

With lap speeds approaching 150mph at the 8.7-mile Spa-Francorchamps circuit, aerodynamics came into play, and several teams' cars, including Brabham, McLaren and Ferrari, sprouted wings over their engines or rear axles. Practice began badly for Hill when his new Hewland gearbox jammed, and on the Saturday, rain hampered the proceedings. He was half a minute off the pace, and started from the sixth row of the three-two-three grid, electing to race without the front fins and rear wedge. On the fifth lap, one of the 49B's driveshafts seized, and Hill walked back to the pits.

In jet-set style, he returned to North America, this time to Canada for a USAC race at Mosport Park in the 56 turbine. Although beset by throttle

Graham Hill at speed in the works Lotus 48 Cosworth FVA at Crystal Palace on Whit Monday 1968. The Holt's Trophy was a round of the European F2 Championship, in two heats and a final, and Hill's race came to an abrupt halt when a driveshaft snapped and the wheel came off. The final was a Jochen Rindt benefit, the Brabham driver winning easily from Redman and Regazzoni. *(PN)*

Hill and Oliver are in discussions, right, as the GLTL mechanics fit gurney flap extensions to the rear spoilers of their cars and Firestone technicians check tyre wear in the Zandvoort pits prior to the 1968 Dutch Grand Prix. *(FMC)*

lag he was pleasantly surprised by how well the 56 performed on a road circuit (as opposed to a banked speedway), and secured a place on the front row. He had discovered at Le Mans in 1963 that the way to get the best out of a gas turbine, with its notoriously long throttle lag, was to balance braking with acceleration. This meant building up throttle pressure long before the exit of a corner, and keeping his foot on the accelerator when on the over-run. But he hit a patch of oil in practice, and the wayward 56 cleared a ditch, travelling unchecked through the rough for some 200 yards. He was thus a non-starter.

Hill discusses problems with his 49/R5 with mechanic Bob Sparshott during practice for the 1968 Dutch Grand Prix. They included faulty ignition timing, and the replacement of some newly-fitted driveshafts with old ones, because the universal joints lacked sufficient angular movement on full suspension travel. *(PN)*

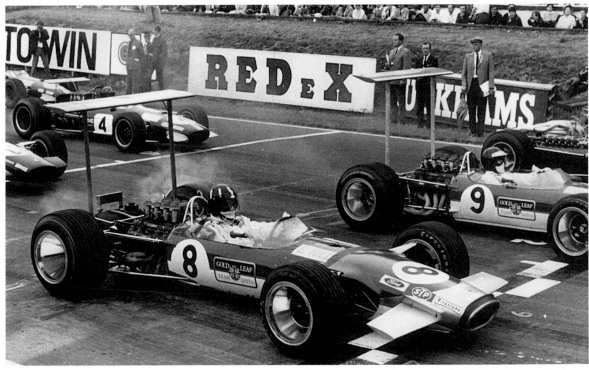

Hill start. The Gold Leaf Lotus 49s of Hill and Jackie Oliver take off at Brands Hatch for the 1968 British Grand Prix, with the Lotus number two driver getting the best traction. Amon's Ferrari is the other front row starter, with Rindt in the Brabham (No.4) behind. Compared with the works Lotus 49 rear wings, everyone else's were quite puny. *(FF)*

In the Dutch Grand Prix at Zandvoort, the 49B's aerodynamics started to make sense and the car had more grip through the corners. This was not enough to prevent Hill from going off twice at Tarzan hairpin during the race, once when the throttle slides jammed with wet sand - it had rained - and then late in the race when he aquaplaned off and a fence post took out the front suspension. In another wet race at Rouen-les-Essarts in the French Grand Prix Hill was let down again by a driveshaft failure, having just passed his old nemesis, Jackie Stewart.

This was the first time that the lofty strut-mounted wings had been used. Mounted on struts taken off the rear uprights, the 49Bs' wings were the biggest yet, and were very effective at producing downforce on the rear of the car and thus better traction in corners. Jackie Oliver's car had a wider rear wing and bigger front fins than Hill's. In practice, Oliver had a colossal accident when a wing support gave way, probably because of turbulence from another car, and his 49B destroyed itself comprehensively against a brick

gatepost. Oliver was extremely fortunate to walk away.

## Leading the Championship

The British Grand Prix at Brands Hatch in July was preceded by an F2 race at the Tüln-Langenlebarn airfield circuit, but Graham's 48 retired with a gearbox oil leak. Things looked promising at Brands for the Grand Prix though, and he secured pole position – winning 100 bottles of champagne in the process – with Oliver alongside in the second 49B, and Siffert's Rob Walker 49B on the second row. Hill led until lap 26 when a knuckle joint in the final drive broke and the whirling driveshaft whipped off the suspension, which in turn caused him to lose the wheel. This was getting to be a bit of a habit, and an alarming one at that. Oliver led until lap 43 when his engine failed, handing the win to Siffert and the Walker team.

The Nürburgring and its setting in the Eifel mountains were shrouded in cloud for most of the German Grand Prix, and it rained intermittently

While Hill took over the lead from teammate Oliver on lap three of the 1968 British Grand Prix, 49/R5's left-hand driveshaft broke a universal joint on lap 26. Oliver then led until lap 44 (out of 80) when his 49/R2's transmission failed, and the race was won by Jo Siffert in Rob Walker's brand new Lotus 49/R7. It was the Walker team's first win since Moss won at the Nürburgring back in 1961. *(CTL)*

during the race. A lap of the 22.8km Nordschleife included 187 corners, equally left and right-handed, with a 1,000ft difference in elevation between the pits at the top and the lowest part of the circuit. There were varying degrees of banking on some corners, such as the Karusell, and cars became airborne on blind crests in some places, damaging the underside of the car as it exceeded the protection of its bump rubbers on landing. Other hazards in these pre-Armco days included slippery sections where resurfacing or patching had taken place and puddles of water could form, and in heavy rain, streams which ran across the track.

Graham's 49B/5 had much bigger driveshafts fitted to reduce the chance of breakages, and in poor driving conditions he put it on the second row alongside Vic Elford's Cooper BRM V12 – the Ferraris of Ickx and Amon were fastest, with Rindt's Brabham-Repco completing the front row. But Stewart in the Matra MS10 got the jump at the start, and Hill found himself battling with Amon for second place. By lap 12 it was raining hard and, as he crested a rise, Hill hit a stream running across the road, aquaplaned and spun to a halt. Amon had gone off himself just before, so there was no immediate danger of him being run into, but Hill had to push his Lotus out of the way and bump start it again. Now it was Rindt who

challenged him hard for the last two laps. Hill came second to Stewart, four minutes in arrears, with Rindt a scant six seconds behind him. It was Hill's first finish since Monaco. Interestingly, the first three cars were fitted with Dunlop, Firestone and Goodyear tyres respectively, suggesting that no one make had a particular advantage in the diverse conditions, although it has been suggested that Stewart's tyres were much the most effective.

Graham then went to Oulton Park for the Guards Gold Cup, but the 49's crown wheel and pinion failed in the Hewland transmission after six laps. Oliver was third behind Stewart and Amon, while Derek Bell made his F1 debut in a works Ferrari. In one of the more peculiar episodes of his career, Graham drove an Alan Mann Escort-FVA in the 19-lap saloon car race. The car was fitted with a blower that allowed it to compete with the Ford Falcons, the idea being that Hill would effectively get among the big V8s of Muir, Hobbs and Pierpoint and take points away from them, to the benefit of Alan Mann's regular driver and tin-top championship contender Frank Gardner in the normally aspirated Escort-FVA. The Hill car was not quick enough to challenge the Falcons however, and he was forced out with a flat tyre, while Gardner finished forth behind the American Fords.

Gold Leaf Team Lotus entered three cars for the Italian Grand Prix – the third was for Mario Andretti, who was disqualified from taking part (as was Bobby Unser) after a promising showing in practice, because he had raced in the USA less than 24 hours before the Italian Grand Prix was due to start. Mario remembers that the transition from USAC to Formula 1 was not difficult:

> The Formula 1 car was so much easier to
> drive, much more agile, nimble and
> balanced, and better brakes. Especially in
> those days, the Indianapolis cars on a road
> course were just cumbersome to say the
> least. The gearbox and everything in the

Formula 1 car was so much better. When I first sat in a little Lotus 49 at Monza, oh man, I felt like I was born in it, and so I loved that. It was great – an easy transition for me.

In the event, both Hill's and Oliver's engines had failed at the end of Monza practice, so Mario would have been effectively without a car anyway. The race was typically a Monza slipstreaming battle, with both Lotuses among the leading bunch. Oliver set fastest lap. Then, on lap 11, Hill's car lost a rear wheel going through the 130mph Lesmo curve, striking the barrier in a cloud of dust. He recovered the errant wheel and carried it back to the pits in his defence. Incredibly, after all his retirements, Graham was still leading the 1968 championship, with Stewart second.

Jackie Stewart won the Formula 2 race at Reims on 15 September in his Matra, while Graham was fourth and Oliver sixth in the Gold Leaf type 48s. The three trans-Atlantic rounds of the World Championship were grouped together for convenience of travelling. The Canadian Grand Prix was staged at the curvaceous St Jovite track some 60 miles north of Montreal, and Graham was fifth fastest in practice. Oliver's 49B/2 was found to have a cracked rear bulkhead, so all three works Lotus chassis were plated accordingly at the weak point. Around lap 22, it became obvious that Hill's number one Lotus was not being thrown around as hard as usual, and sure enough, the gremlins had struck again. This time the pair of top engine mounts had pulled loose in the bulkhead, and only the rigidity of the engine's flush location with the tub kept it from buckling. The effect was that, as he accelerated, the chassis opened in the middle. After a pit stop to assess exactly what the problem was, the mechanics wanted to wheel the car away. But Chapman had other ideas, and Hill was sent out again. This seems an extraordinary risk to ask someone to take, but Hill did as he was told. By nursing the car around the tight circuit for the rest of the 90-lap race, he managed to come in fourth (four laps down), gaining three valuable points towards his championship tally.

Mario Andretti made his Formula 1 race debut at Watkins Glen on 6 October. His Lotus 49B/5 had narrower wings than the other two, but all three Lotuses needed fresh engines, a bombshell delivered by Chapman to the mechanics at 10pm the night before the race. Graham got the brand new motor, Andretti the best of the existing DFVs, and Oliver got the leftovers, something that he was less than happy about. As a rule, they raced brand new engines because they were at their best then, and used tired ones for practice at the following Grand Prix. In the event, the exhausted mechanics had no time to fit new springs or wheels to Oliver's car, and one of his wheels disintegrated in morning's pre-race warm-up, destroying the car against a barrier. There had been a question mark over the quality of the wheels then in use, and Chapman had ordered fresh ones. In fact, their arrival in the Watkins Glen workshops had gone unnoticed by the mechanics, as had the instruction to fit them. Now though, Mario and Graham had them fitted for the race.

The American driver had never even been to Watkins Glen before, let alone raced there, and he promptly went out and set pole time. This spurred Hill to greater efforts, and he logged third quickest time after Stewart – who was now third behind Hill and Hulme in the fight for the title. Andretti recalls the practice sessions and how it felt to be leading the established Lotus number one driver:

It seemed like everything just gelled that particular day. The car really felt good to me, I had such a positive memory of just a couple of weeks before in Monza where we had a very good test. I got a very good tow from Bobby Unser who was driving for BRM specifically for that race. But Watkins Glen was totally foreign to me. I hadn't been there till that weekend, but the car just seemed to be right and I obviously used every possible second of practice learning the circuit. I did quite a bit of running, and I found myself locked in with Jackie Stewart for potential pole. I thought I had a real shot at it, or at least the front row, and I was a bit surprised, quite honestly.

But at the same time, it did feel really good and right, and as to why I was able to pull that off versus Graham, I don't know.

Come the race, after running second for a while, Mario's clutch packed up on lap 32. Graham was subsequently second for much of the race, having begun with a couple of unexpected dramas. Firstly, the car's fuel tanks – an auxiliary one had been fitted for this long race – were over-full and, under acceleration, fuel was pouring down the air intakes, making the engine run so rich that it cut out. Demoted to fourth place, Hill discovered his steering wheel could be pushed against the dashboard, trapping his fingers while cornering. While wrestling with the problem, he inadvertently knocked the fuel pump switches off, losing more ground. The steering wheel continued to move in this alarming fashion on and off for the rest of the race, but as he got the hang of it he began to move back up through the field, and eventually finished second to Stewart. Hulme had crashed, and thus scored no points.

The battle for the World Championship would be decided at Mexico City. The Olympic games were being staged there at the time, so the Grand Prix was postponed until 3 November. In the interim, Graham returned to Europe for a couple of F2 races at Albi and Vallelunga, placing seventh on aggregate at the Rome circuit. Just before the Grand Prix, Chapman's fertile mind hit on a way to gain more pace in a straight line. Overnight, he devised a way to make the 49's rear wing tilt so it would, in effect, have a flatter profile along the straights. In order to counter the drag along the straights, it could be feathered by the driver using a fourth foot pedal, pressed down while travelling along the straight, and then released prior to the corner. That would also conveniently allow him to operate the clutch pedal. The wing was thus tilted for

optimum downforce in the corners. It was operated by means of a Bowden cable connected to the foot pedal and a pair of bungee straps. Tilting rear wings had already been achieved by Chaparral, demonstrated on the 2F that won the BOAC 500 in 1967. An earlier precedent was Porsche's, whose aerodynamicist Michael May had experimented with a strut-mounted wing on a 550 Spyder back in 1956. But these cars' wings had relatively beefy struts compared with those of the Lotus 49B.

In Mexico the mechanics resigned themselves to another all-nighter – a 14-hour stint for four of them in fact – and it meant borrowing hundreds of rivets from other teams. The new wing couldn't be tried because Chapman didn't want to alert their rivals to what they were up to. In a bout of gamesmanship, Team Lotus went the other way, taking all the aerodynamic aids off Hill's car, so that other teams denuded their own cars, believing that Lotus must be on to something.

Because the Magdalena Mixhuca circuit was in a vast public park in Mexico City, unofficial practice was not possible. But the canny Stewart had been there the previous Monday, practising, while Hill was at Vallelunga. At the fifth lap of the

For the Formula 2 race at Albi in October 1968, the Winkelmann team appeared with a massive bi-wing on the rear of Rindt's Brabham BT 23. Graham and Jochen examined the bracing and the dipping mechanism, but despite the complexity, it was inadequate and the concept was dropped. *(FF)*

Mexican Grand Prix, Stewart led Hill and Hulme, the three championship contenders together. By this time, one of the bungee cords that made the Lotus's rear wing flip had come adrift, causing Hill some concern as, without the ability to dip the wing into corners, the car oversteered terribly. Fortunately the other strap held up for the duration of the race and the wing more or less behaved itself. Another factor at Mexico was the kerbs that lined the corners, which most drivers chose to cut across. Graham did not at first, conscious of the harm it might do to his transmission. But once Stewart began to attack in earnest, he followed suit, changing gear on the kerbs in order to minimise the stress on the transmission. Meanwhile, Hulme was out with a broken damper, and Hill re-passed Stewart, who was now being caught by Siffert in the Rob Walker Lotus 49B. The Swiss driver passed Stewart and then took Hill for the lead on lap 22. Hill was able to slipstream the dark-blue Lotus down the straights and pull away from Stewart a little. But three laps later, Siffert's throttle linkage came undone, and Hill was back in front. Stewart's Matra then began to succumb to falling fuel pressure, which took the heat off Hill. The drama was not quite over, however. On the last lap, Hill eased off so that teammate Oliver could overtake him and have one more lap to try and catch Rodriguez. The Mexican driver arrived at the hairpin going far too fast, and Hill, who was cruising for Oliver's benefit, had to swerve out of Pedro's way or else be taken out and lose the title. It was that close. Graham had lost the 1964 world title because Bandini crashed into him at the very same spot. But now, Graham came in to win, and clinch his second World Championship. And Lotus had taken the constructors' title.

Hill the statesman came into his own when he returned to the UK. Not only was there the OBE presentation at Buckingham Palace, there were numerous public appearances, presentations and speeches to be made. He was runner-up on BBC TV's *Sportsview* 'Sports Personality of the Year' contest, (won by David Hemery, an Olympic gold medallist). Perhaps the real implications of his achievement in 1968 were only truly evident to race fans. After all, Graham had, virtually single-handedly, galvanised Team Lotus – and its founder – in the aftermath of Clark and Spence's deaths, and snatched victory out of despair.

## Rindt On Board

Colin Chapman chose to supersede Jackie Oliver with the whirlwind talent of Jochen Rindt for the 1969 season. The Austrian had been virtually invincible in F2, winning 23 F2 races between 1967 and 1970. His nearest rival in terms of results was Stewart, who won nine races. Rindt was dogged by an unreliable Repco engine while driving for Brabham in F1, and might have fared better with mechanical reliability. Rindt was seen as the man most likely to succeed, given the best equipment, though he was the first non-British driver to be given a works F1 contract by Chapman, and his appointment led to frictions within the team, most notably between Chapman and Hill. Aged 27, Rindt was from the new generation of F1 drivers, although he had yet to win a Grand Prix. Now he was accorded joint number one status with the vastly more experienced two-times world champion. The reasoning behind this demeaning – for Hill at least – decision was that Chapman saw in Rindt a driver in Clark's mould. He longed for a natural talent, contrasting with Hill's methodical time-consuming attitude to set-up. Andretti might have provided the answer – as he would do, nearly a decade in the future – but he was committed to USAC racing on more or less a full-time basis. But now, Chapman believed that Rindt had what it took to get straight into a racing car and give it ten-tenths commitment. The attrition rate was particularly high for drivers of that ilk during the 1950s and 1960s, but the analytical Hill suffered only one major accident during his race career, although he was lucky to get away with that, and of course he could have been fatally injured in other crashes caused by mechanical failure.

The driver change also saw chief mechanic Bob Dance transfer to work on the new four-wheel drive type 63 F1 and 64 Indy car projects, and he

A harbinger of the string of catastrophic failures of the struts that carried the 49's rear wing, this time on Hill's 49/R8 during practice for the 1969 Australian Grand Prix at Lakeside, Queensland. As Hill extricates himself from the cockpit, mechanics Roger and Dale Porteous gaze in amazement at the tilted apparatus. It was a bigger wing than had been used in New Zealand, just before, and a smaller, fixed one was fitted for the race, in which Hill finished fourth. *(FF)*

was replaced by Leo Wybrott, while Bob Sparshott quit altogether and Willy Cowe took over as Graham's mechanic with Dave Simms alongside him.

The first contest on the agenda for Team Lotus's 1969 line-up was the seven-race Tasman series, with four events in New Zealand and three in Australia. The three F1 teams to make the trip 'down under' were Gold Leaf Team Lotus, Ferrari (although Amon and Bell had to arrange their own trip) and Frank Williams, who was running Piers Courage in a Brabham BT24 with a 2.5-litre DFV engine like Lotus's. Frank Gardner drove Alec Mildren's Alfa Romeo V8-powered car, which Alan Mann had built. Hill was beset by mechanical misfortune from the outset, with a litany of failures including collapsing front suspension, a broken driveshaft, buckled aerofoil struts,

waterlogged ignition, and disassembled throttle linkage. He did manage second place in the Lady Wigram Trophy at Christchurch, and also at Invercargill, coming fourth at Lakeside in the Australian Grand Prix and sixth at Sandown Park. Rindt came second to Amon at Pukekohe, despite the controls of the aerofoil breaking down, but he totalled the 49B at Levin. The Hethel workshops pulled all the stops out and dispatched the makings of a new car for the Christchurch airfield circuit race, which Rindt duly won. He was on pole for the round at Teretonga (Invercargill) but a driveshaft broke on the line, and Derek Bell's Ferrari rammed him – twice. After the race, Bell reveals in his book *My Racing Life*, Jochen said not a word. But Graham asked Derek, 'What the hell were you up to?' and when Derek tried to make a joke of it, Graham came back with, 'It's not funny. It's just stupid… You don't go when the flag comes down, you go when the bloke in front of you goes!' Away from the circuits Hill was more relaxed – he took up golf, playing between races, along with Rindt, Courage and Frank Gardner, who was already an accomplished golfer.

## Four-Wheel Drive

One of the factors that affected the outcome of the year for Team Lotus was Chapman's decision to produce the four-wheel drive type 63. A year earlier, Lotus had come up with a pure wedge-shaped car – the type 57/8 – intended to function as a DFV-powered F1 car and an FVA Formula 2 car. The shape was akin to the type 56 gas-turbine, and was also adapted for the type 63 four-wheel drive car. It had no fins or rear wing; the doorstop wedge shape providing all the downforce. The type 57/8 was actually due to be tested by Clark on 9 April 1968, two days after he was killed, and although Hill later tested it at Hethel, it was abandoned.

The wedge profile would re-emerge in 1970 as the type 72. Meanwhile the four-wheel drive car was seen as the way forward, and it was anticipated that Team Lotus would convert completely to the type 63 for Grand Prix racing. At the same time, a new chassis, the type 64, was in preparation for Indianapolis in May, and this too had the effect of dissipating Lotus resources. Chapman got Bob Dance to oversee production of the four-wheel drive transmission for the type 63 and the abortive type 64 Indy car, and in the early stages of these projects Bob spent much of his time visiting the ZF and Hewland factories. In the event, four-wheel drive in Formula 1 proved a blind alley. But Hill believed that the Lotus 63 four-wheel drive car was one of the best conceived racing car designs that he had ever seen, and was disappointed that its promise was never fulfilled.

## Wing Ding

The 1969 F1 season began with the South African Grand Prix at Kyalami. Most teams were using 1968 cars because they were dispatched by freighter, a journey of four weeks or so. Gold Leaf Team Lotus fielded three 49Bs for Hill, Rindt and Andretti. That was some driver line-up! But according to Heinz Prüller in his book *Jochen Rindt: The Story of a World Champion*, Chapman was vexed that Rindt out-qualified the other Team Lotus drivers. A tempestuous relationship was developing. The cars were fitted with front wings in a similar fashion to Brabham's the previous season. They were taken off the front uprights, and the driver could flatten both front and rear wings along the straight, using much the same system as pioneered in Mexico in 1968. However, the downforce was so great that the cables stretched and could no longer have any effect on the wings. Both Rindt's and Andretti's wing struts broke in practice, so the uprights were shortened to place them under less load, with commensurate loss of effectiveness. Aerodynamics was very much a black art then, trial and error, because no one really knew what the effects would be. Hill and Rindt chose to run with the new set-up in the race, but Andretti decided to go just with the front nose-fins on R11 and no front wing. Predictably, the Bowden cables operating Hill's wings stretched during the race, costing him straight-line speed. Nevertheless, he still managed to finish second behind Stewart.

It was a similar story at Brands Hatch for the Race of Champions. Hill (from pole) and Rindt ran nose-to-tail in a vain pursuit of Stewart's Tyrrell Matra MS80. The Austrian was held up as they lapped Oliver's BRM, and might have taken his senior teammate but for this. He complained to Chapman after the race that Graham had not let him pass, so Colin diplomatically decreed that each of his drivers had to permit the other to overtake. At Silverstone in the wet International Trophy on 30 March Hill was lapped by Rindt – who disposed of no fewer than four top-class drivers (Ickx, Courage, Hill and Rodriguez) in one passing manoeuvre on his way from 10th to second place. Through the mist and spray, Rindt's drive was astonishing by any standards, much of it sideways under full opposite lock. The writing was now clearly on the wall for the Old Lion.

Now world champion for the second time, Hill drives his Lotus 49/R6, which sports the number 1 for the *Daily Mail* Race of Champions at Brands Hatch in March 1969. Note the cooling ducts in the top of the nose, introduced at Monza the previous year, while the high front wing used at Kyalami had been abandoned. The roll-over hoop now offers Hill's head some protection. He started from pole, and came second, but it did not go unnoticed that his new teammate Rindt was the quicker driver. *(PN)*

Three Formula 2 races followed. The BARC's Easter Monday meeting at Thruxton saw Hill and Rindt driving the brand new Dave Baldwin-designed Lotus type 59B F2 cars under the Winkelmann Racing banner (Rindt's old team), managed by Alan Rees. After spinning at the Esses when opposite locking caught his steering wheel on his thighs, Hill came third in heat one. But the clutch would not disengage at the start of heat two, and that was that. Graham showed well at the following races at Pau and the Nürburgring, retiring from both events, while Rindt won at Thruxton and Pau.

For the Spanish Grand Prix at Barcelona's picturesque Montjuich Park circuit, the Lotus 49Bs flanked Amon's Ferrari on the front row, with Rindt on pole. Chapman had increased the width of the cars' rear wings and added a lip along the trailing edge to make them much more effective. The fact that the modifications were made from cut-down polystyrene packing cases, strips of aluminium and adhesive tape gives a clue as to the nature of the technology involved. An astonished Jackie Stewart was appalled at the size of the 49Bs' modified wings, and is quoted in Michael Oliver's *Lotus 49* book as saying: 'This is ridiculous, you

can't do that.' To which Chapman replied, 'Yes we can, there's nothing in the rules to say we can't.' While Rindt was increasingly uneasy about the wings, both he and Hill were apparently prepared to go along with them, in spite of past failures. When they worked, the downforce they provided was simply irresistible, and each time the wings were enlarged, lap times fell. But now, the wing on Hill's car was even to be seen sagging at the ends in practice. A double Armco barrier had just been installed around most of the hilly circuit, and this proved to be a crucial factor in the race. On lap eight, in hot pursuit of Amon, Hill's Lotus crested a rise just after the pits at about 150mph, its rear wing suddenly folded, and the car careered into the guard-rail, spinning several times down the road and into the opposite barrier, shedding parts as it went along. Hill was wearing lap belts now, and was able to step out when it all came to a halt. The lesson from Hill's accident was that the high-mounted wings were now just too wide and could not take the strain they came under when the cars took off momentarily at the brow of the rise. Hill was unaware that this was the cause of the accident, busy with marshals clearing bits of his car from the racing line. Unable to detect any obvious

This is one of a sequence of well-known shots of Hill's devastating accident at Barcelona's Montjuich Park during the 1969 Spanish Grand Prix. When in the lead, the 49's vast rear wing collapsed at high speed and, with downforce utterly compromised, the helpless Lotus driver was flung from one barrier into another, coming to rest at this point where he protects himself from a wayward wheel. A dozen laps later, Rindt's 49 suffered a similar wing failure with equally catastrophic results. *(PN)*

In spite of the horrendous accidents at Barcelona, all the teams turned up at Monaco with high wings in place, including Graham's 49/R10 (Rindt's Tasman car), and in the first practice session he was second quickest to Stewart. Here, as the oil cooler mounts are checked, Hill jokes with leading *Motor Sport* F1 journalist Denis Jenkinson. (right). (PN)

suspension failure, he began to study his teammate's car as it flashed by to see if anything untoward was happening to that.

Sure enough, there was a crease in the underside of Rindt's rear wing. Graham dispatched Lotus mechanic Dave Simms back to the pits to advise Chapman and give Rindt the 'In' signal. Hill then ran down to the hairpin where Rindt would have been able to see his warning signal. Rindt had also been trying in vain to communicate with Hill to ask what had happened to him, but Hill had been too preoccupied with clearing away his own debris. By then it was too late. On the next lap, exactly the same thing happened to Jochen's car. His rear wing folded, the car rode the top of the barrier, dived across the track and into the remains of Hill's Lotus, flipping it upside down. Just as he had been on the spot when Stewart crashed at Spa in 1966, Graham now directed the marshals to get Rindt's car the right way up. He even stood on the banana-shaped wreck, tugging the steering wheel away from Rindt's body, all the while with fuel flooding out of the ruptured bag-tanks. Eventually they got him out and his injuries were limited to a broken cheekbone and fractured skull. However, it is claimed in the Heinz Prüller book *Jochen Rindt: The Story of a World Champion*, that Rindt felt that Hill (whom he called Pokerface) should have stopped him, something that apparently rankled for a long time. This was in spite of the reassurances of Rindt's manager Bernie Ecclestone that neither Chapman nor Hill knew for certain that the wing struts were about to fail. It was also unlikely that Colin would have brought in a driver who was leading a Grand Prix for the first time in three years.

So, not only were Armco barriers completely vindicated – there was still a strong purist lobby that thought they were for the faint-hearted – it was also the end of the line for strut-mounted aerofoils. The ban did not come into effect immediately. The first day's practice at Monaco was run with wings fitted, but the following day the Commission Sportive Internationale (CSI) declared that rear wings were banned henceforth,

as they were not part of the car's bodywork. For his part, Hill felt the ban was a retrograde step, because the downforce provided by wings was a positive aid to performance. But with two cars totalled at Barcelona, Gold Leaf Team Lotus hurriedly prepared the two Tasman cars and, since Rindt was not yet fit, the previous year's lap record holder, Richard Attwood, was drafted in to drive the second Lotus.

It did not take Hill long to get down to within 0.2 seconds of the time he had set with a wing, although being a relatively slow circuit Monaco

When the CSI met at Monaco and banned any wing that did not form part of the car's bodywork – with immediate effect – Hill practised his 49 shorn of its rear wing, which altered the car's handling dramatically. He was still fourth fastest. *(FF)*

Prior to the Monaco Grand Prix, Ferrari, McLaren and Lotus cobbled together rear spoilers that doubled as engine and transmission covers. In Hill's case, the aluminium for the spoiler was appropriated by the mechanics from the sides of work benches within the Team Lotus transporter. Here in the race, Hill wears his new full-face helmet for the first time, a decision brought about by his experience in Barcelona. *(PN)*

was not ideal for wings. Rear spoilers were allowed, and for the race Hill's car had a makeshift one fitted. Initial leaders Stewart and Amon disappeared into the distance, while Hill was held up by Beltoise for a couple of laps.

Before the race, the feeling was that the Matra and Ferrari transmissions were potentially fragile, evidenced by failures in practice, and Hill played a waiting game until, sure enough, Amon's gearbox played up and Stewart went out with a broken driveshaft. Behind Hill, Courage and Ickx were enjoying themselves and challenged him a few times. He pulled out a 20-second lead by the end, and came in to win his fifth Monaco Grand Prix. This was to be his last world championship Grand Prix win.

By the time of his fifth victory at Monaco, Graham was almost part of the royal family, seen here with Princess Grace and Prince Rainier during the playing of the national anthem in 1969. *(PN)*

For the Lotus team it was a mad scramble to-ing and fro-ing to Indianapolis with the Monaco Grand Prix in the middle of qualifying, and the cars were not ready on time. The type 64 was powered by the turbocharged quad-cam Ford 2.8-litre engine allied to Ferguson-type four-wheel drive. Hill practised his car – 64/2 – but the engine misfired and his lap times were well below Andretti's. Rindt had a misfire as well. Then Mario had a big accident when a hub broke on the right-hand rear wheel and he spun into the wall. The other three cars immediately came under suspicion and were investigated for signs of similar failure. It

Having passed Jean-Pierre Beltoise's Matra-Cosworth MS8 a few laps into the 1969 Monaco Grand Prix, Graham was never overtaken, and here he opposite locks out of Station hairpin. *(P*

was decided that the hubs could indeed be weak and, with insufficient time to make new ones, the STP Lotus entries were withdrawn. The farrago of the aftermath of this event, recorded in the Andrew Ferguson book, has all the makings of a riveting spy thriller.

During the Dutch Grand Prix at Zandvoort, the attention of Team Lotus was divided between the two four-wheel drive type 63s and a pair of 49Bs. It rained in practice, and Hill went out in the 63 but although he could lap just about on the pace, there seemed to be no clear advantage in the four-wheel drive set-up. Unlike Rindt, who would not go near the 63 because of the proximity of the driveline to his groin, Hill enjoyed driving it. Rindt felt that since the 49 was still capable of winning races, it was futile to race an untried car. The 49Bs were used for the race, but the new wing arrangement upset their handling as far as Hill was concerned, and he came a lowly seventh.

At the French Grand Prix at Clermont-Ferrand, Rindt claimed the twisty, hilly circuit made him feel badly queasy, causing his retirement. He cited Bandini's fatal Monaco crash, recalling that the Italian had complained of feeling sick but had carried on racing. John Miles drove the 63, but he also retired with fuel injection maladies. Hill too was off form, and came a lacklustre sixth, a lap down.

Gold Leaf Team Lotus was not a harmonious environment at this stage in the season. Four cars were entered for Silverstone, and the mechanics were overworked as resources were spread too thinly. There was chaos in their paddock enclave. Fed up with mechanical failures that had cost two certain victories and nearly his life, Rindt entered negotiations with Robin Herd to join the nascent March team for 1970. He likened Team Lotus to 'the biggest circus in the world.'

No Lotuses were ready for the morning session of the first day of practice for the Grand Prix at Silverstone, so Graham was invited to try the new Brabham BT26, lapping faster than even Jacky Ickx in the first session. The rumour mill sprang into action, seeing that Rindt had now usurped Hill in terms of race pace. Hill had the use of the

This was the kind of promotional work that Hill was obliged to participate in – he is seen here drawing raffle tickets for a Castrol competition at Silverstone in 1969. He took it all in his stride, encouraged in this instance by commentator Barry Gill (left). *(C)*

63, but he was not as quick as the 4x4 Matra or McLaren. Team Lotus was in the process of selling a 49 to Jo Bonnier, and he kindly lent it back to Hill for the Grand Prix, but a whole litany of problems cropped up. Hill was involved in a battle for much of the race with Amon, Siffert, Courage and Rodriguez, until all three Lotus 49s (Rindt, Hill and Siffert) had to come in for fuel in the closing stages. Hill finished seventh, well out of the running. After the race, Rindt flew home, passing on Hill's traditional post-British Grand Prix party at Mill Hill. At the following race, the German Grand Prix, Chapman offered Rindt the number one seat at Team Lotus for 1970, according to Prüller, promising the Austrian that he would 'organise a Rob Walker contract for Hill,' since he could not 'just kick him out.' Rindt, however, did not actually sign until just before the US Grand Prix.

Graham tried one of the Brabham BT 26s in the first practice session at the 1969 British Grand Prix, since he was ready to go and his Lotus was not, and he was seventh fastest in this session. (FF)

For the 1969 British Grand Prix at Silverstone, Gold Leaf Team Lotus brought along a pair of the new four-wheel drive type 63s. The wedge-shaped cars with their all-enveloping bodywork and state of the art aerodynamics brought a new look to Formula 1. But neither Rindt nor Hill wanted to drive them, and they were not as quick as the four-wheel drive McLaren or Matra. Eventually they raced 49B/6 and 49B/8, Rindt claiming pole, while Miles drove 63/2 into 10th place and Bonnier was lent 63/1, which retired after six laps with engine failure. *(PN)*

At the start of the German Grand Prix at the Nürburgring, Ickx was on pole in the Brabham BT26, but was overhauled by Stewart and Rindt who got away well. Ickx then fell back into the pack, and was passed by Hill in 49B/10, who had started from the fourth row. Jacky staged a recovery, storming back through the field, and Hill was not alone in moving over to let him past. On the day, Ickx was invincible and, in a heroic struggle with Stewart, the Belgian emerged in the lead on the seventh lap, going on to victory. The Lotus drivers were virtual also-rans, although Graham came in fourth, some three and a half minutes later. He had had trouble changing gear. Mario in the type 63 had crashed on the first lap when it bottomed out, and Jochen had ignition trouble.

It was Jochen's turn to drive the four-wheel drive 63 at the Oulton Park Gold Cup, and Graham was without an F1 drive. He got a race in his Roy Winkelmann 59B F2 car however, only to retire, while Ickx won the Gold Cup from Rindt. Other F2 outings during the second half of the season included second place in the first heat at Zolder, retirement at Reims, and third at Tülnbarn.

Langenlebarn. He was second in heat two at Enna-Pergusa, having passed the whole of the leading group on the outside of the last corner of the Sicilian speedbowl. After the Italian Grand Prix came a win at Albi, ahead of Servoz-Gavin and Rindt. Although Stewart had led this race until his engine let go on lap 44, Graham managed to stay in his slipstream despite having too tall a top gear for maximum performance down the straights. Hill led the last 31 laps, proving that he could still cut the mustard. All the F2 cars ran Cosworth FVA engines, and performance was more level than in F1.

For the Italian Grand Prix at Monza, Gold Leaf Team Lotus brought three cars: a pair of 49Bs for Hill and Rindt and a type 63 four-wheel drive car for Miles. Hill's DFV blew up in practice, and he started from the fifth row alongside a miserable Surtees in the V12 BRM P139. Rindt was on pole. They elected to run without wings as the cars were faster down the straight and did not seem to be much slower around the corners. Others, including the McLarens, ran with them. At the start, Rindt hung back anticipating the starter's flag, and Hulme kept back with him. The starter panicked, dropped the flag, and Rindt and Stewart made dragster-like getaways, while Hulme was engulfed by the pack. One of Hill's tail pipes came off at high speed and struck Surtees's engine, knocking off an ignition coil, and making his own DFV slightly down on power. Hill then began sliding around on oil pouring from Brabham's engine. But, rather than give up, he made a concerted effort to haul in the leading group. Slowly but surely, he got back into their slipstream and worked himself up into second place behind Stewart. Like Rindt, he could even pass Stewart at the end of the pit straight and lead him through the Lesmo curves. But the Scot was able to reply down the back straight and retake the lead. Tactics came into play as Hill schemed that he could perhaps pull off an overtaking manoeuvre when they exited the Parabolica on the last lap. But it was a vain hope. With five laps to go, a driveshaft broke, ending what had been one of his finest drives all season. He received a splendid ovation

The reigning world champion relaxes between innings at a Grand Prix drivers' cricket match in 1969, while his youngest daughter Samantha adjusts the Mersham Hatch cricket club's boundary. *(FF)*

from the crowd as he abandoned his car at the Parabolica. It was another nail-biting Monza finish, as Stewart beat Rindt, Beltoise and McLaren with just 19 hundredths of a second between the four cars. Stewart was now unbeatable in the 1969 world championship stakes.

The same Team Lotus cars were on hand at Mosport Park near Toronto for the Canadian Grand Prix, and for the first time, the 63 showed some real potential in John Miles's hands, while Ickx's pole time was way quicker than anybody else. Beltoise and Rindt joined him on the front rank, with Graham on row three. Rindt made an excellent start, but was overtaken by Stewart and then Ickx, and these two proceeded to pull away

from the rest of the field. Their private battle ended with banged wheels and both cars spinning, Stewart sliding into a shallow ditch, while Ickx ended up the less-than-delighted winner. Hill was scrapping with Brabham, and they had passed Rindt when Graham's engine broke a camshaft.

## Hospitalisation

Graham was still reigning world champion when the circus went to Watkins Glen on 5 October for the US Grand Prix. So he was still wearing number one and Jochen was number two, while Mario in the 63 was allocated number nine. Seeing as the first day's practice session was wet, it was hoped that the four-wheel drive car would excel, but this proved not to be the case. Rindt, the eventual winner, took pole from Hulme, Stewart and Hill. His 49B was shod with experimental Firestone tyres, and there was come concern that they might wear badly due to overheating. To offset that possibility, half a degree of camber was taken off the front wheels, which Hill did not like at all, complaining that the handling was upset. Rodriguez had the same type of tyre, and was sufficiently concerned as to have them changed to his regular tyres after 20 laps. On lap 70, Hill was lying fifth when he hit a patch of oil, causing him to spin. His rear tyres had worn badly and had been chunking, which had probably occasioned the spin. The car would not restart on the button, so he got out and pushed it to a downhill section where he could bump start it. Noticing that something was amiss with the tyres – he'd picked up a stone perhaps – he pitted to ask for a fresh set to be prepared to be fitted after he had done another lap. Perhaps what he should have done was asked for assistance doing up his seat belts, which he had taken off to push start the car. But belts were only just starting to be used in F1, and a driver of long standing like Hill was more used to driving without them. He did not complete another lap. As he was travelling along the straight before the loop, the right-hand rear tyre collapsed, and the car veered sideways off the track. It hit an earth bank and overturned, pitching Hill onto the ground while it carried on rolling. He landed on his knees, injuring them very badly. Although Hill did not notice the tyre deflating, mechanics and spectators certainly did, and in what looked like a repeat of Jimmy Clark's fatal accident, when Hill's 49 reached a critical speed of 160mph or so in the bend, the tyre exploded and the accident was inevitable.

Hill had broken his right knee and dislocated the left one with torn ligaments. He was taken to the Arnott Ogden Memorial Hospital in Elmira, and after he was stabilised, flown home to the UK to a celebrity's reception at Heathrow. A long spell in University College Hospital followed. When Rindt opened his annual racing car show in Vienna, he spoke to the recuperating Hill via a phone link. He joked: 'Pity you can't be here in Vienna to open the Show for me, but I can't afford you, Graham.'

# Chapter 7
# A Nicer Class of Person

WITH Graham effectively sidelined for the remainder of 1969 and the first few months of 1970, his place at Team Lotus was taken by John Miles, who is still today associated with Lotus Engineering as a suspension tuning consultant. Having promised Rindt that he would be number one driver for 1970, Chapman offered Hill the role of Lotus team manager, virtually paying him not to go back to driving. It was perhaps fortunate for Chapman that Rob Walker was happy to have Graham drive his Lotus 49C. Jo Siffert had gone to the new STP-March team and, after all, there were only a handful of drivers with experience of the type 49, so Hill was a natural candidate for the Walker drive. Hill wanted to drive, of course, and he applied himself to his rehabilitation as thoroughly as he went testing cars. As he says:

> I'd made up my mind I was going to drive in the South African Grand Prix, and riding a bicycle to and from my therapy (four miles each way), as well as riding a stationary one while there, seemed to me to be the only way to regain knee movement and build up leg muscle to achieve this target.

At the same time, he made a point of condemning the little light-blue invalid tricycles that he saw as unsafe, promoting the need for proper invalid cars.

Rob Walker provided some background to Hill's appointment:

> I was flying to one of the Grands Prix, and as it was a long flight – Canada, possibly – I was walking about in the back of the aircraft, and Colin came up to me and said, 'why don't you get Graham to drive for you next year?' I said, 'Because I've got a perfectly good driver of my own.' Seppe (Siffert) always wanted to join a full works team, although I know he adored being with us. He was paid by Porsche, and whatever they said, he did, and they bought him a drive at March. Well, then, of course, Graham had his accident, but I knew that he intended to drive again whatever happened. Colin didn't want him to drive, and now, with the accident, he'd got a good excuse to get rid of him. He didn't have to bother about getting him into another team. Ford didn't want him to drive either, but he was absolutely determined that he was going to drive. On our Christmas Eve party he crept out of the hospital in the evening and Ford laid on a car and a chauffeur for him to come down. By that time he'd signed on with me. I wanted a good name for my sponsor, Oxo, and I knew Graham very well, and I thought he'd be a very suitable replacement for Seppe.

> Of course, Graham didn't know anything about Colin having written him off. It wasn't to do with the accident. Colin saw that Rindt was the boy, and wanted him instead of Graham, so he wanted to let Graham down gently and get him a good seat. It wasn't the same with Ford, who had a lot of pride in Graham. They just thought it was time he stopped. But when we went

to South Africa, he got into a racing car for the first time since his accident, and within three laps he was going within a fraction of the fastest time, and absolutely flat out down the straight. That really amazed me.

When Hill first approached the Walker 49C/R7 at Kyalami in March 1970, he still had to be lifted into the cockpit of the car. Brian Redman was on hand to take over if he could not manage it. Although he qualified down on the eighth row of the grid, to get there at all was no mean achievement. Stewart and Amon in Marches and Brabham occupied the front row, with Rindt and Ickx, having his first drive for Ferrari, on row two. As it turned out, the old brigade triumphed, with Brabham and Goodyear tyres supreme. Graham finished sixth, just one lap in arrears. His feet were

still very weak, so he couldn't brake hard, and he drove with sheer guts and determination, symptomatic of the willpower and doggedness that powered his racing career. Colin Chapman was one of the first to congratulate him, while at the prize-giving ceremony, the applause from those in attendance was quite moving as Hill struggled up to the rostrum to receive his award.

Back in the UK, Hill was fêted by the press and race fans alike, and he drove Rob Walker's 49C/R7 at Brands Hatch in the Race of Champions. His performance was further confirmation of his tenacity. He was a reasonable eighth fastest in practice and, slowed in the race by a recalcitrant Hewland gearbox, still came in fifth at the end.

The 1970 Spanish Grand Prix was held at Jarama and, despite starting from the penultimate

Driving Rob Walker's Lotus 49C/R7 in the 1970 Spanish Grand Prix at Jarama, Graham negotiates the scene of the first-lap fiery crash when Oliver's BRM pushed off Ickx's Ferrari. The track was awash with water and chemicals used (by poorly trained and equipped fire marshals) to extinguish the blazing cars. Despite his dreadful knee injuries from the previous year's US Grand Prix, Hill came fourth, in a car that had turned white with fire extinguisher foam. *(FF)*

Graham drove in eight Formula 2 races during 1970 for Jochen Rindt's Team Lotus équipe, his Lotus 69 Cosworth FVA resplendent in the pre-Gold Leaf colours of green with yellow stripe. His best result was fourth in the first heat of the Alcoa Trophy at Crystal Palace, with a couple of fifth places at Paul Ricard and the Salzburgring to his credit. *(PN)*

row and having transmission problems, Hill was up to fourth by the finish, one lap behind Stewart, who won and had lapped everybody else.

The *Daily Express* International Trophy was run in two heats and included F5000 cars as well as F1 cars. Graham was delayed in the first heat as the steering column on the Lotus 49C – now bearing Brooke-Bond Oxo sponsorship – was tightened up, but he finished fourth in the second heat in an event dominated by the Marches of Amon and Stewart. At Monaco, Graham had an unaccountable accident in practice, going up the hill towards the Casino, and this caused a problem because, although he was assured of a start at Monaco, his Walker 49C was not. The situation was solved when he was lent the GLTL 49C/R10 that Miles had failed to qualify. Overnight it was painted the dark blue colours of the Rob Walker team and adorned with the Brooke-Bond Oxo colours, and the controls and cockpit were adapted for Graham. Because he had not actually practised the car, however, he was obliged to start from the back. Hampered by over-tight seat belts, Hill ran with the mid-field bunch that included Surtees, Peterson and Oliver. Rindt won after an inspired pursuit of Brabham in the closing laps, Hill finishing fifth, a lap in arrears.

Jochen Rindt was considered pretty much the king of Formula 2 but, as we have seen, Graham was no slouch in F2 either, and Rindt obviously recognised that. He had five races for Jochen Rindt Racing during the season, driving the 1.6 Lotus 69 Cosworth FVA. At Crystal Palace on 25 May he came fourth and fifth in the heats, while later on in the season he took fifth places at Paul Ricard and the Salzburgring. The following year would see something of a revival of Hill's fortunes in Formula 2, driving for Bernie Ecclestone and Ron Dennis.

Back at Spa for the 1970 Belgian Grand Prix, Graham was running the 49C during practice without wing and front fins in a bid to get more straight-line speed, although he reverted to what had become the normal aerodynamic package for the race, which he started from the back row. The DFV engine gave up on lap 19. At Zandvoort he was still in the Walker 49C, with no sign of the anticipated type 72. He started from the back of the grid – in fact, if he had not had a guaranteed start, as he did at Monaco, he would not have qualified, as de Adamich was quicker in practice. In the race, the Lotus 49C was in and out of the pits, and Graham finished 12th and last. Rindt gave the type 72 its first win, but it was a dismal affair, as Piers Courage died in his blazing Williams-run de Tomaso.

## How are the Mighty Fallen

Graham was on the back row of the two-by-two grid alongside George Eaton's V12 BRM 153 for the French Grand Prix, held on the wonderfully undulating Charade circuit above Clermont-Ferrand in the Auvergne. In outdated machinery, there was little he could do except plug away, coming 10th, a lap down, as Rindt notched up another win on his way to his fateful world crown.

The back row of the grid at Brands Hatch for the British Grand Prix was occupied by three Lotus 49s – Graham's R7 flanked by American VW dealer and long-time Lotus devotee Pete Lovely in R11, and new Team Lotus recruit Emerson Fittipaldi in R10. Up at the front, Rindt was on pole in the 72 along with Brabham and Ickx. The battle between Amon and Hill brought them up to fifth and sixth as others fell by the wayside, but there was controversy after Rindt's deserved win over the height of his 72's rear wing.

The GPDA (Grand Prix Drivers' Association), of which Graham was a member, had prevailed upon the organisers of the German Grand Prix to shift the venue from the Nürburgring, which they said was too dangerous without Armco, to Hockenheim. Graham shared the back row of the grid with Peterson in the Antique Automobiles' March 701, but both cars' engines failed. It was Hill's last outing in a 49, and he topped the table of drivers who had raced that model, with 39 outings; next up came Siffert with 22 races.

At Monza for the 1970 Italian Grand Prix, the Rob Walker team had their new Lotus 72/R4, which had made its debut in Brook-Bond Oxo

Hill waits for the start of the Formula 2 race at Hockenheim in June 1970, billed as the 'Internationales DMV Rhein-Pokal-Rennen', in which he was eliminated when the belt operating the Lotus 69's metering unit failed. The winner was Hubert Hahne's BMW 692, marking something of a breakthrough for the Munich company in single-seater racing. *(FF)*

guise at the Oulton Park Gold Cup, where it retired with low oil pressure. The Walker 72 was fitted with a three-tier rear wing, but in Italy several teams had experimented with no wings at all during Monza practice in a bid for greater straight-line speed. It was while running in this format that Rindt had his fatal accident. His car was geared to provide 15mph more than anyone else down the straight, which, with no aerodynamic downforce, probably meant it was going too fast before the tyres had warmed up. Whatever the cause of the crash, which has been widely written about, it was the poorly installed Armco and Rindt's reluctance to wear crotch straps that actually killed him. All Lotuses, including Graham's, were promptly withdrawn from the race. By this time Rindt had accumulated

sufficient points to make him world champion, but for Team Lotus it was another bitter blow.

Another unfamiliar venue for the Formula 1 circus was the Mont Tremblant winter sports centre at St Jovite for the Canadian Grand Prix. Following the Monza tragedy, the Rob Walker Lotus was the only one present, but again Graham was on the last row of the grid. After a pit stop to check the car's handling, Graham was classified 12th, and it was discovered later that a loose wishbone mounting had compromised the entire rear suspension. The F1 cars were then trucked down to Watkins Glen for the US Grand Prix. The works Lotuses were sent over for Fittipaldi and Swedish F3 whirlwind Reine Wisell, Miles having resigned in the wake of Rindt's death. Graham shared the fifth row with Wisell, but just before

Brabham team owner and designer Ron Tauranac takes notes, although he could just as easily be totting up the bill to send to McLaren, since their hard-charging driver Oliver put out Hill's BT 34 on the first lap of the 1971 'Woolmark' British Grand Prix. Hill adopts his typical pensive pose, while at left (in shades) is Eoin Young, freelance consultant, author and erstwhile McLaren director. *(PN)*

half distance, the Walker 72 developed a serious fuel leak that prompted Hill to head for the pits. Once there, he stripped off in order to rid himself of his petrol-soaked overalls, borrowing those of John Surtees who had already retired. The sight of two former world champions entirely naked in the pits is by no means commonplace. Back in the race, the Hill car lost its clutch on lap 73. In Mexico for the final Grand Prix of the year, Graham was eighth fastest in practice, but retired after four laps with engine failure and a puncture.

Rob Walker's opinion of Hill's driving ability is surprisingly blunt:

> My view of Graham as a driver was that he was definitely not talented. He did it by pure hard work and guts and slog. I don't think anyone would ever say that he was talented, although he was world champion and won a lot of races. He wasn't a Stirling or a Rindt or a Senna, it didn't come naturally, it was just hard work. I always used to go everywhere with him during 1970, and I remember a situation where we might well have been completely written off on the road thanks to his driving. He was just not concentrating. We were coming off the aerodrome at Watkins Glen onto the main freeway which was full of traffic, and Graham just didn't see it. I said, 'look out, we're coming to a freeway,' and he jammed on the brakes just in time.

## Brabham Beckons

At the end of the 1970 season, Rob Walker took the Brooke-Bond sponsorship and his Lotus 72 to Team Surtees. One reason why Hill did not carry on with the Walker team was his relationship with the chief mechanic. Rob Walker explained:

> My head mechanic Tony Cleverley didn't get on with Graham. Graham drove very badly in practice at Zandvoort and kept on complaining to the mechanic. If you know Zandvoort, it would take generally an hour to sort out what the settings need to be, and you have to reset the car up because of the sand blowing over the track the whole

time. After he'd complained for the third time about the handling of the car, my mechanic said to him, 'get into the bloody car and drive it, it's your fault, not ours.' I don't think Graham ever forgot that. When we were leaving Canada Graham said, 'What are you going to do next year?' I said 'I don't know.' Graham said, 'If I'm going to drive for you, you'll have to have different mechanics.' I said, 'Well in that case you are not going to drive for me, because my mechanics have been with me always.' And they were bloody good too. We wouldn't have done so well if they hadn't been so good.

Graham joined forces with designer Ron Tauranac who had taken over the Brabham concern from its retiring founder. The deal suited both parties: it gave Graham a decent drive, and opened up the potential of big-time sponsorship for Tauranac – although this never materialised. A less lucrative, but nonetheless convenient benefit for Ron was that he could fly to meetings with Graham, and they got on well. Up-and-coming Aussie Tim Schenken would be Hill's teammate, and the ex-Alan Mann and John Coombs engineer Brian Lewis was appointed chief mechanic for 1971. Bob Dance would fulfil the role in 1972 after his year at March.

The Brabham team operated as Motor Racing Developments and, initially, the cars were the BT33s. Graham's car was BT33/1, which was actually a new monocoque, but built to 1970 spec and designated with an original chassis number.

However, Graham's first foray of the 1971 season was in Formula 2, in the unlikely location of Bogota, Columbia. A local millionaire had funded the construction of a circuit in a quarry near the capital, and a couple of F2 races were staged to get it off the ground. Several of the European F2 regulars were present, including Siffert, Bell, Pescarolo and Hill, who was entered by Bernie Ecclestone and driving his regular Lotus 69. He was second on aggregate to Siffert in the first event and fifth in heat one of the second event a week later.

At the Race of Champions on 21 March, Hill had the new Tauranac-designed BT34 at his disposal. This car was known affectionately as the 'Lobster Claw' Brabham, because of its distinctive split-radiator arrangement either side of the nose, which, at a pinch, resembled the crustacean's twin talons. An aerofoil between the radiator pods provided frontal downforce, but the chassis and rear suspension were similar to the outgoing model, with a conventional front end instead of an inboard system with rocker arms. It was an auspicious beginning. Graham set fastest race lap in his harrying of a dogged Stewart, but retired with a broken valve spring on lap 35. Teammate Tim Schenken, who drove the old BT33 all year, came fourth after nipping by Howden Ganley's BRM on the last lap.

Graham set fastest lap in the 1971 *Daily Mail* Race of Champions at Brands Hatch, driving the works Brabham BT 34/1 (1min 26.7sec – 177.071kph). He harassed Stewart in his quest for the lead, but the Brabham's Cosworth engine gave out at 34 laps. *(PN)*

A potentially lucrative non-championship event called the Questor Grand Prix was staged on the new Ontario Motor Speedway, 40 miles east of Los Angeles in California. Nineteen F1 cars lined up against 11 Formula A (F5000) 5-litre cars with USAC drivers like Mark Donohue, A.J. Foyt and the Unsers at the wheel. The race was divided into two 32-lap heats, since the F5000 cars lacked the range to go the full Grand Prix distance. With few exceptions, the F1 cars were predictably quicker than the F5000 machines. For an Indy veteran like Hill, it could have been a breeze up on the banked turns. But sadly the Brabham's DFV engine failed when he was well placed in the early stages. Mario Andretti was overall victor for Ferrari, having won both heats.

The second outing for Hill in the unique 'Lobster Claw' Brabham BT 34 was the 1971 Questor Grand Prix at Ontario Motor Speedway, California, on 28 March. The Tauranac-designed car was so named because of the unusual location of the radiators either side of the nose, linked by a frontal spoiler. In this non-championship event, the engine failed early on when he was well placed, while Andretti won for Ferrari. *(PN)*

Hill and Schenken teamed up to race the Brabham BT36 in Formula 2, driving for Rondel Racing. This highly competitive outfit was run by former Brabham F1 mechanics Neil Trundel and Ron Dennis, later of McLaren fame, and the cars were painted light blue with dark blue and red stripes. Graham came second to Cevert in the Jim Clark Memorial Trophy at Hockenheim (having won heat two) with Tim fifth. At Thruxton a week later for the *Yellow Pages* Trophy race, Hill got pole in the 28-lap first heat, and Schenken was on the front row for heat two. In the final, the battle was between Hill and F2 ace Ronnie Peterson, and the wily Hill pipped the Swede on the penultimate lap. Schenken came fifth again.

Hill's major F1 triumph of the season was the non-title GKN International at Silverstone. It was run in two heats of 26 laps, making a race distance of 152 miles, so that the entry could include the F5000 cars. Potential winners looked like being the V12 Matras of Amon and Beltoise, Stewart's

The 1968 Monaco Grand Prix saw Graham notch up his fourth victory at the principality, making it two wins on the trot that season. Here he steers Lotus 49B/R5 around the Station hairpin in one of its transitional phases. *(FMC)*

A typical Monaco procession as Hill's Lotus 49B leads Siffert in the Rob Walker car (49/R2), Surtees's Honda RA301 V12, Rindt's Brabham BT24 Repco, and Attwood's BRM P126 V12 in 1968. The latter would come to exert pressure on Hill, who kept the lead to the finish. *(FMC)*

Graham Hill and his new teammate Jackie Oliver listen attentively as a gesticulating Piers Courage makes a point in the Monaco pits, 1968. Bob Sparshott, right, looks bemused. *(IC)*

Having sold off two of the 49s to Bonnier and John Love, Chapman told his drivers they had to race the Type 63 four-wheel drive cars for the British Grand Prix at Silverstone. As demonstrated here, Graham practised the Lotus 63 four-wheel drive car but persuaded Bonnier to lend back his 49B/R8 for the race. *(IC)*

The fact that he couldn't land his plane because of fog and had to divert to Gatwick may have accounted for Hill's dour look at Brands Hatch prior to the 1969 Race of Champions. Hill started 49/R6 from pole but was obliged to pursue Stewart's leading Tyrrell-Matra MS80 in vain. He also staved off the attentions of teammate Rindt, much to the Austrian's annoyance. (FMC)

Graham's winning car at Monaco in 1969 was 49B/R10, refettled from its Tasman format as a substitute for his regular car following the crash at Barcelona when the rear wing collapsed. Wings were banned for the Monaco race, but on Thursday's practice session when this picture was taken, all the teams still had them fitted. (PN)

Having qualified 12th fastest at Monaco in 1970, Hill slid into the barriers on the wet track going up the hill after St Devote, seriously damaging the front of the chassis of 49B/R7. Since Miles didn't qualify, Team Lotus lent the Walker team his car – 49C/R10, and it was hastily repainted dark blue with all the appropriate sponsor decals. It was nicely ironic that this had been chassis R5 (later renumbered R10), Hill's winning car in 1968 and '69. He came fifth in 1970. (PN)

During the 1971 season, Hill drove the unique Brabham BT34 'lobster claw' car for Ron Tauranac's Motor Racing Developments. His only success was a win on aggregate in the *Daily Express* International Trophy at Silverstone, while he came seventh here at Watkins Glen. *(FMC)*

Graham's association with Brabham lasted two seasons, the first of which was spent almost entirely at the wheel of the Formula 1 BT34 'lobster claw' car. He drove a Brabham BT36 in F2 for Rondel Racing, and enjoyed more success than in F1, where his young teammate Tim Schenken enjoyed a rather better rapport with Ron Tauranac. *(IC)*

During the 1972 season, Hill drove the Brabham BT38 FVA in Formula 2 events, with sponsorship from the German Jaegermeister drinks concern. He is pictured here in the fifth and final round of the John Player F2 series at Oulton Park, where he came 10th having lost several laps with fuel pressure problems. The top three finishers were Peterson, Lauda and Hunt. *(IC)*

Having decided to set up his own team for 1973, Hill commissioned a car from the new Shadow concern. Using Shadow componentry, the chassis was built by TC Prototypes and assembled by Hill's own mechanics to Shadow's specifications. Hill is pictured at Anderstorp during the Swedish Grand Prix, where he retired on lap 18 with electrical trouble. *(IC)*

Frustrated by a lack of reliability and hence results, the Embassy Hill Racing Team switched to Lola chassis for 1974. The T370 was based on Lola's Formula 5000 chassis, so it was rather overweight. Although there were more finishes, they couldn't be described as successes. One failure was here at Jarama, where the Lola suffered a succession of engine blow-ups. *(IC)*

Standing in the Zandvoort pits, Graham doesn't look too unhappy with prospects for the 1974 Dutch Grand Prix. But he was out-qualified by his teammate Guy Edwards, and in the race, the clutch housing bolts came undone on Hill's Lola on lap 17, while Edwards's fuel system packed up on lap 37. *(PN)*

Hill practising at the Nürburgring in 1974, prior to taking ninth place in the Lola T370. The Embassy Team's main drama here was that number two driver Guy Edwards had to pull out of the race because of a wrist injury, incurring the wrath of the team principal. *(IC)*

Impressed with his showings in Formula 3 and Formula Atlantic, Graham decided to offer the number one seat in the Embassy Hill Team to Tony Brise, who made his debut at Zolder in 1975. Brise is pictured here during practice for the British Grand Prix, where his times were very consistent. The race was a wash out, with 13 cars crashing, including Brise. *(IC)*

Having made his F1 debut at Barcelona in the Harry Stiller-entered Hesketh 308, Alan Jones drove the second Hill GH1/3 at Zandvoort (seen here ahead of Watson's Surtees TS16) and also in the French, British and German Grand Prix before handing it back to the recovered Stommelen. *(PN)*

175

Graham finally decided to make his retirement official and call it a day at the British Grand Prix. He did a celebratory lap in the Hill GH1, without helmet, and received a tremendous ovation from the spectators. *(IC)*

Graham found that running his own team was far from plain sailing, having to keep his sponsors happy despite poor results, develop cars that were effectively brand new designs, fire his first team manager, switch chassis, and manage a string of number two drivers. He kept on racing because it was what he loved. *(PN)*

No fewer than 40 Formula 2 cars entered the *Yellow Pages* Trophy at Thruxton on 12 April 1971. Run in two heats and a final, Graham won the first heat in the Rondel Racing Brabham BT36 FVA from Derek Bell's March, and is pictured at the chicane on his way to winning the final ahead of Jabouille's Tecno-Pederzani TF71 and Peterson's March 712M-FVA. It was Hill's first win since his F2 victory at Albi in 1969. *(PN)*

new Tyrrell 003 and, as an outside chance, Fittipaldi's Lotus 56B turbine. The first heat was dominated by Stewart in the Tyrrell, while Hill and Rodriguez had a mighty battle, which Pedro eventually won by a scant second. The same thing looked set to happen in heat two, but Stewart's throttle stuck wide open and he crashed, leaving Hill and Rodriguez to fight it out once more. The matter was settled when the Mexican's BRM picked up a puncture, and Graham was then the undisputed winner, with Schenken in the older Brabham third. This was Graham's last Formula 1 victory.

Despite a string of failures, crashes and mediocre placings, Hill still took things very seriously. In testing at the Österreichring during practice for the Austrian Grand Prix he completed no fewer than 55 laps of the fast, undulating Styrian circuit during the afternoon of second day's practice, for a race that was of 54 laps duration. Out of this he recorded eighth fastest time, placing him on row four, with Schenken alongside, having taken half the number of practice laps to achieve it. As the race settled down, Hill sparred with Wisell in the Lotus 72 for fifth place, while Schenken disputed third spot with Fittipaldi. Those were the Brabham drivers' finishing positions and, not for the first time in his career, Graham was overshadowed by his young teammate. Notwithstanding, Tim Schenken had this to say about his relationship with Graham:

First of all, I remember Graham as a great

Hill hurls the BT 34 'Lobster Claw' Brabham (minus engine cover) round the old Station hairpin at Monaco during practice for the 1971 Grand Prix, which was in the wet on the Thursday. Hill was one of only a handful of drivers to brave the conditions. *(FF)*

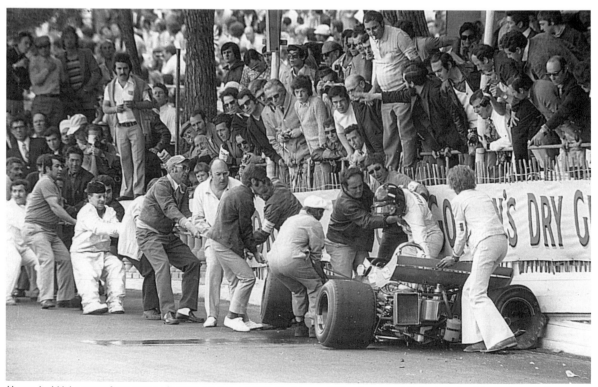

Heave-ho! Volunteers form a tug-of-war team to haul Hill's Brabham off the Armco, while he is helped from the car after making a rare mistake at the Tabac at the end of the second lap of the 1971 Monaco Grand Prix. *(PN)*

person who was extremely funny and good company. His face was known almost everywhere he travelled, and even on the odd occasion when he was not recognised, people seemed to know he was somebody famous. Regarding his driving ability, I am definitely in the camp with those who think he had to work at it. My view is that he was not a natural in the same mould as Clark and Stewart, but more like Mansell and even his son, Damon.

Between the two North American Grands Prix, the Brabham teammates had flown back to Europe to take part in the Albi Grand Prix for F2 cars. There was still an outside chance that Schenken could grasp the F2 championship from under Peterson's nose, but such hopes ended when he

collided with Hill's spinning Rondel BT36, deranging the back end of his own car. Hill then soldiered on to fifth place. It was a season best summarised by a catalogue of lowly placings and retirements, with just the non-championship win at Silverstone and an F2 victory at Thruxton. In 1971, he was 21st in the World Championship table with two points.

## Management Shakeout

A change of management at Brabham's Motor Racing Developments for 1972 found Bernie Ecclestone at the helm, along with motorcycle racing and tuning specialist Colin Seeley and ex-McLaren designer Ralph Bellamy, with Keith Greene as team manager. Ron Tauranac left the team to concentrate on designing F1 cars for

At the Rothmans International Trophy, a 40-lap non-championship race for Formula 2 cars at Brands Hatch on August bank holiday 1971, Graham got the jump on pole-man Ronnie Peterson at the start in his Rondel Racing Brabham BT36 FVA. But by lap four, Peterson had recovered from a poor start and taken the lead, beating Graham by 14.8 seconds. *(FF)*

In the days when anyone with a track pass could risk life and limb standing on the Monte Carlo pavement as Formula 1 cars flashed by, Hill negotiates the Station hairpin in the Motor Racing Developments Brabham BT37. In appalling conditions, he came 12th in the 1972 Grand Prix, four laps behind Beltoise (BRM) and Ickx (Ferrari). *(PN)*

Trojan, Theodore, and his own highly successful Ralt F2 cars. At the last minute, Graham re-signed for 1972, with the Argentinean Reutemann alongside him. The cars were now painted white, and Graham elected to race the old 1970 model BT33/3 as raced by Tim Schenken, although it had been re-skinned in 16swg aluminium and fitted with updated bodywork, new dampers and brakes. Reutemann got to drive the BT34 'Lobster Claw' car, which had also been updated in the winter period. In practice for his home Grand Prix – and indeed his world championship debut – Carlos claimed pole position in an astonishing effort that completely eclipsed his veteran teammate, who languished in 16th spot on the grid after knocking a corner off the car. After 12 laps, Hill retired with broken fuel pump drive.

A new F1 Brabham, the BT37, was unveiled for Graham to drive at the GKN *Daily Express* International at Silverstone on 23 April. Conceived by Tauranac and completed by Bellamy, the twin radiators were replaced by a single frontal item, but little else was changed from the BT34. Hill ran in close company with Gethin and Graham McRae, bringing the new and unsorted car home in seventh place.

Graham Hill drove more Formula 2 races during the 1971 and 1972 seasons than at any other time in his career, taking in the South American Torneio series at the end of 1971. During 1972 he drove the Jaegermeister-sponsored Brabham BT38 Cosworth in nine European events, and he is pictured here at Rouen, where he was seventh on aggregate. *(PN)*

The first European round of the 1972 World Championship was at Jarama, where the sponsorship gravy train was getting up steam. The Brabhams looked positively discreet in their white livery in among the panoply of commercially orientated colour schemes that bedecked the rest of the field. In a first corner mêlée caused by an over-enthusiastic Peterson, Hill was punted off and stalled his engine.

Regulations for the incoming Formula 2 called for engines of 2-litres with homologated production cylinder heads. The Rondel squad now comprised Reutemann, Pescarolo and Schenken in BT38s, so Graham was reduced to racing an old Brabham BT36 Cosworth under the Tate of Leeds banner with sponsorship from the German Jaegermeister brewery and he endorsed Esso's Uniflow oil in contemporary motoring magazine adverts. At Pau, for the demanding round-the-houses F2 Grand Prix, possibly the last significant race on this circuit, Graham's orange Jaegermeister BT38 was seventh in heat one, but dropped all the oil from its FVA engine in the second race, causing several cars to slide off. A couple of his subsequent F2 results demonstrated that the fire still burned, however – he was seventh on aggregate at Rouen, fifth at Imola, and took a well-deserved win in both heats at the slipstreaming Monza Lottery Grand Prix.

## The Triple Crown

The Le Mans 24 Hours was shaping up to be a battle between championship leaders Ferrari, who were sweeping all before them that season with the flat-12 powered 312Ps, the works Matra team, who were keeping their powder dry for this one event, Alfa Romeo and JW Automotive's Gulf Mirages. A week before the race, Ferrari withdrew his four cars, possibly because he thought the F1-derived engines would not last 24 hours – although they were perfectly capable of going 1,000km. John Wyer pulled the DFV-powered Mirages at the last moment, so Matra had to beat the Alfas and a couple of Lola T280 DFVs entered by Jo Bonnier. Like Ferrari, the French team employed a strong driver line-up for its Bernard Boyer-designed MS670s, encompassing young hot-shoes, hard-bitten veterans and all-weather experts. Hired for the Matra team by Jabby Crombac, the driver pairings were Amon/Beltoise, Cevert/Ganley, Hobbs/Jabouille, and Hill/Pescarolo. Having been sacked from the Matra F1 team at the end of the 1970 season, Pescarolo was in bullish mood. He was not keen on having Graham as his co-driver, anticipating that Graham was, if not exactly past it, then not up to the particular challenge presented by the 24-hour marathon. Crombac, whose relationship with Graham was more than professional – Hill had been best man at his wedding – sought to reassure his bearded countryman, citing Hill's desire to fulfil his ambition to lift the sport's triple crown as evidence of the Englishman's determination and dedication to the Matra cause. Graham got wind of this, and sent up Pescarolo by acting out the part of an old man when they began the lengthy test programme at Paul Ricard. But Hill was actually very much into it and treated the whole affair most professionally. At the helm was the guiding hand of Gerard Ducarouge (who went on to design the

Lotus-Renault F1 cars) and, in practice, Cevert in the long-tail MS670 narrowly beat Pescarolo in the short-tail, high-downforce version, for the pole, with the Amon/Beltoise partnership in another long-tail MS670 third fastest. The fourth Matra, an updated MS660, of Jabouille/Hobbs was seventh fastest behind the Alfa Romeo trio.

In the race, the mighty Matra squad was reduced to three on only the second lap as the Beltoise car blew its engine very publicly in front of the pits. This was despite the assurances from Matra boffins that the engines would last the distance even if full revs were used. Then, on the third lap, the leading car was Bonnier's little yellow Lola. A lap later the other Lola took the lead while, further back in the GT category, a Corvette (astonishingly) was leading Ferrari Daytonas. However, the status quo was restored after an hour or so when the Lolas had to refuel their thirsty DFV engines, which proved to be a slow and laborious process. For the next 23 hours, the race was led by one or other of the Matras. Surreptitiously, a lone Porsche 908 long-tail coupé, an ex-works car driven by Jöst/Casoni/Weber, crept up the running order, and emerged in third place. Its 3-litre flat-eight was just as fast as the Matra's V12 down the Mulsanne straight – clocking 198.7mph.

Rivalry between the Matra crews was strong, as each one wanted the win. Pit signals to cool it were studiously ignored by the two fastest crews, who later claimed they could not read them because of the spray. Twice Hill passed Ganley for the lead, once when he elected to switch from slicks to intermediate tyres in the early morning as he perceived that rain was on the way. This allowed him to catch and pass Ganley when the New Zealander had to change tyres. Then at midday on Sunday, Ganley's leading Matra was rear-ended by a Corvette as he was driving steadily through a rain shower, handing the lead to Hill/Pescarolo while repairs were carried out. Reliability did not forsake the new leaders and, for the first time since 1950 when the Rosiers (father and son) won in a Talbot, a French car scooped the honours at Le Mans. They had covered 4,691.343km averaging

Hill's victory in the 1972 Le Mans 24 Hours gained him the so-called triple crown, a combination of the F1 World Championship, Indianapolis 500 and this French marathon. Hill and Pescarolo had a secure lead for the final four hours, and here, the Englishman guides the howling Matra MS670 through a Mulsanne chicane during a rain shower. *(LAT)*

195.472kph, or 343 laps, 10 more than the other surviving Matra of Cevert/Ganley. After the Jöst Porsche came the single surviving Alfa 33TT3 of de Adamich/Vaccarella, then a bevy of five Daytonas and then two of the Capris.

Now Graham had achieved what no one else has managed – victories in the F1 World Championship, the Indianapolis 500, and the Le Mans 24 Hours. But for Graham, his most recent victory was tempered with sadness because of the death of his former teammate, Jo Bonnier. Around 8am on the Sunday, Bonnier's Lola had collided with a Ferrari Daytona and plunged over the barrier and into the trees alongside the Mulsanne

straight at 160mph. The news of his death was not spoken about in the Matra camp until after the race, although it was fairly clear to all competitors that a devastating accident must have occurred. Bonnier had been Hill's co-driver in Porsche and Ferrari sports cars, and the pair drove briefly together at BRM. The two men got on well, perhaps because they were both naval men, Bonnier having done his national service for Sweden on board a destroyer.

Despite the loss of his colleague, Hill still managed to be the life and soul of Matra's post-race celebrations, held at Genissel's Mulsanne hostelry.

Hill delivers an amusing line to Henri Pescarolo on the Le Mans podium after their triumph in the 1972 24-hour epic in the Matra MS 670. *(PN)*

## True Grit

Three Brabhams were present at Brands Hatch for the John Player-sponsored British Grand Prix and again, Reutemann was much the fastest of the trio. Graham had put in more practice laps than all but Cevert, but his race ended on lap 48 when he moved over to let the leaders Ickx and Emerson Fittipaldi through at Paddock Bend, got on the marbles on the outside of the track and slid off into the Armco at the bottom of the hill. He remarked acidly afterwards, 'From a gentleman to a twit in a tenth of a second...'

The relative lap times of the three Brabham drivers at the Nürburgring provide an assessment of Graham's standing in the hierarchy of F1 performance. On pole was Ickx's 312B2 Ferrari, on 7min 7.0sec, while Reutemann in BT37/2 was sixth quickest at 7min 12.4sec. Hill's BT37/1 was 15th quickest, on 7min 18.4sec, and Wilson Fittipaldi was 21st on the grid in BT34/1 with 7min 24.8secs. So, although not exactly in the 'also ran' category, they were hardly 'on the pace'. In fact, 1971 and 1972 were two of the marque's leanest years. What they did excel at during the early 1970s was presentation, the cars being clean and invariably well turned out. Graham's sixth place at the Nürburgring earned him a single

world championship point and effectively doubled his score in the table – about which he remarked, 'Big deal!'

For the first time, chicanes were installed at Monza, which meant that lap times were increased and brakes had to work much harder. Graham was one of a small number of drivers – Andretti, Cevert, Regazzoni – who chose to appear from the main gate from paddock to pits and thus earn the adulation of the tifosi. They chose to appear as celebrities, and accept the cheers of the crowd, rather than simply drive out of the paddock in their cars. At 43, Hill was, of course, very much the veteran.

He shared row seven on the grid with Cevert, Reutemann in front of him by a few tenths and Wilson Fittipaldi a row behind. While the younger drivers tended to smite the chicanes and put themselves out, the experienced Hill kept on going, and was up to fourth before his brakes gave up with only five laps to go. He nursed the Brabham round and took a well-deserved fifth place, which was to be his best Grand Prix result of the year.

There was a contretemps in Canada between Graham and Ronnie Peterson. The Swede had started from the front row at Mosport, and was running second to Stewart at half distance when he got held up lapping a bunch including Schenken, Wisell, Hill, Pace and Ganley. Graham refused to let him through, and after four laps trying, while Stewart opened up a 30-second gap, Peterson lunged through just after the pits, but was cut off by Hill. The Brabham carried on while the March, steering deranged, was pushed back to the pits. After repairs had been carried out, Peterson rejoined the fray, giving Hill a taste of his own medicine until he was black-flagged for the reverse push in the pit lane.

There is a strong sense that by this stage Hill was going against the flow. His season ended with just four world championship points, making him 12th in the title standings. But that has to be weighed against one of his most important victories, the Le Mans 24 Hours.

# Chapter 8
# Playing His Own Game

LATE in 1972, with no realistic prospect of a works drive with another team, Graham decided to set up on his own. He ordered one of the new Tony Southgate-designed Shadow DN1s, which were being built at Northampton to be run as works cars with UOP (Universal Oil Products) sponsorship for Jackie Oliver and the American George Follmer.

The deal Graham struck with cigarette sponsors W.D. & H.O. Wills for its Embassy brand had already been mooted in 1972, and involved setting up workshops for his brand new Embassy Racing team at Feltham, near Heathrow airport. The team manager was Alain de Cadanet, no mean competitor himself, who would race his own DFV-powered de Cadanet sports prototype at Le Mans in 1973. While the works UOP cars were painted unremitting black, Hill's Shadow would be finished in the altogether more agreeable white and red striped livery of the Embassy cigarette packet.

Another driver who set up his own F1 team was John Surtees, in 1970, and he spoke about the importance of funding.

> Frankly, Graham set the team up because there was nowhere else for him to go. That was the next stage. My own position was somewhat different, in that I was so disillusioned after a year dealing with the politics at BRM (which was totally different then to the team that existed in the early '60s) and since we had all the designs, we decided to make our own F1 car. We didn't have a big sponsor like Graham did. But of course we did actually build our car, whereas Graham went along to Shadow and Lola. Brooke-Bond Oxo's sponsorship was peanuts compared to what Embassy was paying. We never had a budget over £300,000, and that was to run F2, F1, and F5000, and in 1971 with the TS9B, the budget was in the region of £100,000. It all comes down to budgets.

However, the Shadow operation was behind with its own programme, and Graham's chassis was not ready on time, so he missed the first three Grands Prix of the 1973 season.

The Embassy Racing team made its debut at Montjuich Park in the Spanish Grand Prix on 29 April 1973. Hill's new Shadow DN1/3A was something of a kit car, since the chassis was built by John Thompson's TC Prototypes of Northampton (who also built the Ferrari and Tecno tubs because of strikes by Italian sheet-metal workers). The car was assembled by Hill's own mechanics to Shadow's specifications, using Shadow components. The newness of the Embassy-Hill project was manifest in the car's back row starting position, almost nine seconds off the pace, set by the in-form Peterson's Lotus. While Follmer in one of the works Shadows came third, Graham retired his car at 28 laps with a lack of brakes.

With the magnificent Spa circuit excluded from the F1 calendar for being too dangerous, the Belgian Grand Prix alternated briefly between the new but insipid Nivelles-Baulers autodrome south of Brussels and the slightly more pleasant Zolder circuit in Flanders. Another dispute erupted. The GPDA complained that the newly-laid tarmac

For 1973, Graham set up his own Embassy Racing Team with backing from the Wills tobacco company, a had a Shadow DN1 built at his own Feltham workshops using factory components. Here he drives under the bridge spanning the Monaco track between Loews hairpin and th Portier. He retired on lap 63 with a broken suspension mounting. *(IC)*

surface was breaking up, and insisted that the event should be relocated to Nivelles. Hailwood and Ickx provided the voice of reason, declaring that everyone was in the same boat, so they should just get on with it. Graham once again started from the back of the grid but, amid many retirements, he trailed home in ninth place, five laps in arrears. And that was the highest he finished all season.

At Monaco, where the sea-front section of the circuit had been changed quite radically to include a new portion around the swimming pool, Hill shared the penultimate row of the grid with David Purley. Oliver, in the surviving works Shadow, was on the row ahead of Graham, so there was no disgrace in being so far back. It was Hill's 150th Grand Prix, but there was little to celebrate about the outcome. Having made several pit stops to try and improve the car's handling, the Shadow's left rear radius rod's forward mounting broke on lap 63, causing the entire corner to move forward by a few inches. The Monte Carlo race witnessed the demise of de Cadenet as team manager. Frustrated by delays and breakdowns, Hill's irritation boiled over and he fired de Cadenet for driving the Shadow racing car from paddock to pits – something that was actually not at all out of the ordinary.

Hill was deep in the twilight of his career, and the frustrations of running his own team made him especially prickly. Rob Walker cast some light on the darker side of Hill's personality: 'Graham could be frightfully abrupt. He never was with me,

Hill's Shadow DN1/3A leads Rickky von Opel's Mo Nunn-built Ensign MN01 at Monza early on during the 1973 Italian Grand Prix. Hill went on to finish 14th, while the German driver, a scion of the eponymous car company, retired on lap 10. *(FMC)*

but one time the chauffeur lost his way to the hotel, and I never heard anyone give a tearing off like Graham gave that chauffeur. He could do this often if he was stressed.' Perhaps Hill felt sufficiently confident of his standing to castigate a servant, but not exalted enough to turn on someone of higher status.

Apart from a drive for Matra in the Spa 1000km, Hill was doing only the Grands Prix. 1973 was a season of retirements and lowly placings, in which Hill scored not a single world championship point.

## Lola Chassis

Hill, who had been at the forefront of motor racing and done more than his fair share of winning, was not going to accept lowly grid positions and tail-end finishes for very long. His sponsors too were desperate for some success that would reflect a positive return on their investment. As the season progressed, Hill tried to elicit some support from Shadow principal Don Nichols to overcome teething troubles with the car, but without much success. Other works Shadow personnel including Oliver and team manager Alan Rees were equally frustrated. So Graham decided to abandon his Shadow and try a Lola chassis. This was on the basis that Eric Broadley's concern made excellent sports racing chassis (T70, T212, T280) and, although their F1 days were from another era, back in 1962 when Hill won his first world championship, (not to mention his Indy win in 1966), Lola made good contemporary Formula 5000 (T330) single-seater chassis.

So the Embassy Racing Team's cars for 1974 were a pair of specially commissioned Lola T370s. They used the Ford-Cosworth DFV engine, and were conventional and on the heavy side for F1 cars, due to their origins in the F5000 design. They were always immaculately turned out, as befitted a team boss who strove for excellence in all things. Graham was to drive T370/HU2, and his new recruit from F5000 and 2-litre sports racers, Guy Edwards, got chassis T370/HU3. Graham had also considered hiring Tim Schenken, Peter Gethin and Howden Ganley for the job, but

Hill rounds Loews hairpin in the Lola T370/HU2 during the 1974 Monaco Grand Prix. He finished seventh, a lap ahead of teammate Guy Edwards in the second Embassy Racing Lola. There were just nine finishers out of 25 starters, so the Lolas had at least proved reliable. *(FF)*

Edwards ostensibly came to the table with £25,000-worth of sponsorship from Amoco petroleum. That was his particular forte, finding wealthy sponsors, and it was this anticipated injection of finance that clinched the deal, since the funding from Embassy had been badly underestimated. But no sooner was the matter apparently settled than Amoco decided they were not up for it after all. Edwards retained his place in the team by the skin of his teeth.

## Over-commitment

Hill was not only over-committed on his innumerable public appearances, but had also succeeded Hulme as president of the GPDA on 1 April 1974, with its attendant responsibilities. He was fast getting out of his depth. Here was a man who'd gone from being a mechanic in the relaxed, if not amateurish, Fangio epoch, to Formula 1 team owner at the dawn of the big-business era. As a racing driver he had always been used to working under the protective penumbra of BRM,

Lotus or Motor Racing Developments, as well as private entrants, where management decisions and finance were not his responsibility. Now he had to make those kinds of decisions himself, oversee the building and running of the cars, and he had to drive them. Wisely, he formed an alliance with big-time sports manager Mark McCormack. He would do a small number of charity appearances for free, on the understanding that he would take a fee for anything else.

The new cars were ready for their debut at Buenos Aires on 13 January. Work on the cars must have begun at Lola's Huntingdon plant in early autumn of the previous year. Hill put in a lot of practice laps to acclimatise himself to the new car, qualifying 17th on the grid, while Edwards played himself into the new environment. In the race, the DFV in Hill's car overheated on lap 48, but Edwards did not disgrace himself with 11th place. As the man in charge, Hill commandeered Edwards's car in practice for the Brazilian Grand Prix a fortnight later, and chose to stick with it for

Frustrated by his Shadow, Hill elected to use a Lola T370 for the 1974 season, powered by the ubiquitous Cosworth-Ford DFV V8 engine. Three cars were built specially for the Embassy Hill Racing Team, but they were on the heavy side, being based on the Lola T330 F5000 chassis. *(FF)*

Man of the people. Graham signs an autograph for a young fan in the Brands Hatch paddock during the wet Race of Champions meeting at Brands Hatch in March 1974. *(PN)*

the race. The Lolas were well off the pace though, handling badly on Interlagos's bumpy surface. Edwards's race ended on lap four with a broken aerofoil, but Hill kept going and finished 11th ahead of Hulme's McLaren.

Now entered as Embassy-Hill Lola-Ford DFVs, the Feltham team was back in force at Silverstone for the *Daily Express* race. Hill reverted to the second chassis, with Edwards in the first one, and a third chassis was assembled in the paddock. All three differed markedly in suspension layout, indicating a lack of coherence in the design detail. Hill's scrap with Redman and Migault ended when Redman was pushed off, and then the Lola was damaged as Hill went off the road when chasing the Frenchman.

Regularity and consistency at Nivelles brought Hill up to eighth place in the Belgian Grand Prix, albeit a couple of laps down. Both Lolas finished at Monaco, in seventh and eighth places, Hill beating Edwards by a lap, but two laps behind Peterson's winning Lotus 72. While the Tyrrells of Scheckter and Depailler dominated in Sweden, the Lola pair enjoyed another finish, this time with Hill scoring a point for sixth place and Edwards behind him in seventh. That was as good as it got.

At Dijon-Prenois for the French Grand Prix, Hill had done far more practice laps than anybody else – 193 all told – thought to have been a record at the time. But for a shower of rain, he might have completed a full 200, and all for an 80-lap race. Both Lolas had tyre trouble in the race, and the rewards for perseverance were 13th and 15th places, in another race where Peterson wrung the best out of an ageing Lotus 72 chassis to gain another victory.

## Out of Favour

Guy Edwards's fall from grace began when he injured his wrist in a F5000 race at Mallory Park the week before the British Grand Prix. Hill was not impressed, taking a different view to one he would have held a decade earlier, when he regularly raced cars other than F1. Edwards's wrist was strapped up, and he found it impossible to control the Lola around Brands Hatch in that

condition. So it was handed over to Peter Gethin, who shared the penultimate row of the grid with his new boss. Unfortunately he was consigned to Hill's spare car (T370/HU3), since the ex-Edwards car (T370/HU1) blew its engine on the warm-up lap. But, being smaller in stature than Hill, he was not comfortable in his new seating position. So rather than risk everything in the race, Gethin retired after one lap. Hill went on to finish 13th, six laps behind.

Edwards was again in trouble at the Nürburgring. After a few slow, exploratory laps, he tried a quick lap in the Lola with his wrist still bandaged. But when the car landed after taking off at the Flugplatz, he realised that a whole race was out of the question and, thinking discretion was the better part of valour, withdrew from the race. Hill was unsympathetic. The team boss was 15 seconds off the pace himself, placing him three-quarters of the way down the grid. He came in ninth, just failing to catch Jarier's Shadow. As Edwards sat out the Austrian Grand Prix, his place was taken by the bespectacled German sports car ace, Rolf Stommelen, past winner of events like the Targa Florio and Daytona 24 Hours. The newcomer was three-tenths faster than Hill in practice, making him four rows in front and half-way down the grid, instead of two rows from the back where the boss was. But Stommelen crashed when a tyre blew on lap 15, while Hill too pitted with tyre trouble.

In a season characterised by few mechanical failures but lowly finishes, Hill scored a single point for 18th place in the 1974 World Championship. By 1975, Graham was being described in the media as a 'veteran', and at 45, he certainly was, in contemporary F1 terms, even though five-times world champion Fangio was at his absolute peak at a comparable age, 20 years earlier.

For Argentina, Graham had T370/HU2 and Rolf had T370/HU3. The third car was back at Feltham being fitted with a flat-12 Alfa Romeo engine, thanks to Stommelen's sports car racing connections with Autodelta. In this, the first round of the 1975 season, held in Buenos Aires at the

Parque Amiralte Brown, Hill was 10th and Stommelen 13th.

A lot of drivers have found themselves in the right car or the right team at the wrong time, and at Sao Paulo for the Brazilian race, Jarier put the works Shadow on pole. Such a transformation must have caused the Embassy team to wonder what might have been had they stuck with the Northampton marque. It was Graham's 176th Grand Prix, a record surpassed only in 1989 by Patrese. He could do no better than 12th though, a lap down, and Stommelen came 14th.

At Kyalami, the Embassy squad had a new T371 for Stommelen, which featured revised suspension geometry and repositioned fuel tanks. Hill relied on his regular T370, but spun off in practice, collecting copious amounts of catch fencing and comprehensively destroying the left rear corner and the gearbox. Since there was no spare, he was a non-starter. It had been another of those accidents caused by a puncture that only manifested itself when the car changed direction and the punctured tyre came under load. Rolf finished an unlapped seventh in T370/HU1, their best result for nearly a year, and in what was basically the first 'Hill' car, as opposed to a Lola. The transition was enabled to a certain extent by Eric Broadley himself.

As team principal, it was Graham's somewhat nerve-racking first taste of watching 'his car' do an entire race from the pits. Stommelen raced the singleton Embassy Hill entry at the Race of

The Embassy Racing Team modified the Lola T370 to such an extent under designer Andy Smallman that the cars became known as Hill-Lolas with a GH designation. *(FMC)*

Champions in March, but finished a dismal ninth, five laps behind.

The Feltham workshop had built a second Hill for the *Daily Express* International Trophy meeting on 12 and 13 April. Rolf's car was re-designated GH1/1, while the new one was GH1/2. This was the singleton entry at Silverstone, with Graham at the wheel. It was the last race he competed in. He came 11th, a lap down, pressured for much of the race by Lella Lombardi in a March 751. A harbinger of things that might come to pass, was that the Formula Atlantic support race was won by Tony Brise in the Modus M1. His progress had been under scrutiny for over a season, since he blew the John Player-sponsored Formula Atlantic hierarchy apart at the British Grand Prix meeting at Silverstone in 1974 with the little cream and orange Modus. Most of the regular Formula Atlantic front runners were somewhat miffed at the performance of this interloper in what was ostensibly a Formula 3 chassis – their Marches and Chevrons being F2 chassis. Now Brise was set to make his Formula 1 debut in a Williams FW03 in the Spanish Grand Prix, as was another F3 and Formula Atlantic front runner, Alan Jones.

## Calamity at Barcelona

At Barcelona's Montjuich Park for the Spanish Grand Prix, Stommelen handled GH1/2, while GH1/1 was given to François Migault, a promising French F3 and F2 driver. Graham Hill managed the operation. The German qualified as high as the fifth row, his French teammate back on the penultimate rank and, by comparison, Brise's Williams was two rows further forward. As a prelude to the race, world champion Emerson Fittipaldi declared that he thought the circuit was unsafe, and an inspection of the barriers and catch fencing showed his assessment to be completely accurate. There was a strong move not to race, but team principals feared legal retribution or worse if they pulled out. Last minute repairs were carried out by circuit staff and race-team personnel, but there were still doubts about the safety arrangements.

Twenty-six laps into an eventful race, Stommelen, amazingly, was leading, with Pace right up behind him. Past the pits they went at 150mph, and up the long uphill left-hander. As they crested the notorious brow, Stommelen's rear wing suddenly came off. Deprived of downforce, and with a left-hand bias to its steering, the car shot into the left-side guard-rail. The barrier stood firm, but GH1/2 ricocheted back across the track, still going at about 130mph. Pace's Brabham was also involved, similarly destroying itself against the Armco. Unluckily for Stommelen, his car was now travelling at the same height as the top of the barrier, having been virtually airborne at the brow of the hill when the wing came off. The car careered along the top of the guard-rail, removing a lamp-post and wire fencing as it disintegrated. When it came to rest, the hapless driver was unconscious and badly injured, while a fire marshal and four spectators lay dead. The race was stopped so emergency vehicles could attend the scene, and Mass was declared the winner of the abandoned Grand Prix. Even at an abbreviated 29 laps, there were only 10 finishers out of 25 starters.

Monte Carlo offers a racing environment not so dissimilar to Barcelona, so it was pretty obvious that the repercussions following on from the Spanish disaster would make themselves felt at the Monaco Grand Prix. The obvious modifications were made to the Armco: a third layer was installed here and there, the two lower sections joined with additional plates so the nose of a car could not penetrate, and all bolts were tightened up. Stommelen was still recovering from his massive accident, so Hill himself was the driver of the only Embassy car at the event – T371 or GH1/1. Unfortunately his engine died before he had put in a decent time in the already restricted first practice session. He thus missed the second session and, with Saturday declared a free day, his time set on the Friday was not quick enough to get him onto the grid for the race. Because of the Spanish tragedy the number of starters was reduced to just

The final curtain. Because of fears of a repeat of the carnage at the preceding round at Barcelona, entries for the 1975 Monaco Grand Prix were restricted to just 18 starters. A good qualifying time was therefore crucial but, along with seven other aspiring entrants, Hill failed to make the cut, by less than a quarter of a second. It was his last appearance in a Grand Prix. *(FMC)*

18 instead of the normal 23. Graham thus failed to start (as did BRM, also five-times winners at the principality). So, apart from waving to his adoring public, Hill had time to see the traditional Formula 3 epic and witness Brise charge from the back of the grid in the final to challenge Ribeiro for the lead, which he would almost certainly have taken if the two cars had not collided. Hill's mind was made up. He would step down, and hire the capable Brise to carry the torch.

## Brise Promise

Twenty-three-year-old Tony Brise made his debut in the Embassy-Hill team at Zolder for the Belgian Grand Prix. The former British karting and JPS Formula 3 Champion handled it with the same aplomb with which he threw his GRD and Modus around in F3 and Formula Atlantic. Amazingly, he was up on the fifth row alongside Emerson Fittipaldi. His engine failed in a big way on lap 18, but not before he had given notice that the Hill outfit was potentially a force to be reckoned with. Migault had not impressed in the newer car, and for the next race in Sweden, his place was taken by Australian driver Vern Schuppan, another amiable exile from Formula Atlantic, BRM and Gulf Mirage sports cars.

At Anderstorp Brise made his way up through the field after a lowly grid position based on only a handful of practice laps in GH1/1 and a set-up based on guesswork. He did very well under the circumstances to finish sixth and earn his first world championship point. At Zandvoort, just three-quarters of a second covered the 10 fastest drivers' practice lap times, and that included Brise. The second Embassy-Hill car was being driven by Alan Jones, Vern Schuppan going on to race in USAC events with Dan Gurney's Eagle operation. In wet, then dry conditions, Brise came seventh, and Jones 13th, albeit five laps behind.

Tony Brise had a new car – GH1/4 – built up for him for the French Grand Prix, while Jones was in GH1/3. The young Englishman was consistently faster than the Australian recruit around the Paul Ricard circuit, and from 12th on the grid he ran seventh during the race ahead of such stars as

The makings of a great team: Hill's new recruit Tony Brise in GH1/2 with chief mechanic Ray Brimble (standing) and designer Andy Smallman. *(PN)*

Andretti, Reutemann and Peterson. That was where he finished, while Jones came home 16th, lapped just once.

The time had come for Graham Hill to bow out officially, for him to confirm once and for all that he wouldn't drive an F1 car again. He decided to announce if formally at Silverstone, in front of his home crowd. At the British Grand Prix, he drove a valedictory lap of honour.

There were plenty of pundits who thought that he should have retired much sooner. After Watkins Glen '69, maybe, or on the crest of the Le Mans wave in '72. Rob Walker, for one, thought so: 'I think it did surprise me very much that he carried on. He should have stopped earlier than he did.' Sir Louis Stanley observed:

> Physically he could cope with the strain. A younger generation of drivers in spite of their painstaking efforts were still a long way short of his resilient driving, judgement and skill. But once the edge had worn off and lesser fry were beating him he should have withdrawn. But I have never met anyone in the sport who was fairer or more sincere. Abroad he was motor-racing's finest ambassador.

A fair epitaph.

## Fabulous Career

Mario Andretti had an extraordinarily long career, and he gives an insight into Hill's motivation during those final disappointing years of competition:

It's a very difficult assessment, because it's so personal. But its fair enough to comment on, and I have used Graham as a personal example of drivers with just tremendously fabulous careers, who I don't think were very happy when they finally retired, because during their last couple of seasons they were not really competitive. I don't think he would have been enjoying that. But some of those who did keep going did so because they just didn't want to let go of something that they loved so much. That's what I think about Graham. He was one of those that purely loved to drive, no question, and he tried to milk the thing as long as he felt it was reasonable. I have

followed Graham's career closely and I have felt that, when things were slipping, that this might be okay for some, but it's time to quit. So, yes, I think Graham might have been happier with himself if he would have retired maybe two years sooner, I would venture to say that.

Andretti thought Hill must have been a frustrated man by 1975:

I am sure that his standard was much higher than what he was able to produce at the time, as far as results go. And again, the ultimate satisfaction out of driving is results, winning and being able to feel that you are still a force to be reckoned with. When that disappears, then it's not fun anymore. No matter what passion, or how much you love the driving, then it's not fun anymore.

Graham determined that the Embassy-Hill Racing torch would be carried by Formula 1 debutant Tony Brise, seen here in his Modus-Ford BDA (left) on the front of the grid for the 1974 Dublin Grand Prix. The event was a qualifying round of the John Player Formula Atlantic series, and behind him are such luminaries as Alan Jones, Jim Crawford, Dave Morgan and John Nicholson. This extraordinary event was staged on the Phoenix Park, where crowd protection was scant and lamp posts and park benches were cushioned by straw bales. *(JT)*

Alan Jones's temporary contract terminated with the return to form of Rolf Stommelen, making his comeback in the Austrian Grand Prix at the wheel of GH1/3. Brise handled GH1/4 and in the race was measurably quicker. But on lap 10 he lost a balance weight off one of the wheels and had to pit for a replacement. From the outset, the track had been in the grip of a deluge, with several inevitable spin-offs. After pressure from the GPDA and FOCA (Formula One Constructors' Association), the race was stopped after 29 laps, and the surprising winner was Vittorio Brambilla. Brise came 14th and Stommelen 15th.

At Monza, Brise had GH1/4 and Stommelen had GH1/3, with the old Lola T370 HU3 acting as a spare. Brise qualified sixth fastest, although his colleague was back on the penultimate rank of the grid. The race was a shambles. The electrics failed in Evans's BRM and he hit Stommelen, who hit Jim Crawford's Lotus 72. Scheckter missed his braking for the chicane, spun his Tyrrell, and Andretti, Peterson, Mass and Brise were all out as a result of the subsequent fracas.

Behind the scenes at the Embassy-Hill workshops at Feltham, a new car was being prepared. This was GH2, designed by former Lola employee Andy Smallman, following the principals of the GH1 design but incorporating new regulations. Tony Brise gave it its shakedown run at Silverstone, prior to it going to Paul Ricard for the test session in late November.

## Catastrophe

The sudden and awful demise of the Hill squad is well known. Graham was flying key members of the operation back home from Paul Ricard on 29 November, via Marseilles for refuelling. Aboard the Aztec were star driver Tony Brise, team manager Ray Brimble, designer Andy Smallman, mechanics Terry Richards and Tony Alcock, and of course Hill himself. It was the end of a highly promising race team. Flying through fog on its approach to Elstree airfield, the aeroplane clipped the tree-tops on Arkley golf course, crashed in flames, and they were all killed.

Bette Hill voiced her own views succinctly in a *Motor Sport* interview in December 1999: 'I didn't want Graham to build a team,' she admitted. 'There wasn't sufficient support or finance. It was the biggest heartbreak and toughest job he ever took on. The saddest thing is he was just getting it together when he had the crash.'

There are mixed accounts of Graham's flying abilities. Former Team Lotus and Brabham chief mechanic Bob Dance told how they were once flying back from Marseilles. He was up in the front of the cockpit, with Graham at the controls, and Bob's wife Mary and Bette Hill were behind in the cabin. During the flight, Graham had been fiddling with the mixture settings for each engine to see whether he could get them even. As an indicator, he had to allow each one to run dry, and then switch onto the reserve tank. The first engine ran out over the Channel, causing the plane to do a swooping dive, much to the alarm of the passengers in the rear, picking up again when the reserve feed came in. Very soon afterwards, the process was repeated for the second engine.

According to Team Lotus racing manager Jim Endruweit, Graham was a considerate flyer. He recalled:

It was difficult to feel confident with some people. The Old Man (Chapman) was one that you could, although the journey to Panshanger (Herts) by car with him was far more worrying than the subsequent flight. Jimmy was OK to fly with as well. But I remember flying to Monza with Chapman one year, and having flown over the Alps at 12,000ft, he dropped very steeply down into Milan. That night at dinner I really felt quite ill, I think because of it. The following year, I flew to Jarama with Graham, and we spent about an hour descending gradually from the Pyrenees, circling round and round. After we'd landed I asked him why it had taken so long to come down. 'That was for your benefit,' he said. And he'd remembered how bad I'd felt after the steep descent into Milan the previous year. He was pretty considerate like that. Another time we

Both two-times world champion, Hill and Emerson Fittipaldi confer at Silverstone in 1975. It was here that Graham made the official announcement of his retirement. (IC)

were flying with him into Gatwick. It was dark and ten-tenths cloud right down to a few hundred feet. The controller asked him if he could land on instruments. 'Yes,' he said. And every so often the controller's voice would come on, very calm, giving him a new heading because he kept wandering off course. It was pretty tense, and you could actually cut the silence in the cabin. After we landed, the relief was also tangible. Graham asked if anyone wanted to go on to Panshanger with him. All of a sudden, everyone found they'd got a car waiting or were staying the night near Gatwick! But he took off again. He was just extremely self-confident. He was known as 'Zoomer' Hill to the lads.

This confidence in the air was corroborated by Rob Walker:

I often used to fly with him and we went all over the place. He was a frightfully good flyer. Once we went into Southend, and the fog was so thick that the commercial airlines weren't allowed to fly, and we had to check customs there. Hill dropped it down, and many of the passengers on the commercials who were stuck there were looking daggers at us as we flew off again. Another time, four of us were going to

With the proceeds of his victory in the Indianapolis 500 in 1966, Graham was able to buy himself the Piper Aztec 45 Yankee, and it is ironic that he should have survived two decades in the most dangerous of sports, yet lose his life needlessly in a flying accident. *(PN)*

Hockenheim in three separate planes – Colin's, Brabham's and Graham's – and the only one who found the field was Graham. I said to him, 'how do you always manage to find exactly where you are?' and he said, 'Oh, well I fly down the crease of the map!' A typical Graham remark. But I reckon he was a very good pilot.

Jackie Stewart took a rather different view:

I flew with Graham a lot. But racing drivers are not generally very good pilots. Niki Lauda was very competent – certainly the best pilot among them. David Hobbs was a professional airline pilot, but among the drivers in the '60s there was Chris Irwin, Jim Clark, Colin Chapman, Jack Brabham, Pete Arundell, Innes Ireland... some of them were real mavericks in the air, and there was some very bad behaviour! The FAA would not have appreciated some of the goings on! But it was so sad that Graham died in an air crash when the altimeter was set for the wrong airport. That surprised me. You know, racing drivers are not disciplined enough to be commercial pilots. There's a few of them around, but it was never my opinion they were that good. I learned to fly, but I gave it up immediately. Graham, Jim Clark and I learned at the same place in Australia. We were taught by an Australian pilot of enormous experience called Jim Hazel. We learned in the outback at Orange, which was a lot quieter. I got my licence and then packed it in. I recognised very early on I shouldn't be doing it.

## Barometric Pressure

Hill had taken up flying in a big way in 1965, and took the controls of a Lear jet – along with Tony Rudd and Jackie Stewart – for the first time on the way from Watkins Glen to New York. Tony Rudd remembers Hill's flying career:

Graham was very interested in people flying. We used to get a lift with Innes Ireland sometimes in 1962, but it was not

Damon seems intent on getting back on board the Aztec, while his father struggles with the luggage. Hill relied on the aircraft to commute to most events in the UK and Europe. *(PN)*

until about '64 that Graham had the idea of having his own aeroplane. He learned to fly, and he had a Cessna 175 that he kept at Elstree. He flew himself about in that, mainly in this country, to Snetterton and places like that, but he wasn't a serious aviator. Then, when he won at Indianapolis, he bought an Aztec, which was an American-registered plane. And that was his undoing, because I don't think it was a properly certified aeroplane. The first trip he did in it, we went to Zandvoort in '66, and he had a professional pilot to fly it there, and he flew it back. That was his first serious trip on his own. He didn't know whether he liked me going with him or not, because I'd got a lot more flying experience than he had. But he was pretty happy-go-lucky towards his flying. We came up to Lincolnshire one weekend to go wildfowling, and he flew back to Elstree later than he intended. He'd forgotten to tell them what time he was coming in and wanted the runway lights on, and the controller was asleep and didn't hear the radio. Graham claimed he took turnips with him and threw them out to wake him up! But the time when he bought it in the crash, it was a very common mistake not to reset the altimeters.

Rudd expanded on the function of an altimeter: The barometric pressure changes from hour to hour and from place to place. Barometric pressure here (in Norfolk) might not be the same as the barometric pressure in the South of France or even in Elstree. You fly from the South of France in five hours, and you've got two things to take into account: time and barometric pressure, which can drop quite quickly, or rise quite quickly. That's all an altimeter is, it's a barometer calculating or calibrating an altitude. He set his altimeters on taking off in France, and there were two of them,

Profile of Hill c.1967: although he was widely regarded as the archetypal debonair English racer, he did not suffer fools. (RP)

side by side. Quite often you have one that you set to the airport you are going to, and one set to the information you are getting en route. Ground control says, 'maintain 10,000 feet QNH1828', which is millibars, and you set your altimeter to that, and fly at 10,000 feet. And his course was pretty accurate at that, within a couple of hundred feet. It was only six feet that did it when he hit the top of the tree coming into Elstree. I think he thought he was at 1,000 feet and he was actually at 500 feet or so. It was dark and foggy, and he could have safely gone to Luton, which was open and had all the navigation aids and equipment. But he was determined to go into Elstree; they had their cars there, and he knew his way around. He was just over-confident, and that's really what did it. In my Rolls-Royce days, I used to investigate accidents, and it was nearly always the pilot's over-confidence; he thinks, 'I've done it before and that will be alright,' and he leaves out a check that catches him.

The other dreadful check that Graham forgot to make was to see to it that his pilot's licence was up to date. At the time of the crash, it was not, so the insurance company refused to pay out, which meant that the relatives of those who lost their lives in the crash had no alternative but to sue the Hill estate for compensation, with devastating financial effect.

The Elstree plane crash signals a full stop in the story of Graham Hill the racing driver. But there is a postscript. Apart from giving tremendous pleasure to so many enthusiasts over the two decades of his career – which included feats of courage and heroism, as well as increasing the safety aspect through his presidency of the GPDA – Graham Hill's lasting legacy (in the context of the sport) is, of course, his son Damon. Damon's career in motorcycling and motor sport is a salutary lesson in gutsy self-reliance in the absence of his father and in the face of the financial consequences that the plane crash had on the family. That he emulated his father by winning the

World Championship in 1996 suggests that there was something exceptional in the genes. Damon Hill buoyed up his team when the star was killed – Ayrton Senna in 1994 in a Williams – just as his father had done at Lotus after Clark was killed in 1968. The difference between father and son is that, while Graham founded a team in his name when he finally stepped out of the cockpit, Damon has yet to commit to a similar involvement in the sport.

In an interview in *Motor Sport* magazine (December 1999) Damon highlighted the difference between his own career and that of his father:

> When John Surtees won the title from my Dad in 1964 it was claimed that Lorenzo Bandini was sent to take off my father. There was uproar but it was a storm in a tea cup compared to how they reacted when Schumacher hit me. It went on for

Graham never forgot his roots in motorcycling, and here he discusses the attributes of the 750 Norton Commando with daughter Samantha in 1972 beside their family home, Lyndhurst, at Shenley, near Elstree. *(FF)*

Like father, like son. Damon Hill drives a BRM P57 at the Goodwood Revival in 1998. *(FF/Philip Johnson)*

days. The upside was the incident defined my career and became a talking point beyond the fairly limited area of motor sport. It became an international incident. The downside is that I learnt the pressure of the media. You're never off duty. My father was able to get beneath those pressures, be himself and do whatever Graham Hill did in his spare time without worrying about having every dimension of his life covered. I think he quite liked the publicity, so maybe he'd have preferred it as is now, but his way of coping was to have a few beers, take his trousers down and dance on the table. Do that today and you're in big trouble.

# Bibliography

APART from Hill's own *Life at the Limit*, there are a few other books about the man. Bette Hill's *Other Side of the Hill* was written a couple of years after she lost him. Then there's a rather chaotic summary of Graham's life story, a book entitled *Graham*, ostensibly written by Hill 'with' Neil Ewart. It has a foreword by Prince Charles, and dips into all the social, or at least, non-motor racing aspects of Hill's life. There's rowing, flying (he took up helicopters in 1974), religion (he wasn't a practising Christian), the parties, his children (and their mostly absent father), the celebs (the Rainiers, Paul Newman), the golf, shooting, horses, a film biography (*Graham*), and so on. I mention this because it provides a personal account of his lifestyle, often skirting away from motor sport. But the most poignant chapter in the Hill/Ewart book is the last one, written by Bette after Graham's death. Unlike the rest of the book, suddenly everything is very focused, now the star of the show is no longer with us.

The Tony Rudlin book *Mr Monaco* tells it as he saw it, in flamboyant style with more levity and, after a briefing on the bulk of his career, it takes up Hill's life story after the 1969 Watkins Glen accident. It is strong on lightweight anecdotal material between races, such as this or that girl fancied Graham, or they played golf here or there. It also portrays the downside of the Hill character: the angry, frustrated, impatient beast as well as the sharp, tactical, child-friendly, immaculately-groomed people's hero.

Yet the widely-held public perception of the former world champion is of the debonair archetypal Englishman. The reason why lies in Rudlin's remark that the producer of the *Graham* film had great difficulty in getting anyone to say anything in the slightest bit uncomplimentary about Hill, let alone dish any dirt, so strong was the bond of friendship among his family and friends.

The Rudlin book contains an interesting transcript of an interview Hill gave him for *Motor* magazine, but which was largely unpublished. Here, Hill bares his soul, championing the role of the racing driver over all others involved in the sport. There's also a hint as to why he kept going, perhaps for longer than he should have – the financial rewards that the sport brought him, which allowed him to maintain and sustain the life-style to which he had become accustomed. Tony Rudlin's book concludes with a reconstruction of Graham Hill's last flight, which he made with Bette Hill on board his aeroplane to help exorcise at least some of the grief. He too makes a case for the altimeter in the Aztec having the wrong setting, making the pilot believe that he was some 300ft higher than he actually was on his approach to the tiny Elstree landing strip.

Arron, Simon (with statistics by Steve Small) *Graham Hill* Hazleton, 1992

Bell, Derek with Alan Henry *Derek Bell* PSL, 1988

Bluemel, Keith with Jess Pourret *Ferrari 250 GTO* Bay View Books, 1998

Crombac, Jabby *Colin Chapman, the Man and his Cars* PSL, 1986

Ferguson, Andrew *Team Lotus: the Indianapolis Years* PSL, 1996

Henry, Alan *Damon Hill* PSL, 1994

Hill, Graham *Life at the Limit* William Kimber, 1969

Hill, Graham with Neil Ewart *Graham* Book Club Associates, 1977

Hilton, Christopher *Champions*

Moss, Stirling *All But My Life*

Oliver, Michael *Lotus 49: The Story of a Legend* Veloce, 1999

Prüller, Heinz *Jochen Rindt* William Kimber, 1971

Rudd, Tony *It Was Fun* Haynes, 1993

Rudlin, Tony *Mr Monaco* PSL, 1983

Smith, Ian H. *The Story of Lotus 1947-1960 Birth of a Legend* MRP, 1970

Stanley, Sir Louis *Strictly off the Record*

Tipler, John *Lotus 25 & 33* Sutton Publishing, 2001

Weitmann, Julius *Porsche Story* PSL, 1985

*Graham Hill Grand Prix Racing Book,* Shell, 1966

*Autosport* magazine

*Motor Sport* magazine

Graham Hill's success and extrovert personality won him close friends of celebrity status, and here at Watkins Glen in 1990 he shares a joke with actress Britt Ekland.

# Appendices

## Graham Hill's Racing Cars

Cooper-JAP Mk IV F3 (1954)

Kieft 500cc F3 (1955)

Aston Martin DB3S (Tommy Atkins's 1957)

Connaught F2 (Atkins's, 1957)

Tojeiro-Jaguar (John Ogier, 1957)

Austin A35 (Speedwell) *c.*1958

Lotus Eleven ('Yellow Peril', 1956)

Lotus Seven (1958)

Lotus 12 (1958 – F1/F2)

Lotus 15 (1958; 1959 Le Mans)

Lotus 16 (F1, 1958/59)

Lotus 17 (1959)

Austin-Healey Sprite (Speedwell, 1960)

Maserati T61 Birdcage (Sebring, 1961)

Porsche RS60 (Le Mans 1960, Targa Florio, Nürburgring 1000km, 1962)

Porsche Carrera RSK (Goodwood TT, 1960)

Ferrari 250 Testa Rossa (Scuderia Serenissima, 1961)

BRM P48 four-cylinder

BRM P61 V8

BRM P57 V8

Jaguar Mk II (Equipe Endeavour, John Coombs)

Jaguar E-type

Ferrari 250GT (Rob Walker, Le Mans 1961)

Ferrari 250GTO (Maranello Concessionaires, John Coombs)

Aston Martin 212 (Le Mans 1962)

Porsche F8 (Nürburgring 1000km, 1962)

Lotus 19 (UDT-Laystall, 1962)

Rover-BRM gas-turbine (Le Mans, 1963, 1965)

Ferrari 330LM SP (NART, 1963)

Ferrari 330P3 (Le Mans 1964 etc, Maranello Concessionaires)

BRM P61 V8

Ferguson FF P99 (Rob Walker, Tasman series, 1963)

Lotus 23B (Roy Winkelmann, Ian Walker, 1963)

Ford Galaxie (John Willment, 1963)

BRM P26 monocoque (1964)

Cooper T72 Cosworth (Coombs, 1964)

Brabham BT10 (F2, Coombs, 1964)

Brabham BT11 (Willment, Rand GP etc)

Brabham BT3 (Scuderia Veloce 1965 Tasman series)
Brabham BT16 (F2, Coombs)
McLaren Elva-Oldsmobile (Group 7, Coombs)
Ferrari 275P (Maranello, 1965)
Lotus 35-BRM (F2, Coombs, 1965)
Brabham BT16 (F2, Coombs)
Ford GT40 (Alan Mann, 1966, Sebring)
Ford Mk II (Alan Mann, Le Mans, 1966)
Lola T70-Chevrolet (Team Surtees, Guard's Trophy, 1966)
Matra MS5-BRM (F2, Coombs, 1966)
Lola T90-Ford (John Mecom, Indianapolis, 1966)
BRM P261 Tasman (1965/66)
BRM P115 (one-off H-16 engine)
BRM T83 H-16 (1966)
Lotus 33 Climax/BRM (1967)
Lotus 43 H-16 BRM (1967)
Lotus 49/49B/49C/49T Cosworth (1967–70, Team Lotus, GLTL, Rob Walker/Brooke-Bond Oxo)
Lotus 48 (F2, 1967–68 Team Lotus, Gold Leaf Team Lotus)
Lotus Cortina (1967)
Porsche 910 (BOAC 500, 1967)
Lotus 56 gas-turbine (Indianapolis, 1968)
Ford Escort Twin-Cam (Alan Mann, 1968)
Lotus 63 Cosworth V8 4x4 (1969)
Lotus 64 Ford V8 (1969, abandoned STP Indianapolis car)
Lotus 59B Cosworth (F2, Roy Winkelmann, 1969)
Ford Capri 3000GT (Ford Motor Co., 1970, 1971)
Lotus 69 Cosworth (Jochen Rindt Racing, F2, 1970, Bernie Ecclestone, 1971)
Lotus 72 (Rob Walker/Brooke-Bond Oxo, 1970)
Brabham BT33 Cosworth V8 (F1, Motor Racing Developments, 1971, 1972)
Brabham BT34 (F1, Motor Racing Developments, 1971)
Brabham BT36 Cosworth (Rondel Racing, F2, 1971; Graham Hill Racing, 1972, Jaegermeister)
Brabham BT37 Cosworth V8 (F1, Motor Racing Developments, 1972)
Brabham BT38 Cosworth (F2, Jaegermeister Racing, 1972)
Matra MS670-V12 (1972, Le Mans, 1973, Spa)
Shadow DN1 Cosworth V8 (F1, 1973, Embassy Racing)
Lola T370 Cosworth V8 (F1, 1974/75, Embassy Racing)
Hill GH1 Cosworth V8 (F1, 1975, Embassy Racing)

# Hill Statistics

| | |
|---|---|
| Grand Prix starts: | 176 (1958–75) |
| Grand Prix wins: | 14 (percentage of races: 7.95) |
| GP second places: | 15 |
| GP third places: | 7 |
| World championship points: | 289 |
| GP pole positions: | 13 |
| GP front rows: | 42 |
| Successive GP starts: | 90 (from the US in 1960 to US 1969) |
| GP starts with Team Lotus: | 49 (plus 12 with Rob Walker racing team) |
| GP starts with BRM: | 63 |
| GP starts with Brabham: | 23 |
| GP starts with Embassy Hill Racing Team: | 29 |
| GP starts with Cosworth-Ford DFV engine: | 94 |
| GP fastest laps: | 10 |
| GP laps led: | 1,105 from 32 races |
| Total number of race starts (inc. heats) 1956–75: | 607 |
| Le Mans 24 Hours: | 10 (winner in 1972) |
| Indianapolis 500: | 3 (winner in 1966) |
| Targa Florio: | 5 |

Hill liked to have his cars set up with virtually no suspension movement, and the 2-litre P261 V8 lifts its nose under acceleration up Beau Rivage during practice for the 1966 Monaco Grand Prix. *(PN)*

# Racing Record

## 1956

| Race | Circuit | Date | Entrant | Car | Result |
|---|---|---|---|---|---|
| Up to 1200cc Sports Cars | Brands Hatch | 29/04/56 | Team Lotus | Lotus Eleven-Climax | 1st |
| Up to 1500cc Sports Cars | Brands Hatch | 29/04/56 | Team Lotus | Lotus Eleven-Climax | 2nd, *broke 1500cc lap record* |
| Farningham Trophy | Brands Hatch | 21/05/56 | Equipe Endeavour | Cooper-Climax | 3rd |
| Wrotham Cup | Brands Hatch | 21/05/56 | Equipe Endeavour | Cooper-Climax | 6th, *handicap race* |
| Anerley Trophy | Crystal Palace | 22/05/56 | Tommy Sopwith | Lotus Eleven-Climax | 3rd |
| Norbury Trophy | Crystal Palace | 22/05/56 | Tommy Sopwith | Lotus Eleven-Climax | 3rd |
| Up to 1200cc Production Race | Mallory Park | 08/06/56 | J.J. Richards | Lotus Eleven-Ford | 1st |
| *Autosport* Championship Race | Aintree | 23/06/56 | J.J. Richards | Lotus Eleven-Ford | 1st |
| Sports and F2 Race | Silverstone | 14/07/56 | J.J. Richards | Lotus Eleven-Ford | 7th |
| *Autosport* Trophy Race | Brands Hatch | 06/08/56 | J.J. Richards | Lotus Eleven-Ford | DSQ, *too many spins* |
| Class 1B Hillclimb | Prescott | 08/09/56 | J.J. Richards | Lotus Eleven-Ford | 3rd |
| *Autosport* 3-Hour Race | Oulton Park | 22/09/56 | J.J. Richards | Lotus Eleven-Ford | *Engine, retired* |
| Sports Car Race | Snetterton | 07/10/56 | Tommy Sopwith | Lotus Eleven-Ford | *Bent steering arm, retired* |
| Sports/Formula 2 Race | Brands Hatch | 14/10/56 | J.J. Richards | Lotus Eleven Ford | 5th |
| Up to 1200cc Sports Car Race | Brands Hatch | 14/10/56 | J.J. Richards | Lotus Eleven-Ford | 2nd |

## 1957

| Race | Circuit | Date | Entrant | Car | Result |
|---|---|---|---|---|---|
| Up to 1100cc Sports Car Race | Brands Hatch | 31/03/57 | Dr E. Manton | Lotus Eleven-Climax | 1st |
| Up to 1200cc Sports Car Race | Oulton Park | 06/04/57 | Dr E. Manton | Lotus Eleven-Climax | 5th |
| Lavant Cup | Goodwood | 22/04/57 | Tommy Atkins | Connaught F2 | 4th |
| Chichester Cup | Goodwood | 22/04/5/ | Dr E. Manton | Lotus Eleven-Climax | 1st, *1100cc class, 4th overall* |
| Sussex Trophy | Goodwood | 22/04/57 | Tommy Atkins | Aston Martin DB3S | 9th |
| Up to 1100cc Sports Car Race | Brands Hatch | 19/05/57 | Dr E. Manton | Lotus Eleven-Climax | 1st |
| Sports Car Race | Brands Hatch | 19/05/57 | Tommy Atkins | Aston Martin DB3S | 3rd |
| Up to 1100cc Sports Car Race | Brands Hatch | 09/06/57 | Dr E. Manton | Lotus Eleven-Climax | 4th |
| Anerley Trophy | Crystal Palace | 10/06/57 | Dr E. Manton | Lotus Eleven-Climax | 4th |
| Up to 1100cc Sports Car Race | Snetterton | 28/07/57 | Dr E. Manton | Lotus Eleven-Climax | Retired |
| Vanwall Formula Libre Trophy | Snetterton | 28/07/57 | Dr E. Manton | Lotus Eleven-Climax | 5th |
| Up to 1100cc Sports Car Race | Brands Hatch | 05/08/57 | Dr E. Manton | Lotus Eleven-Climax | 1st |
| Up to 1500cc Sports Car Race | Brands Hatch | 05/08/57 | John Willment | Willment 1500cc | 2nd |
| Kingsdown Trophy | Brands Hatch | 05/08/57 | John Ogier | Tojeiro-Jaguar | 2nd |
| Up to 1250cc Sports Car Race | Goodwood | 31/08/57 | Dr E. Manton | Lotus Eleven-Climax | 2nd |
| Over 1500cc Sports Car Race | Silverstone | 14/09/57 | John Ogier | Tojeiro-Jaguar | *Suspension failure, retired* |
| International Trophy, Heat 2 | Silverstone | 14/09/57 | John Willment | Cooper-Climax F2 | *4th F2 class, 8th overall* |
| International Trophy, Final | Silverstone | 14/09/57 | John Willment | Cooper Climax F2 | *5th F2 class, 13th overall* |
| Woodcote Cup | Goodwood | 28/09/57 | Team Lotus | Lotus 12-Climax F2 | 5th |
| International Gold Cup | Oulton Park | 05/10/57 | Team Lotus | Lotus 12-Climax F2 | 11th, *fastest lap* |
| Christmas Trophy | Brands Hatch | 26/12/57 | Dr E. Manton | Lotus Eleven-Climax | 1st |

## 1958

| Race | Circuit | Date | Entrant | Car | Result |
|---|---|---|---|---|---|
| Lavant Cup, F2 | Goodwood | 07/04/58 | Team Lotus | Lotus 12-Climax F2 | 2nd |
| Glover Trophy, F1/F2 | Goodwood | 07/04/58 | Team Lotus | Lotus 12-Climax F2 | Retired |
| Sussex Trophy | Goodwood | 07/04/58 | Team Lotus | Lotus 15-Climax | *Gearbox, retired* |
| British Empire Trophy | Oulton Park | 12/04/58 | Team Lotus | Lotus 15-Climax | 6th overall, *fastest lap in heat 2* |
| Over 1100cc Sports Car Race | Aintree | 19/04/58 | Team Lotus | Lotus 15-Climax | *Gearbox failure, retired* |
| Aintree 200 | Aintree | 19/04/58 | Team Lotus | Lotus 16-Climax F2 | 4th in F2 class |
| Sports Car Race | Silverstone | 03/05/58 | Team Lotus | Lotus 15-Climax | 1st |
| *Daily Express* International Trophy | Silverstone | 03/05/58 | Team Lotus | Lotus 12-Climax | 8th |
| Saloon Car Race | Silverstone | 03/05/58 | Speedwell Racing | Austin A35 | 3rd |
| **Monaco GP** | **Monte Carlo** | **18/05/58** | **Team Lotus** | **Lotus 12-Climax** | *Lost wheel, retired* |
| **Dutch GP** | **Zandvoort** | **25/05/58** | **Team Lotus** | **Lotus 12-Climax** | *Engine failure, retired* |
| Coupe de Vitesse | Reims | 06/06/58 | Team Lotus | Lotus 16-Climax F2 | Retired |
| Rouen GP | Rouen | 08/06/58 | Team Lotus | Lotus 15-Climax | 2nd |
| **Belgian GP** | **Spa-Francorchamps** | **16/06/58** | **Team Lotus** | **Lotus 12-Climax** | *Engine failure, retired* |
| Le Mans 24-Hours | Le Mans | 21-22/06/58 | Team Lotus | Lotus 15-Climax 2.0 | *c/d Allison. Overheating, retired* |

| | | | | | |
|---|---|---|---|---|---|
| **French GP** | Reims | **06/07/58** | **Team Lotus** | **Lotus 16-Climax** | *Engine failure, retired* |
| **British GP** | Silverstone | **19/07/58** | **Team Lotus** | **Lotus 16-Climax** | *Low oil pressure, retired* |
| *Daily Express* Sports Car Race | Silverstone | 19/07/58 | Team Lotus | Lotus 15-Climax | *Conrod failed, retired* |
| Saloon Car Race | Silverstone | 19/07/58 | Speedwell Racing | Austin A35 | *Overheating, retired* |
| Birkett 6-Hour relay | Silverstone | 16/8/58 | Speedwell Racing | Austin A35 | 1st. *Team members: Sprinzel/Adams/Hulbert* |
| **German GP** | **Nürburgring** | **03/08/58** | **Team Lotus** | **Lotus 16-Climax** | *Oil pipe split, retired* |
| **Portuguese GP** | **Porto** | **28/08/58** | **Team Lotus** | **Lotus 16-Climax** | *Spun off, retired* |
| Kentish Trophy | Brands Hatch | 30/08/58 | Team Lotus | Lotus 16-Climax | *Gearbox, retired heat 2* |
| Farningham Trophy | Brands Hatch | 30/08/58 | Team Lotus | Lotus 15-Climax | 2nd |
| **Italian GP** | **Monza** | **07/09/58** | **Team Lotus** | **Lotus 16-Climax** | **6th** |
| Tourist Trophy | Goodwood | 13/09/58 | Team Lotus | Lotus 15-Climax | *c/d Allison. Dropped valve, retired* |
| Sports Car Race | Oulton Park | 20/09/58 | Team Lotus | Lotus 15-Climax | *Ignition failure, retired* |
| Over 1100cc Sport Car Race | Snetterton | 11/10/58 | Team Lotus | Lotus 15-Climax | 1st |
| **Moroccan GP** | **Casablanca** | **19/10/58** | **Team Lotus** | **Lotus 16-Climax** | **16th** |
| Sports Car Race | Brands Hatch | 26/12/58 | Team Lotus | Lotus Seven | 1st |
| Formule Libre | Brands Hatch | 26/12/58 | Team Lotus | Lotus 16-Climax F2 | 1st |
| | | | | | |
| **1959** | | | | | |
| International 100 | Goodwood | 30/03/59 | Team Lotus | Lotus 16-Climax Fl | *Brake failure, retired* |
| Lavant Cup | Goodwood | 30/03/59 | Team Lotus | Lotus 16-Climax F2 | 4th |
| British Empire Trophy | Oulton Park | 11/04/59 | Team Lotus | Lotus 16-Climax F2 | *Severe vibrations, retired* |
| Unlimited Sports Car Race | Oulton Park | 11/04/59 | Team Lotus | Lotus 17-2.0 | 4th |
| Over 1500cc Sports Car Race | Aintree | 18/04/59 | Team Lotus | Lotus 17-2.0 | 4th |
| Aintree 200 | Aintree | 18/04/59 | Team Lotus | Lotus 16-Climax Fl | 5th |
| Syracuse GP | Syracuse | 25/04/59 | Team Lotus | Lotus 16-Climax F2 | *Broken rear hub, retired* |
| 1100-3000cc Sports Car Race | Silverstone | 02/05/59 | Team Lotus | Lotus 17-2.0 | *Crownwheel & pinion, retired* |
| *Daily Express* International Trophy | Silverstone | 02/05/59 | Team Lotus | Lotus 16-Climax Fl | *Brake pipe split, retired* |
| **Monaco GP** | **Monte Carlo** | **10/05/59** | **Team Lotus** | **Lotus 16-Climax Fl** | *Car caught fire, retired* |
| Over 1500cc Sports Car Race | Crystal Palace | 18/05/59 | Team Lotus | Lotus 17-2.0 | 3rd |
| Formula 2 Race | Mallory Par | 25/05/59 | Team Lotus | Lotus 16-Climax F2 | *Engine failure, retired* |
| Up to 1100cc Sports Car Race | Mallory Par | 25/05/59 | Team Lotus | Lotus Eleven-Climax | 3rd |
| Over 1100cc Sports Car Race | Mallory Park | 25/05/59 | Team Lotus | Lotus 15-Climax | 1st |
| **Dutch GP** | **Zandvoort** | **31/05/59** | **Team Lotus** | **Lotus 16-Climax Fl** | **7th** |
| Le Mans 24-Hours | Le Mans | 20-21/06/59 | Team Lotus | Lotus 17-Climax | *c/d Jolly. Retired* |
| Coupe de Vitesse | Reins | 04/07/59 | Team Lotus | Lotus 16-Climax F2 | *Engine failure, retired* |
| **French GP** | **Reins** | **05/07/59** | **Team Lotus** | **Lotus 16-Climax Fl** | *Radiator split, retired* |
| Sports Car Race | Rouen | 12/07/59 | Team Lotus | Lotus Eleven-Climax | *Steering failure, retired* |
| Rouen GP | Rouen | 12/07/59 | Team Lotus | Lotus 16-Climax F2 | 7th |
| **British GP** | **Aintree** | **18/07/59** | **Team Lotus** | **Lotus 16-Climax Fl** | **9th** |
| Sports Car Race | Aintree | 18/07/59 | Team Lotus | Lotus 17-2.0 | 1st |
| Auvergne Trophy | Clermont-Ferrand | 26/07/59 | Team Lotus | Lotus 16-Climax F2 | 6th |
| **German GP** | **Avus** | **02/08/59** | **Team Lotus** | **Lotus 16-Climax Fl** | *Gearbox failed in heat 1, retired* |
| Wrotham Trophy | Brands Hatch | 03/08/59 | Team Lotus | Lotus Eleven-Climax | 3rd |
| Kingsdown Trophy | Brands Hatch | 03/08/59 | Team Lotus | Lotus 17-Climax | 1st |
| John Davy Trophy | Brands Hatch | 03/08/59 | Team Lotus | Lotus 16-Climax F2 | *Burst oil-cooler, retired* |
| **Portuguese GP** | **Monsanto** | **23/08/59** | **Team Lotus** | **Lotus 16-Climax Fl** | *Spun off on oil, retired* |
| Kentish 100, Heat 1 | Brands Hatch | 29/08/59 | Team Lotus | Lotus 16-Climax F2 | 2nd |
| Kentish 100, Heat 2 | Brands Hatch | 29/08/59 | Team Lotus | Lotus 16-Climax F2 | 2nd overall |
| Rochester Trophy | Brands Hatch | 29/08/59 | Team Lotus | Lotus 17-Climax | 3rd |
| Farningham Trophy | Brands Hatch | 29/08/59 | Team Lotus | Lotus 17-2.5-litre | 1st |
| Tourist Trophy | Goodwood | 05/09/59 | Team Lotus | Lotus 17-2.0 | *c/d Stacey. Accident, retired* |
| **Italian GP** | **Monza** | **13/09/59** | **Team Lotus** | **Lotus 16-Climax Fl** | *Transmission failure, retired* |
| Gold Cup | Oulton Park | 26/09/59 | Team Lotus | Lotus 16-Climax Fl | 5th |
| Up to 1100cc Sports Car Race | Brands Hatch | 04/10/59 | Team Lotus | Lotus Eleven-Climax | 1st |
| Saloon Car Race | Brands Hatch | 04/10/59 | Speedwell Racing | Austin A35 | 1st |
| Silver City Trophy | Snetterton | 10/10/59 | Team Lotus | Lotus 16-Climax Fl | *Broken driveshaft, retired* |
| | | | | | |
| **1960** | | | | | |
| Buenos Aires 1000Kms | Buenos Aires | 31/01/60 | Porsche System Engineering | Porsche RSK | *c/d Bonnier. 3rd overall, 1st in class* |
| **Argentine GP** | **Buenos Aires** | **07/02/60** | **BRM/Owen Racing Organisation** | **BRM P25** | *Broken valve spring, retired* |
| Sebring 12-Hours | Sebring | 26/03/60 | Porsche System Engineering | Porsche RSK | *c/d Bonnier. Conrod failure, retired* |
| International 100 | Goodwood | 18/04/60 | BRM/Owen Racing Organisation | BRM P48 | 5th |
| Aintree 200 | Aintree | 30/04/60 | Porsche System Engineering | Porsche F2 | 3rd |
| Targa Florio | Piccolo Madonie | 08/05/60 | Porsche System Engineering | Porsche RSK | *c/d Barth. 3rd* |

| | | | | | |
|---|---|---|---|---|---|
| *Daily Express* International Trophy | Silverstone | 14/05/60 | BRM/Owen Racing Organisation | BRM P48 | 3rd |
| Nürburgring 1000Kms | Nürburgring | 22/05/60 | Porsche System Engineering | Porsche RSK | *c/d Barth. Crashed, retired* |
| **Monaco GP** | **Monte Carlo** | **29/05/60** | **BRM/Owen Racing Organisation** | **BRM P48** | **Crashed, retired** |
| **Dutch GP** | **Zandvoort** | **05/06/60** | **BRM/Owen Racing Organisation** | **BRM P48** | **3rd** |
| Rouen GP | Rouen | 07/06/60 | Speedwell Racing | Speedwell Sprite | *2nd in up to 1100cc class* |
| **Belgian GP** | **Spa-Francorchamps** | **19/06/60** | **BRM/Owen Racing Organisation** | **BRM P48** | **Engine failure, retired** |
| Le Mans 24-Hours | Le Mans | 25-26/06/60 | Porsche System Engineering | Porsche RSK | *c/d Bonnier. Engine failure, retired* |
| **French GP** | **Reims** | **03/07/60** | **BRM/Owen Racing Organisation** | **BRM P48** | **Accident on grid, retired** |
| **British GP** | **Silverstone** | **16/07/60** | **BRM/Owen Racing Organisation** | **BRM P48** | **Set fastest lap, spun off, retired** |
| Solitude GP | Solitude | 24/07/60 | Porsche System Engineering | Porsche F2 | 4th |
| German GP | Nürburgring | 31/07/60 | Porsche System Engineering | Porsche F2 | 4th |
| Silver City Trophy | Brands Hatch | 01/08/60 | BRM/Owen Racing Organisation | BRM P48 | 2nd |
| Saloon car race | Brands Hatch | 01/08/60 | Speedwell Racing | Jaguar Mk II | *Fastest lap, crashed, retired* |
| **Portuguese GP** | **Porto** | **14/08/60** | **BRM/Owen Racing Organisation** | **BRM P48** | **Gearbox failure, retired** |
| Tourist Trophy | Goodwood | 20/08/60 | Porsche System Engineering | Porsche Carrera | *c/d Abarth. 4th overall, 1st in class* |
| Kentish 100 | Brands Hatch | 27/08/60 | Porsche System Engineering | Porsche F2 | 4th |
| Lombank Trophy | Snetterton | 17/09/60 | BRM/Owen Racing Organisation | BRM P48 | *Engine failure, retired* |
| Gold Cup | Oulton Park | 24/09/60 | BRM/Owen Racing Organisation | BRM P48 | 3rd |
| 1000Km de Paris | Montlhéry | 23/10/60 | Porsche System Engineering | Porsche Carrera | *c/d Von Hanstein. 7th* |
| **US GP** | **Riverside** | **20/11/60** | **BRM/Owen Racing Organisation** | **BRM P48** | **Gearbox problems, retired** |

**1961**

| | | | | | |
|---|---|---|---|---|---|
| New Zealand GP | Ardmore | 07/01/61 | Owen Racing Organisation | BRM P48 | 3rd |
| International 100 | Warwick Farm | 05/02/61 | Owen Racing Organisation | BRM P48 | *Leaking fuel tank, retired* |
| Formule Libre, Heat 1 | Ballarat | 12/02/61 | Owen Racing Organisation | BRM P48 | 1st |
| Formule Libre, Final | Ballarat | 12/02/61 | Owen Racing Organisation | BRM P48 | 1st |
| Sebring 12 Hours | Sebring | 25/03/61 | Camoradi International | Maserati T61 | *c/d Moss. Exhaust manifold problem, retired* |
| Lavant Cup | Goodwood | 03/04/61 | Owen Racing Organisation | BRM P48-Climax | 3rd |
| St Mary's Trophy | Goodwood | 03/04/61 | Equipe Endeavour | Jaguar 3.8 | 2nd |
| Glover Trophy | Goodwood | 03/04/61 | Owen Racing Organisation | BRM P48/57-Climax | 2nd |
| GT Race | Oulton Park | 15/04/61 | Equipe Endeavour | Jaguar E-type | 1st |
| Sports Car Race | Oulton Park | 15/04/61 | UDT-Laystall Racing | Lotus 19-Climax | 2nd |
| Aintree 200 | Aintree | 22/04/61 | Owen Racing Organisation | BRM P48/57-Climax | 3rd |
| Syracuse GP | Syracuse | 25/04/61 | Owen Racing Organisation | BRM P48/57-Climax | *Engine trouble, retired* |
| Production Car Race | Silverstone | 06/05/61 | Equipe Endeavour | Jaguar 3.8 | 1st |
| *Daily Express* International Trophy | Silverstone | 06/05/61 | Owen Racing Organisation | BRM P48/57-Climax | Retired |
| **Monaco GP** | **Monte Carlo** | **14/05/61** | **Owen Racing Organisation** | **BRM P48/57-Climax** | **Fuel pump failure, retired** |
| **Dutch GP** | **Zandvoort** | **22/05/61** | **Owen Racing Organisation** | **BRM P48/57-Climax** | **8th** |
| Nürburgring 1000Kms | Nürburgring | 28/05/61 | Porsche S.E./Camoradi Racing | Porsche RSK | *c/d Moss. Engine failure, retired* |
| Nürburgring 1000Kms | Nürburgring | 28/05/61 | Porsche System Engineering | Porsche Carrera P | *c/d Moss/Linge/Greger. 8th* |
| Silver City Trophy | Brands Hatch | 03/06/61 | Owen Racing Organisation | BRM P48/57-Climax | 13th |
| Peco Trophy GT Race | Brands Hatch | 03/06/61 | Equipe Endeavour | Jaguar E-type | 3rd |
| Le Mans 24-Hours | Le Mans | 09-10/06/61 | NART | Ferrari 250GT | *c/d Moss. Water leak, retired* |
| **Belgian GP** | **Spa-Francorchamps** | **18/06/61** | **Owen Racing Organisation** | **BRM P48/57-Climax** | **Oil leak, retired** |
| Targa Florio | Piccolo Madonie | 30/06/61 | Camoradi International | Porsche RSK | *c/d Moss. Broken differential, retired* |
| **French GP** | **Reins** | **02/07/61** | **Owen Racing Organisation** | **BRM P48/57-Climax** | **6th** |
| British Empire Trophy | Silverstone | 08/07/61 | Owen Racing Organisation | BRM P48/57-2.5 | 3rd |
| Saloon Car Race | Silverstone | 08/07/61 | Equipe Endeavour | Jaguar 3.8 | 2nd |
| GT Race | Silverstone | 08/07/61 | Equipe Endeavour | Jaguar E-type | Retired |
| **British GP** | **Aintree** | **15/07/61** | **Owen Racing Organisation** | **BRM P48/57-Climax** | **Broken valve spring, retired** |
| **German GP** | **Nürburgring** | **06/08/61** | **Owen Racing Organisation** | **BRM P48/57-Climax** | **Accident, retired** |
| Peco Trophy | Brands Hatch | 07/08/61 | Equipe Endeavour | Jaguar E-type | *Puncture, retired* |
| Guards Trophy | Brands Hatch | 07/08/61 | Owen Racing Organisation | BRM P48/57-2.5 | 3rd |
| Tourist Trophy | Goodwood | 19/08/61 | Porsche System Engineering | Porsche Abarth | *6th overall, 1st in class* |
| Modena GP | Modena | 03/09/61 | Owen Racing Organisation | BRM P48/57-Climax | 7th |
| **Italian GP** | **Monza** | **10/09/61** | **Owen Racing Organisation** | **BRM P48/57-Climax** | **Engine failure, retired** |
| Gold Cup | Oulton Park | 23/09/61 | Owen Racing Organisation | BRM P48/57-Climax | Retired |
| Production Sports Car Race | Oulton Park | 23/09/61 | Equipe Endeavour | Jaguar E-type | 2nd |
| **US GP** | **Watkins Glen** | **08/10/61** | **Owen Racing Organisation** | **BRM P48/57-Climax** | **5th** |
| Paris 1000Kms | Montlhéry | 15/10/61 | Scuderia Serenissima | Ferrari 250GT | *c/d Bonnier. 12th* |
| Nassau Trophy | Nassau | 10/12/61 | Scuderia Serenissima | Ferrari 250 TR | 5th |
| Christmas Trophy | Brands Hatch | 26/12/61 | Scuderia Serenissima | Ferrari 250 TR | 1st |

## 1962

| | | | F1 World Champion driver | | |
|---|---|---|---|---|---|
| Monte Carlo Rally | Monte Carlo | –/01/62 | Rootes Group | Sunbeam Rapier | *c/d Peter Jopp. 10th* |
| Sebring 12-Hours | Sebring | 24/03/62 | Scuderia Serenissima | Ferrari 250 TR/I | NS, *injured back* |
| Brussels GP, Heat 1 | Heysel | 01/04/62 | Owen Racing Organisation | BRM P57-V8 | 1st |
| Brussels GP, Heat 2 | Heysel | 01/04/62 | Owen Racing Organisation | BRM P57-V8 | DSQ, *push-start* |
| GT Race | Oulton Park | 07/04/62 | John Coombs | Jaguar E-type | 2nd |
| Touring Car Race | Snetterton | 14/04/62 | John Coombs | Jaguar Mk II 3.8 | 3rd |
| Lombank Trophy | Snetterton | 14/04/62 | Owen Racing Organisation | BRM P57-V8 | 2nd |
| Glover Trophy | Goodwood | 23/04/62 | Owen Racing Organisation | BRM P57-V8 | 1st |
| St Mary's Trophy | Goodwood | 23/04/62 | John Coombs | Jaguar Mk II 3.8 | 1st |
| Saloon Car Race | Aintree | 28/04/62 | John Coombs | Jaguar Mk II 3.8 | 1st |
| Aintree '200' | Aintree | 28/04/62 | Owen Racing Organisation | BRM P57-V8 | Retired |
| Targa Florio | Piccolo Madonie | 06/5/62 | Scuderia Serenissima | Porsche-Abarth Carrera | *c/d Vaccarella/Bonnier. 3rd (practiced but didn't drive in race)* |
| *Daily Express* International Trophy | Silverstone | 12/05/62 | Owen Racing Organisation | BRM P57-V8 | |
| GT Race | Silverstone | 12/05/62 | John Coombs | Jaguar E-type | 3rd |
| Saloon Car Race | Silverstone | 12/05/62 | John Coombs | Jaguar Mk II 3.8 | 1st |
| **Dutch GP** | **Zandvoort** | **20/05/62** | **Owen Racing Organisation** | **BRM P57-V8** | **1st** |
| Nürburgring 1000Kms | Nürburgring | 27/05/62 | Porsche System Engineering | Porsche F8 | *c/d Herrmann. 3rd overall, 1st in class* |
| **Monaco GP** | **Monte Carlo** | **03/06/62** | **Owen Racing Organisation** | **BRM P57-V8** | ***Engine failure, retired, classified 6th*** |
| International 2000 Guineas | Mallory Park | 11/06/62 | Rob Walker | Lotus 18/21-Climax | 3rd |
| GT Race, Heat 3 | Mallory Park | 11/06/62 | John Coombs | Jaguar E-type | 2nd |
| GT Race, Final | Mallory Park | 11/06/62 | John Coombs | Jaguar E-type | 2nd |
| **Belgian GP** | **Spa-Francorchamps** | **17/06/62** | **Owen Racing Organisation** | **BRM P57-V8** | **Pole position, 2nd** |
| Le Mans 24-Hours | Le Mans | 23-24/06/62 | David Brown | Aston Martin 4.0 | *c/d Ginther. Oil pipe split, retired* |
| Reims GP | Reims | 01/07/62 | Owen Racing Organisation | BRM P57-V8 | 2nd |
| **French GP** | **Rouen** | **08/07/62** | **Owen Racing Organisation** | **BRM P57-V8** | ***Fastest lap, fuel injection problems, classified 9th*** |
| Scott-Brown Memorial race | Snetterton | 15/07/62 | UDT-Laystall | Lotus 19-Climax | 1st |
| Saloon Car Race | Snetterton | 15/07/62 | John Coombs | Jaguar Mk II 3.8 | 1st |
| **British GP** | **Aintree** | **21/07/62** | **Owen Racing Organisation** | **BRM P57-V8** | **4th** |
| **German GP** | **Nürburgring** | **05/08/62** | **Owen Racing Organisation** | **BRM P57-V8** | **1st, *fastest lap*** |
| Peco Trophy Race | Brands Hatch | 06/08/62 | John Coombs | Jaguar E-type | 4th |
| Molyslip Trophy saloon car race | Brands Hatch | 06/08/62 | John Coombs | Jaguar Mk II 3.8 | *Crashed, retired* |
| Kanonloppet | Karlskoga | 12/08/62 | Rob Walker | Lotus 18/21-Climax | *Oil leak, retired* |
| Tourist Trophy | Goodwood | 18/08/62 | John Coombs | Ferrari 250GTO | 2nd |
| Saloon Car Race | Oulton Park | 01/09/62 | John Coombs | Jaguar Mk II 3.8 | 1st |
| Gold Cup | Oulton Park | 01/09/62 | Owen Racing Organisation | BRM P57-V8 | 2nd |
| **Italian GP** | **Monza** | **16/09/62** | **Owen Racing Organisation** | **BRM P57-V8** | **1st, *fastest lap*** |
| US GP | Watkins Glen | 07/10/62 | Owen Racing Organisation | BRM P57-V8 | 2nd |
| Riverside GP | Riverside | 14/10/62 | Bill Sturgis | Cooper T61-Monaco | *Gear linkage failed, retired* |
| Pacific GP | Laguna Seca | 21/10/62 | Bill Sturgis | Cooper T61-Monaco | *Gearbox problems, retired* |
| Rand GP | Kyalami | 15/12/62 | Owen Racing Organisation | BRM P57-V8 | Retired |
| Natal GP, Heat 1 | Westmead | 22/12/62 | Owen Racing Organisation | BRM P57-V8 | 2nd |
| Natal GP, Final | Westmead | 22/12/62 | Owen Racing Organisation | BRM P57-V8 | *Ignition trouble, 15th* |
| **South African GP** | **East London** | **29/12/62** | **Owen Racing Organisation** | **BRM P57-V8** | **1st** |

## 1963

| | | | | | |
|---|---|---|---|---|---|
| New Zealand GP | Pukekohe | 05/01/63 | Rob Walker | Ferguson P99 4WD | *Gearbox, retired* |
| Australian GP | Warwick Farm | 10/02/63 | Rob Walker | Ferguson P99 4WD | *Carburation problems, 6th* |
| Lakeside International Trophy | Lakeside | 17/02/63 | Rob Walker | Ferguson P99 4WD | 2nd |
| Sebring 3-Hours | Sebring | 22/03/63 | Speedwell Racing | MG Midget | *Transmission failure, retired* |
| Sebring 12-Hours | Sebring | 23/03/63 | NART | Ferrari 330LM/SP | *c/d Rodriguez. 3rd* |
| Lombank Trophy | Snetterton | 30/03/63 | Owen Racing Organisation | BRM P57-V8 | 1st |
| GT Race | Snetterton | 30/03/63 | John Coombs | Jaguar E-type | 1st |
| Saloon Car Race | Snetterton | 30/03/63 | John Coombs | Jaguar Mk II 3.8 | 2nd |
| Saloon Car Race | Oulton Park | 06/04/63 | John Coombs | Jaguar Mk II 3.8 | 1st |
| St Mary's Trophy | Goodwood | 15/04/63 | John Coombs | Jaguar Mk II 3.8 | 1st |
| Sussex Trophy | Goodwood | 15/04/63 | John Coombs | Jaguar E-type | 1st |
| Glover Trophy | Goodwood | 15/04/63 | Owen Racing Organisation | BRM P57-V8 | 9th |
| Aintree '200' | Aintree | 27/04/63 | Owen Racing Organisation | BRM P57-V8 | 1st |
| Saloon Car Race | Aintree | 27/04/63 | John Coombs | Jaguar Mk II 3.8 | 1st |
| GT Race | Silverstone | 11/05/63 | John Coombs | Jaguar E-type | 1st |
| *Daily Express* International Trophy | Silverstone | 11/05/63 | Owen Racing Organisation | BRM P57-V8 | Retired |
| **Monaco GP** | **Monte Carlo** | **26/05/63** | **Owen Racing Organisation** | **BRM P57-V8** | **1st** |
| Player's 200 | Mosport Park | 01/06/63 | British Racing Partnership | Lotus 19-Climax | *Holed piston, retired* |

| Race | Circuit | Date | Entrant | Car | Result |
|---|---|---|---|---|---|
| Saloon Car Race | Crystal Palace | 03/06/63 | John Coombs | Jaguar Mk II 3.8 | 3rd |
| **Belgian GP** | **Spa-Francorchamps** | **09/06/63** | **Owen Racing Organisation** | **BRM P57-V8** | *Pole position, gearbox failure, retired* |
| Le Mans 24-Hours | Le Mans | 15-16/06/63 | Owen Racing Organisation | Rover-BRM turbine | *c/d Ginther. Not classified, but 7th on road* |
| **Dutch GP** | **Zandvoort** | **23/06/63** | **Owen Racing Organisation** | **BRM P57-V8** | *Overheating, retired* |
| **French GP** | **Reims** | **30/06/63** | **Owen Racing Organisation** | **BRM P61-V8** | *Push-start, 1 minute penalty, 3rd* |
| Grovewood Trophy | Mallory Park | 13/07/63 | John Coombs | Jaguar E-type | 1st |
| **British GP** | **Silverstone** | **20/07/63** | **Owen Racing Organisation** | **BRM P61-V8** | *Ran out of fuel on last lap, 3rd* |
| **German GP** | **Nürburgring** | **04/08/63** | **Owen Racing Organisation** | **BRM P61-V8** | *Gearbox failure, retired* |
| Guards Trophy | Brands Hatch | 05/08/63 | Maranello Concessionaires | Ferrari 250 GTO | *Broken throttle pedal, retired* |
| Molyslip Trophy 'B' | Brands Hatch | 05/08/63 | John Coombs | Jaguar E-type | 2nd |
| Tourist Trophy | Goodwood | 24/08/63 | Maranello Concessionaires | Ferrari 250 GTO | 1st |
| Canadian GP | Mosport Park | 28/08/63 | Ian Walker | Lotus 23B-Climax | *2nd overall, 1st in class* |
| Northwest GP, Heat 1 | Kent, Seattle | 29/08/63 | Winkelmann Racing | Lotus 23B-Climax | 3rd |
| Northwest GP, Heat 2 | Kent, Seattle | 29/08/63 | Winkelmann Racing | Lotus 23B-Climax | *Gearbox failure, retired* |
| **Italian GP** | **Monza** | **08/09/63** | **Owen Racing Organisation** | **BRM P61-V8** | *Clutch failure, retired* |
| Saloon Car Race | Oulton Park | 21/09/63 | John Willment | Ford Galaxie | 2nd |
| Gold Cup | Oulton Park | 21/09/63 | Owen Racing Organisation | BRM P57-V8 | 3rd |
| **US GP** | **Watkins Glen** | **06/10/63** | **Owen Racing Organisation** | **BRM P57-V8** | *Pole position, 1st* |
| Riverside GP | Riverside | 13/10/63 | Ian Walker | Lotus 23B-Climax | *10th overall, 4th in class* |
| Monterey Pacific GP | Laguna Seca | 20/10/63 | Ian Walker | Lotus 23B-Climax | *12th overall, 4th in class* |
| **Mexican GP** | **Mexico City** | **27/10/63** | **Owen Racing Organisation** | **BRM P57-V8** | **4th** |
| **South African GP** | **East London** | **28/12/63** | **Owen Racing Organisation** | **BRM P57-V8** | **3rd** |
| | | | | | |
| **1964** | | | | | |
| Monte Carlo Rally | Monte Carlo | –/01/64 | Ford Motor Company | Ford Falcon V8 | *All 8 Falcons finished* |
| International 100 | Warwick Farm | 16/02/64 | Scuderia Veloce | Brabham BT3-Climax | 4th |
| South Pacific Trophy | Longford | 02/03/64 | Scuderia Veloce | Brabham BT3-Climax | 1st |
| *Daily Mirror* Trophy | Snetterton | 14/03/64 | Owen Racing Organisation | BRM P261-V8 | *Lost wheel, crashed, retired* |
| Sebring 12-Hours | Sebring | 21/03/64 | Maranello Concessionaires | 4.0 Ferrari 330 | *c/d Bonnier. Gearbox failure, retired* |
| *News of the World* Trophy | Goodwood | 30/03/64 | Owen Racing Organisation | BRM P261-V8 | *Broken rotor arm, retired* |
| Sussex Trophy | Goodwood | 30/03/64 | Maranello Concessionaires | 3.0 Ferrari GTO | 1st |
| Pau GP | Pau | 05/04/64 | Jean Redelé | Alpine-Renault F2 | *NS, car unprepared* |
| Aintree 200 | Aintree | 18/04/64 | Owen Racing Organisation | BRM P261-V8 | 2nd |
| Targa Florio | Piccolo Madonie | 26/04/64 | Maranello Concessionaires | Porsche 718/8 | *c/d Bonnier. Driveshaft broke, retired* |
| GT Race | Silverstone | 02/05/64 | Maranello Concessionaires | 3.0 Ferrari GTO | 1st |
| *Daily Express* International Trophy | Silverstone | 02/05/64 | Owen Racing Organisation | BRM P261-V8 | 2nd |
| **Monaco GP** | **Monte Carlo** | **10/05/64** | **Owen Racing Organisation** | **BRM P261-V8** | *1st, fastest lap* |
| London Trophy F2, Heat 1 | Crystal Palace | 18/05/64 | John Coombs | Cooper T72-Cosworth | 1st |
| London Trophy F2, Final | Crystal Palace | 18/05/64 | John Coombs | Cooper T72-Cosworth | 2nd |
| **Dutch GP** | **Zandvoort** | **24/05/64** | **Owen Racing Organisation** | **BRM P261-V8** | **4th** |
| Nürburgring 1000Kms | Nürburgring | 31/05/64 | Maranello Concessionaires | 3.3 Ferrari 275P | *c/d Ireland. Refueled out on circuit, DSQ* |
| **Belgian GP** | **Spa-Francorchamps** | **14/06/64** | **Owen Racing Organisation** | **BRM P261-V8** | *5th, ran out of fuel on last lap, retired* |
| Le Mans 24-Hours | Le Mans | 20-21/06/64 | Maranello Concessionaires | 4.0 Ferrari 330P3 | *c/d Bonnier. 2nd* |
| **French GP** | **Rouen** | **28/06/64** | **Owen Racing Organisation** | **BRM P261-V8** | **2nd** |
| Reims GP F2 | Reims | 05/07/64 | John Coombs | Brabham BT10-Cosworth | Retired |
| Reims 12-Hours | Reims | 05/07/64 | Maranello Concessionaires | 3.3 Ferrari 250LM | *c/d Bonnier. 1st* |
| **British GP** | **Brands Hatch** | **11/07/64** | **Owen Racing Organisation** | **BRM P261-V8** | **2nd** |
| Solitude GP | Solitude | 19/07/64 | Owen Racing Organisation | BRM P261-V8 | *Spun off on wet track, retired* |
| **German GP** | **Nürburgring** | **02/08/64** | **Owen Racing Organisation** | **BRM P261-V8** | **2nd** |
| British Eagle Trophy F2 | Brands Hatch | 03/08/64 | John Coombs | Brabham BT10-Cosworth | 3rd |
| Guards International Trophy | Brands Hatch | 03/08/64 | Maranello Concessionaires | 4.0 Ferrari 330P | 4th |
| **Austrian GP** | **Zeltweg** | **23/08/64** | **Owen Racing Organisation** | **BRM P261-V8** | *Pole position. Distributor drive broken, retired* |
| Tourist Trophy | Goodwood | 29/08/64 | Maranello Concessionaires | 4.0 Ferrari 330P | 1st |
| **Italian GP** | **Monza** | **06/09/64** | **Owen Racing Organisation** | **BRM P261-V8** | *Clutch failed on grid, retired* |
| Gold Cup | Oulton Park | 19/09/64 | John Coombs | Brabham BT10-Cosworth F2 | *Engine failure, retired* |
| *Autosport* 3-Hours | Snetterton | 26/09/64 | Maranello Concessionaires | Ferrari 250LM | *Low oil pressure, retired* |
| Grand Prix de L'Isle de France, F2 | Montlhéry | 27/09/64 | John Coombs | Brabham BT10-Cosworth | *Brake fade, 9th* |
| **US GP** | **Watkins Glen** | **04/10/64** | **Owen Racing Organisation** | **BRM P261-V8** | **1st** |
| Paris 1000Kms | Montlhéry | 11/10/64 | Maranello Concessionaires | Ferrari 330P | *c/d Bonnier. 1st* |
| **Mexican GP** | **Mexico City** | **25/10/64** | **Owen Racing Organisation** | **BRM P261-V8** | *Hit by Bandini, 11th* |
| Rand GP, Heat 1 | Kyalami | 12/12/64 | John Willment | Brabham BT11-BRM V8 | 1st |
| Rand GP, Heat 2 | Kyalami | 12/12/64 | John Willment | Brabham BT11-BRM V8 | *(1st on aggregate)* |

**1965**

| | | | | | |
|---|---|---|---|---|---|
| **South African GP** | **East London** | **01/01/65** | **Owen Racing Organisation** | **BRM P261-V8** | **3rd** |
| New Zealand GP, Heat 2 | Pukekohe | 09/01/65 | Scuderia Veloce | Brabham BT3-Climax | 1st |
| New Zealand GP, Final | Pukekohe | 09/01/65 | Scuderia Veloce | Brabham BT3-Climax | *Fastest lap, 1st* |
| International 100 | Warwick Farm | 14/02/65 | Scuderia Veloce | Brabham BT3-Climax | 5th |
| International Cup | Sandown Park | 21/02/65 | Scuderia Veloce | Brabham BT3-Climax | *cylinder head problem, retired* |
| *Launceston Examiner* Race | Longford | 27/02/65 | Scuderia Veloce | Brabham BT3-Climax | 1st |
| Australian GP | Longford | 03/03/65 | Scuderia Veloce | Brabham BT3-Climax | 4th |
| Race of Champions, Heat 1 | Brands Hatch | 13/03/65 | Owen Racing Organisation | BRM P261-V8 | 5th |
| Race of Champions, Heat 2 | Brands Hatch | 13/03/65 | Owen Racing Organisation | BRM P261-V8 | *Overheating, retired* |
| Sports Car Race | Silverstone | 20/03/65 | John Coombs | McLaren Elva-Oldsmobile | *Engine failure, retired* |
| Sebring 12 Hours | Sebring | 27/03/65 | John Mecom | Ferrari 330P | *c/d Rodriguez. Clutch failure, retired* |
| *Daily Express* Cup, F2 | Oulton Park | 03/04/65 | John Coombs | Brabham BT16-BRM | *Engine failure, retired* |
| *Autocar* Trophy F2, Heat 1 | Snetterton | 10/04/65 | John Coombs | Brabham BT16-BRM | 1st |
| *Autocar* Trophy F2, Heat 2 | Snetterton | 10/04/65 | John Coombs | Brabham BT16-BRM | *(1st on aggregate)* |
| *Sunday Mirror* Trophy | Goodwood | 19/04/65 | Owen Racing Organisation | BRM P261-V8 | 2nd |
| Pau GP, F2 | Pau | 25/04/65 | John Coombs | Brabham BT16-BRM | *Engine seized, retired* |
| Guards Trophy, Heat 1 | Mallory Park | 06/05/65 | John Coombs | McLaren Elva-Oldsmobile | 1st |
| Guards Trophy, Heat 2 | Mallory Park | 06/05/65 | John Coombs | McLaren Elva-Oldsmobile | NS, *Engine problem* |
| Targa Florio | Piccolo Madonie | 09/05/65 | Porsche System Engineering | Porsche 904 flat-8 Coupé | *c/d Bonnier, 4th* |
| *Daily Express* International Trophy | Silverstone | 15/05/65 | Owen Racing Organisation | BRM P261-V8 | *Camshaft failure, retired* |
| Nürburgring 1000Km | Nürburgring | 23/05/65 | Maranello Concessionaires | 3.3 Ferrari 275P2 | *c/d Stewart. Electrical problem, retired* |
| **Monaco GP** | **Monte Carlo** | **30/05/65** | **Owen Racing Organisation** | **BRM P261-V8** | *Pole position  Fastest lap, 1st* |
| London Trophy, Heat 1 | Crystal Palace | 07/06/65 | John Coombs | Brabham BT16-BRM F2 | 2nd |
| London Trophy, Heat 2 | Crystal Palace | 07/06/65 | John Coombs | Brabham BT16-BRM F2 | *(2nd on aggregate)* |
| **Belgian GP** | **Spa-Francorchamps** | **13/06/65** | **Owen Racing Organisation** | **BRM P261-V8** | *Pole position, 5th* |
| Le Mans 24 Hours | Le Mans | 19-20/06/65 | Owen Racing Organisation | Rover-BRM gas-turbine | *c/d Stewart 10th on the road* |
| **French GP** | **Clermont-Ferrand** | **27/06/65** | **Owen Racing Organisation** | **BRM P261-V8** | **5th** |
| Reims GP, F2 | Reims | 03/07/65 | John Coombs | Brabham BT16-BRM | *Engine failure, retired* |
| Reims 12 Hours | Reims | 03-04/07/65 | Maranello Concessionaires | 4.0 Ferrari 330P2 | *c/d Bonnier. Transmission problem, retired* |
| **British GP** | **Silverstone** | **10/07/65** | **Owen Racing Organisation** | **BRM P261-V8** | *Fastest lap, 2nd* |
| Rouen GP, F2 | Rouen | 11/07/65 | John Coombs | Brabham BT16-BMW | 2nd |
| **Dutch GP** | **Zandvoort** | **18/07/65** | **Owen Racing Organisation** | **BRM P261-V8** | *Pole position, 4th* |
| **German GP** | **Nürburgring** | **01/08/65** | **Owen Racing Organisation** | **BRM P261-V8** | **2nd** |
| Kanonloppet, F2 | Karlskoga | 08/08/65 | John Coombs | Brabham BT16-BMW | Retired |
| Guards International Trophy, Heat 1 | Brands Hatch | 30/08/65 | John Coombs | McLaren Elva-Oldsmobile | NC |
| Guards International Trophy, Heat 2 | Brands Hatch | 30/08/65 | John Coombs | McLaren Elva-Oldsmobile | NC |
| British Eagle Trophy | Brands Hatch | 30/08/65 | John Coombs | Lotus 35-BRM F2 | 4th |
| **Italian GP** | **Monza** | **12/09/65** | **Owen Racing Organisation** | **BRM P261-V8** | **2nd** |
| Gold Cup | Oulton Park | 18/09/65 | John Coombs | Lotus 35-BRM F2 | *Drove Ron Harris/Team Lotus spare car, 3rd* |
| Albi GP | Albi | 26/09/65 | John Coombs | Lotus 35-BRM F2 | *Fuel pump failure, retired* |
| **US GP** | **Watkins Glen** | **03/10/65** | **Owen Racing Organisation** | **BRM P261-V8** | *Pole position. Fastest lap, 1st* |
| **Mexican GP** | **Mexico City** | **24/10/65** | **Owen Racing Organisation** | **BRM P261-V8** | *Broken conrod, retired* |
| *Los Angeles Times* GP | Riverside | 31/10/65 | | McLaren Elva-Oldsmobile | *Lost wheel, retired* |

**1966**

| | | | | | |
|---|---|---|---|---|---|
| New Zealand GP | Pukekohe | 08/01/66 | Owen Racing Organisation | BRM P261T-V8 | 1st |
| International 100 | Warwick Farm | 13/02/66 | Owen Racing Organisation | BRM P261T-V8 | 2nd |
| Australian GP | Lakeside | 20/02/66 | Owen Racing Organisation | BRM P261T-V8 | 1st |
| Exide International 100 | Sandown Park | 27/02/66 | Owen Racing Organisation | BRM P261T-V8 | 3rd |
| *Launceston Examiner* Race | Longford | 05/03/66 | Owen Racing Organisation | BRM P261T-V8 | 2nd |
| South Pacific Trophy | Longford | 07/03/66 | Owen Racing Organisation | BRM P261T-V8 | 2nd |
| Sebring 12 Hours | Sebring | 26/03/66 | Alan Mann Racing | Ford GT40 | *c/d Stewart. Car caught fire, retired* |
| BARC 200, F2 | Oulton Park | 02/04/66 | John Coombs | Brabham BT16-BRM | NS, *Meeting abandoned, snow* |
| Archie Scott-Brown Trophy | Snetterton | 08/04/66 | Team Surtees | Lola T70-Chevrolet V8 | *Transmission failure, retired* |
| *Sunday Mirror* Trophy, F2 | Goodwood | 11/04/66 | John Coombs | Brabham BT16-BRM | 5th |
| Pau GP, F2 | Pau | 17/04/66 | John Coombs | Brabham BT16-BRM | 3rd |
| Juan Jover Trophy, F2 | Barcelona | 25/04/66 | John Coombs | Brabham BT16-BRM | 6th |
| Limbourg GP | Zolder | 08/05/66 | John Coombs | Matra MS5-BRM F2 | Retired |
| **Monaco GP** | **Monte Carlo** | **22/05/66** | **Owen Racing Organisation** | **BRM P261-V8 2.0** | **3rd** |
| Indianapolis 500 | Indianapolis | 30/05/66 | John Mecom | Lola T90-Ford 4.2 | 1st |
| **Belgian GP** | **Spa-Francorchamps** | **12/06/66** | **Owen Racing Organisation** | **BRM P261-V8 2.0** | *Stopped to help Stewart, retired* |
| Le Mans 24 Hours | Le Mans | 18-19/06/66 | Alan Mann | Ford Mk II 7.0 | *c/d Muir. Font suspension broke, retired* |
| Reims GP | Reims | 02/07/66 | John Coombs | Matra MS5-BRM F2 | Retired, *classified 11th* |

| French GP | Reims | 03/07/66 | Owen Racing Organisation | BRM P261-V8 2.0 | *Camshaft failure, retired* |
|---|---|---|---|---|---|
| Rouen GP | Rouen | 10/07/66 | John Coombs | Matra MS5-BRM F2 | 5th |
| **British GP** | **Brands Hatch** | **16/07/66** | **Owen Racing Organisation** | **BRM P261-V8 2.0** | **3rd** |
| **Dutch GP** | **Zandvoort** | **24/07/66** | **Owen Racing Organisation** | **BRM P261-V8 2.0** | **2nd** |
| **German GP** | **Nürburgring** | **07/08/66** | **Owen Racing Organisation** | **BRM P261-V8 2.0** | **4th** |
| Guards International Trophy | Brands Hatch | 29/08/66 | Team Surtees | Lola T70 Mk 2-Chevrolet V8 | 3rd |
| **Italian GP** | **Monza** | **04/09/66** | **Owen Racing Organisation** | **BRM T83-H16 3.0** | *Engine failure, retired* |
| GP de l'Isle de France | Montlhéry | 11/09/66 | John Coombs | Matra MS5-BRM F2 | 8th |
| Gold Cup | Oulton Park | 17/09/66 | Owen Racing Organisation | BRM T83-H16 3.0 | *Camshaft failure, retired* |
| Trophée Craven A | Le Mans | 18/09/66 | John Coombs | Matra MS5-BRM F2 | *Camshaft failure, retired* |
| Albi GP | Albi | 25/09/66 | John Coombs | Matra MS5-BRM F2 | 10th |
| **US GP** | **Watkins Glen** | **02/10/66** | **Owen Racing Organisation** | **BRM T83-H16 3.0** | *Gearbox failure, retired* |
| Mt Fuji Race | Fuji Speedway | 09/10/66 | John Mecom | Lola T90-Ford 4.2 | 5th |
| *Los Angeles Times* GP | Riverside | 30/10/66 | Team Surtees | Lola T70 Mk 2-Chevrolet V8 | 3rd |
| **Mexican GP** | **Mexico City** | **23/10/66** | **Owen Racing Organisation** | **BRM T83-H16** | *Engine misfire, retired* |

**1967**

| **South African GP** | **Kyalami** | **02/01/67** | **Team Lotus** | **Lotus 43-BRM H16** | *Suspension failure, retired* |
|---|---|---|---|---|---|
| Australian GP | Warwick Farm | 19/02/67 | Team Lotus | Lotus 48-Cosworth F2 | *Transmission failure, retired* |
| Lombank Trophy | Brands Hatch | 12/03/67 | Team Lotus | Lotus Cortina | *2nd overall, 1st up to 2000cc class* |
| Guards 100 F2 | Snetterton | 24/03/67 | Team Lotus | Lotus 48-Cosworth | 2nd |
| Group 5 Saloons | Snetterton | 24/03/67 | Team Lotus | Lotus Cortina | 4th |
| Group 5 Saloons | Silverstone | 27/03/67 | Team Lotus | Lotus Cortina | 2nd |
| Group 5 Saloons | Oulton Park | 17/09/67 | Team Lotus | Lotus Cortina | Retired |
| Wills Trophy F2, Heat 1 | Silverstone | 27/03/67 | Team Lotus | Lotus 48-Cosworth | Retired |
| Wills Trophy F2, Heat 2 | Silverstone | 27/03/67 | Team Lotus | Lotus 48-Cosworth | 2nd |
| Pau GP F2 | Pau | 02/04/67 | Team Lotus | Lotus 48-Cosworth | *Transmission failure, retired* |
| Juan Jover Trophy F2 | Barcelona | 09/04/67 | Team Lotus | Lotus 48-Cosworth | *Metering unit failed, retired* |
| Spring Cup, F2 | Oulton Park | 15/04/67 | Team Lotus | Lotus 48-Cosworth | 8th |
| Eifelrennen, F2 | Nürburgring | 23/04/67 | Team Lotus | Lotus 48-Cosworth | 15th |
| *Daily Express* International Trophy | Silverstone | 29/04/67 | Team Lotus | Lotus 33-BRM V12 2.0 | 4th |
| **Monaco GP** | **Monte Carlo** | **07/05/67** | **Team Lotus** | **Lotus 33-BRM V12 2.0** | **2nd** |
| Indianapolis 500 | Indianapolis | 30-31/05/67 | STP-Team Lotus | Lotus 42-Ford 4.2 | *Piston failure, retired* |
| **Dutch GP** | **Zandvoort** | **04/06/67** | **Team Lotus** | **Lotus 49-Cosworth V8** | *Pole position. Timing gear failure, retired* |
| **Belgian GP** | **Spa-Francorchamps** | **18/06/67** | **Team Lotus** | **Lotus 49-Cosworth V8** | *Gearbox failure, retired* |
| Reims GP, F2 | Reims | 25/06/67 | Team Lotus | Lotus 48-Cosworth | 2nd |
| **French GP** | **Le Mans 'Bugatti'** | **02/07/67** | **Team Lotus** | **Lotus 49-Cosworth V8** | *Pole position. Fastest lap, gearbox failure, retired* |
| Rouen GP, F2 | Rouen | 09/07/67 | Team Lotus | Lotus 48-Cosworth | 4th |
| **British GP** | **Silverstone** | **15/07/67** | **Team Lotus** | **Lotus 49-Cosworth V8** | *Engine failure, retired* |
| Flugplatzrennen, F2 | Tülln Langenlebarn | 16/07/67 | Team Lotus | Lotus 48-Cosworth | 6th |
| Madrid GP, F2 | Jarama | 23/07/67 | Team Lotus | Lotus 48-Cosworth | *Electrical problem, retired* |
| BOAC 500 | Brands Hatch | 30/07/67 | Porsche System Engineering | Porsche 910 F8 | *c/d Rindt. Dropped valve, retired* |
| **German GP** | **Nürburgring** | **06/08/67** | **Team Lotus** | **Lotus 49-Cosworth V8** | *Suspension failure, retired* |
| Swedish GP, F2 | Karlskoga | 13/08/67 | Team Lotus | Lotus 48-Cosworth | 5th |
| Mediterranean GP, F2 | Enna-Pergusa | 20/08/67 | Team Lotus | Lotus 48-Cosworth | 7th |
| **Canadian GP** | **Mosport Park** | **27/08/67** | **Team Lotus** | **Lotus 49-Cosworth V8** | **4th** |
| Guards Trophy, F2 | Brands Hatch | 28/08/67 | Team Lotus | Lotus 48-Cosworth | 7th |
| Suomen GP, F2 | Keimola | 03/09/67 | Team Lotus | Lotus 48-Cosworth | 3rd |
| Hämeenlinnan Ajot, F2 | Ahvenisto | 05/09/67 | Team Lotus | Lotus 48-Cosworth | 5th |
| **Italian GP** | **Monza** | **10/09/67** | **Team Lotus** | **Lotus 49-Cosworth V8** | *Engine failure, retired* |
| Gold Cup | Oulton Park | 17/09/67 | Team Lotus | Lotus 48-Cosworth | 3rd |
| Saloon car race, Group 5 | Oulton Park | 17/09/67 | Team Lotus | Lotus Cortina Mk 2 | *Crashed, retired* |
| Albi GP, F2 | Albi | 24/09/67 | Team Lotus | Lotus 48-Cosworth | Retired |
| **US GP** | **Watkins Glen** | **01/10/67** | **Team Lotus** | **Lotus 49-Cosworth V8** | *Pole position. Fastest lap, 2nd* |
| Rome GP, F2 | Vallelunga | 08/10/67 | Team Lotus | Lotus 48-Cosworth | 8th |
| **Mexican GP** | **Mexico City** | **22/10/67** | **Team Lotus** | **Lotus 49-Cosworth V8** | *Broken UJ, retired* |
| Spanish GP | Jarama | 12/11/67 | Team Lotus | Lotus 49-Cosworth V8 | 2nd |

**1968** F1 World Champion driver

| **South African GP** | **Kyalami** | **01/01/68** | **Team Lotus** | **Lotus 49-Cosworth V8** | **2nd** |
|---|---|---|---|---|---|
| Rothmans International 100 | Surfer's Paradise | 11/02/68 | Gold Leaf Team Lotus | Lotus 49T-Cosworth V8 | 2nd |
| International 100 | Warwick Farm | 18/02/68 | Gold Leaf Team Lotus | Lotus 49T-Cosworth V8 | 2nd |
| Australian GP | Sandown Park | 25/02/68 | Gold Leaf Team Lotus | Lotus 49T-Cosworth V8 | 3rd |
| South Pacific Trophy | Longford | 04/03/68 | Gold Leaf Team Lotus | Lotus 49T-Cosworth V8 | 6th |

| Race | Circuit | Date | Team | Car | Result |
|---|---|---|---|---|---|
| *Daily Mail* Race of Champions | Brands Hatch | 17/03/68 | Gold Leaf Team Lotus | Lotus 49-Cosworth V8 | *Broken driveshaft, retired* |
| Juan Jover Trophy, F2 | Barcelona | 31/03/68 | Gold Leaf Team Lotus | Lotus 48-Cosworth | *Engine failure, retired* |
| Deutschland Trophy, F2, Heat 1 | Hockenheim | 07/04/68 | Gold Leaf Team Lotus | Lotus 48-Cosworth | 12th |
| Deutschland Trophy, F2, Heat 2 | Hockenheim | 07/04/68 | Gold Leaf Team Lotus | Lotus 48-Cosworth | NS, *Team Lotus withdrew after Clark's death* |
| *Daily Express* International Trophy | Silverstone | 20/04/68 | Gold Leaf Team Lotus | Lotus 49-Cosworth V8 | *Fractured fuel line, retired* |
| Gran Premio de Madrid, F2 | Jarama | 28/04/68 | Gold Leaf Team Lotus | Lotus 48-Cosworth | *Broken wheel studs, retired* |
| **Spanish GP** | **Jarama** | **12/05/68** | **Gold Leaf Team Lotus** | **Lotus 49-Cosworth V8** | **1st** |
| **Monaco GP** | **Monte Carlo** | **26/05/68** | **Gold Leaf Team Lotus** | **Lotus 49B-Cosworth V8** | **Pole position, 1st** |
| Indianapolis 500 | Indianapolis | 30/05/68 | STP-Team Lotus | Lotus 56 turbine | *Hit wall, retired* |
| Holts Trophy, F2 | Crystal Palace | 28/04/68 | Gold Leaf Team Lotus | Lotus 48-Cosworth | *Lost wheel, retired* |
| **Belgian GP** | **Spa-Francorchamps** | **09/06/68** | **Gold Leaf Team Lotus** | **Lotus 49B-Cosworth V8** | **Transmission failure, retired** |
| Canadian Telegram Trophy | Mosport Park | 15/06/68 | STP-Team Lotus | Lotus 56 turbine | NS, *Practice accident* |
| **Dutch GP** | **Zandvoort** | **23/06/68** | **Gold Leaf Team Lotus** | **Lotus 49B-Cosworth V8** | **Spun off, retired, classified 9th** |
| **French GP** | **Rouen** | **07/07/68** | **Gold Leaf Team Lotus** | **Lotus 49B-Cosworth V8** | **Driveshaft failure, retired** |
| OAMTC Flugplatzrennen, F2 | Tülln Langenlebarn | 14/07/68 | Gold Leaf Team Lotus | Lotus 48-Cosworth | *Gearbox oil leak, retired* |
| **British GP** | **Brands Hatch** | **20/07/68** | **Gold Leaf Team Lotus** | **Lotus 49B-Cosworth V8** | **Pole position, broken universal joint, retired** |
| **German GP** | **Nürburgring** | **04/08/68** | **Gold Leaf Team Lotus** | **Lotus 49B-Cosworth V8** | **2nd** |
| Gold Cup | Oulton Park | 17/08/68 | Gold Leaf Team Lotus | Lotus 49B-Cosworth V8 | *Crownwheel and Pinion failed, retired* |
| Saloon Car Race | Oulton Park | 17/08/68 | Alan Mann | Ford Escort-FVA | *Puncture, retired* |
| **Italian GP** | **Monza** | **08/09/68** | **Gold Leaf Team Lotus** | **Lotus 49B-Cosworth V8** | **Lost wheel, retired** |
| Trophée de France, F2 | Reims | 15/09/68 | Gold Leaf Team Lotus | Lotus 48-Cosworth | 4th |
| **Canadian GP** | **Mont Tremblant** | **22/09/68** | **Gold Leaf Team Lotus** | **Lotus 49B-Cosworth V8** | **4th** |
| **US GP** | **Watkins Glen** | **06/10/68** | **Gold Leaf Team Lotus** | **Lotus 49B-Cosworth V8** | **2nd** |
| Grand Prix d'Albi, F2 | Albi | 20/10/68 | Gold Leaf Team Lotus | Lotus 48-Cosworth | *Brake caliper seal failed, retired/classified 14th* |
| Rome GP, F2, Heat 1 | Vallelunga | 27/10/68 | Gold Leaf Team Lotus | Lotus 48-Cosworth | 7th |
| Rome GP, F2, Heat 2 | Vallelunga | 27/10/68 | Gold Leaf Team Lotus | Lotus 48-Cosworth | *(7th on aggregate)* |
| **Mexican GP** | **Mexico City** | **03/11/68** | **Gold Leaf Team Lotus** | **Lotus 49B-Cosworth V8** | **1st** |

**1969**

| Race | Circuit | Date | Team | Car | Result |
|---|---|---|---|---|---|
| New Zealand GP | Pukekohe | 04/01/69 | Gold Leaf Team Lotus | Lotus 49T-Cosworth V8 | *Suspension failure, retired* |
| Rothmans International 100 | Levin | 11/01/69 | Gold Leaf Team Lotus | Lotus 49T-Cosworth V8 | *Driveshaft failure, retired* |
| Lady Wigram Trophy, Heat 2 | Christchurch | 18/01/69 | Gold Leaf Team Lotus | Lotus 49T-Cosworth V8 | 1st |
| Lady Wigram Trophy, Final | Christchurch | 18/01/69 | Gold Leaf Team Lotus | Lotus 49T-Cosworth V8 | 2nd |
| Rothmans International 100, Heat 1 | Invercargill | 25/01/69 | Gold Leaf Team Lotus | Lotus 49T-Cosworth V8 | 6th |
| Rothmans International 100, Final | Invercargill | 25/01/69 | Gold Leaf Team Lotus | Lotus 49T-Cosworth V8 | 2nd |
| Australian GP | Lakeside | 02/02/69 | Gold Leaf Team Lotus | Lotus 49T-Cosworth V8 | 4th |
| International Tasman 100 | Warwick Farm | 09/02/69 | Gold Leaf Team Lotus | Lotus 49T-Cosworth V8 | 11th |
| Sandown Park International | Sandown Park | 16/02/69 | Gold Leaf Team Lotus | Lotus 49T-Cosworth V8 | 6th |
| **South African GP** | **Kyalami** | **01/03/69** | **Gold Leaf Team Lotus** | **Lotus 49B-Cosworth V8** | **2nd** |
| *Daily Mail* Race of Champions | Brands Hatch | 19/03/69 | Gold Leaf Team Lotus | Lotus 49B-Cosworth V8 | 2nd |
| *Daily Express* International Trophy | Silverstone | 30/03/69 | Gold Leaf Team Lotus | Lotus 49B-Cosworth V8 | 7th |
| Wills Trophy, F2, Heat 1 | Thruxton | 07/04/69 | Roy Winkelmann Racing | Lotus 59B-Cosworth | 3rd |
| Wills Trophy, F2, Final | Thruxton | 07/04/69 | Roy Winkelmann Racing | Lotus 59B-Cosworth | *Clutch failed, retired* |
| Pau GP, F2 | Pau | 20/04/69 | Roy Winkelmann Racing | Lotus 59B-Cosworth | *Fuel injection metering belt broke, retired* |
| ADAC Eifelrennen, F2 | Nürburgring | 27/04/69 | Roy Winkelmann Racing | Lotus 59B-Cosworth | *Broken front wishbone, retired* |
| **Spanish GP** | **Barcelona** | **04/05/69** | **Gold Leaf Team Lotus** | **Lotus 49B-Cosworth V8** | **Rear wing collapsed, crashed, retired** |
| **Monaco GP** | **Monte Carlo** | **18/05/69** | **Gold Leaf Team Lotus** | **Lotus 49B-Cosworth V8** | **1st** |
| Limbourg GP, F2, Heat 1 | Zolder | 08/06/69 | Roy Winkelmann Racing | Lotus 48-Cosworth | 2nd |
| Limbourg GP, F2, Heat 2 | Zolder | 08/06/69 | Roy Winkelmann Racing | Lotus 48-Cosworth | *Rear suspension failure, retired* |
| **Dutch GP** | **Zandvoort** | **21/06/69** | **Gold Leaf Team Lotus** | **Lotus 49B-Cosworth V8** | **7th** |
| Trophée de France, F2 | Reims | 29/06/69 | Roy Winkelmann Racing | Lotus 48-Cosworth | *Accident with Galli, retired* |
| **French GP** | **Clermont-Ferrand** | **06/07/69** | **Gold Leaf Team Lotus** | **Lotus 49B-Cosworth V8** | **6th** |
| Flugplatzrennen, F2, Heat 1 | Tülln Langenlebarn | 13/07/69 | Roy Winkelmann Racing | Lotus 48-Cosworth | 3rd |
| Flugplatzrennen F2, Heat 2 | Tülln Langenlebarn | 13/07/69 | Roy Winkelmann Racing | Lotus 48-Cosworth | *(3rd on aggregate)* |
| **British GP** | **Silverstone** | **19/07/69** | **Gold Leaf Team Lotus** | **Lotus 49B-Cosworth V8** | **7th** |
| **German GP** | **Nürburgring** | **03/08/69** | **Gold Leaf Team Lotus** | **Lotus 49B-Cosworth V8** | **4th** |
| Gold Cup | Oulton Park | 16/08/69 | Roy Winkelmann Racing | Lotus 59B-Cosworth | *Oil leak, retired* |
| Enna GP, F2, Heat 1 | Enna-Pergusa | 24/08/69 | Roy Winkelmann Racing | Lotus 59B-Cosworth | 7th |
| Enna GP, Heat 2 | Enna-Pergusa | 24/08/69 | Roy Winkelmann Racing | Lotus 59B-Cosworth | 2nd *(6th on aggregate)* |
| **Italian GP** | **Monza** | **07/09/69** | **Gold Leaf Team Lotus** | **Lotus 49B-Cosworth V8** | **Driveshaft failure, retired, classified 9th** |
| Albi GP, F2 | Albi | 14/09/69 | Roy Winkelmann Racing | Lotus 59B-Cosworth | 1st |
| **Canadian GP** | **Mosport Park** | **20/09/69** | **Gold Leaf Team Lotus** | **Lotus 49B-Cosworth V8** | **Camshaft failure, retired** |
| **US GP** | **Watkins Glen** | **05/10/69** | **Gold Leaf Team Lotus** | **Lotus 49B-Cosworth V8** | **Tyre deflated, crashed, sustained serious leg injuries** |

**1970**

| | | | | | |
|---|---|---|---|---|---|
| **South African GP** | **Kyalami** | **07/03/70** | **Rob Walker Racing Team** | **Lotus 49C-Cosworth V8** | **6th** |
| *Daily Mail* Race of Champions | Brands Hatch | 22/03/70 | Rob Walker Racing Team | Lotus 49C-Cosworth V8 | 5th |
| **Spanish GP** | **Jarama** | **19/04/70** | **Rob Walker Racing Team** | **Lotus 49C-Cosworth V8** | **4th** |
| *Daily Express* International Trophy, Heat 1 | Silverstone | 26/04/70 | Rob Walker Racing Team | Lotus 49C-Cosworth V8 | *Delayed by pit stop, 14th* |
| *Daily Express* International Trophy, Heat 2 | Silverstone | 26/04/70 | Rob Walker Racing Team | Lotus 49C-Cosworth V8 | 4th *(9th on aggregate)* |
| **Monaco GP** | Monte Carlo | 10/05/70 | Brooke Bond Oxo/Rob Walker | Lotus 49C-Cosworth V8 | 5th |
| Ford Capri 3000 GT Race | Brands Hatch | 24/05/70 | Ford Motor Company | Ford Capri 3000 GT | 9th |
| Alcoa Trophy, F2, Qualifying Heat 1 | Crystal Palace | 25/05/70 | Jochen Rindt Team Lotus | Lotus 69-Cosworth | 4th |
| Alcoa Trophy, F2, Final | Crystal Palace | 25/05/70 | Jochen Rindt Team Lotus | Lotus 69-Cosworth | 5th |
| **Belgian GP** | **Spa-Francorchamps** | **07/06/70** | **Brooke Bond Oxo/Rob Walker** | **Lotus 49C-Cosworth V8** | *Engine failure, retired* |
| Rhine Cup, F2 | Hockenheim | 14/06/70 | Jochen Rindt Team Lotus | Lotus 69-Cosworth | *Metering unit belt broke, retired* |
| **Dutch GP** | **Zandvoort** | **21/06/70** | **Brooke Bond Oxo/Rob Walker** | **Lotus 49C-Cosworth V8** | **12th** |
| Rouen GP, F2, Heat 1 | Rouen | 28/06/70 | Jochen Rindt Team Lotus | Lotus 69-Cosworth | 8th |
| Rouen GP, F2, Final | Rouen | 28/06/70 | Jochen Rindt Team Lotus | Lotus 69-Cosworth | DNQ |
| **French GP** | **Clermont-Ferrand** | **05/07/70** | **Brooke Bond Oxo/Rob Walker** | **Lotus 49C-Cosworth V8** | **10th** |
| **British GP** | **Brands Hatch** | **19/07/70** | **Brooke Bond Oxo/Rob Walker** | **Lotus 49C-Cosworth V8** | **6th** |
| Trophée de France, F2 | Paul Ricard | 26/07/70 | Jochen Rindt Racing Team | Lotus 69-Cosworth | 5th |
| **German GP** | **Hockenheim** | **02/08/70** | **Brooke Bond Oxo/Rob Walker** | **Lotus 49C-Cosworth V8** | *Engine failure, retired* |
| Gold Cup, Heat 1 | Oulton Park | 22/08/70 | Brooke Bond Oxo/Rob Walker | Lotus 72C-Cosworth V8 | *Engine failure, retired, classified 18th* |
| Preis von Salzburg, F2, Heat 1 | Salzburgring | 30/08/70 | Jochen Rindt Racing Team | Lotus 69-Cosworth | 5th |
| Preis von Salzburg, F2, Heat 2 | Salzburgring | 30/08/70 | Jochen Rindt Racing Team | Lotus 69-Cosworth | 6th *(5th on aggregate)* |
| **Italian GP** | **Monza** | **06/09/70** | **Brooke Bond Oxo/Rob Walker** | **Lotus 72C-Cosworth V8** | NS, *All Lotuses withdrawn after Rindt's fatal practice accident* |
| **Canadian GP** | **Mont Tremblant** | **20/09/70** | **Brooke Bond Oxo/Rob Walker** | **Lotus 72C-Cosworth V8** | NC, *Gearbox problems* |
| **US GP** | **Watkins Glen** | **04/10/70** | **Brooke Bond Oxo/Rob Walker** | **Lotus 72C-Cosworth V8** | *Clutch failure, retired* |
| **Mexican GP** | **Mexico City** | **25/10/70** | **Brooke Bond Oxo/Rob Walker** | **Lotus 72C-Cosworth V8** | *Engine failure, retired* |

**1971**

| | | | | | |
|---|---|---|---|---|---|
| Colombian GP, F2, Heat 1 | Bogota | 04/02/71 | Bernie Ecclestone | Lotus 69-Cosworth | 3rd |
| Colombian GP, F2, Heat 2 | Bogota | 04/02/71 | Bernie Ecclestone | Lotus 69-Cosworth | 4th *(2nd on aggregate)* |
| Bogota GP, F2, Heat 1 | Bogota | 07/02/71 | Bernie Ecclestone | Lotus 69-Cosworth | *Fuel metering unit failed, retired* |
| Bogota GP, F2, Heat 2 | Bogota | 07/02/71 | Bernie Ecclestone | Lotus 69-Cosworth | 5th |
| **South African GP** | **Kyalami** | **06/03/71** | **Motor Racing Developments** | **Brabham BT33-Cosworth V8** | **9th** |
| *Daily Mail* Race of Champions | Brands Hatch | 21/03/71 | Motor Racing Developments | Brabham BT34-Cosworth V8 | *Engine failure, retired* |
| Questor GP, Heat 1 | Ontario Speedway | 28/03/71 | Motor Racing Developments | Brabham BT34-Cosworth V8 | *Split oil line, retired* |
| Jim Clark Trophy, F2, Heat 1 | Hockenheim | 04/04/71 | Rondel Racing | Brabham BT36-Cosworth | 3rd |
| Jim Clark Trophy F2, Heat 2 | Hockenheim | 04/04/71 | Rondel Racing | Brabham BT36-Cosworth | 1st *(2nd on aggregate)* |
| Yellow Pages Trophy, F2, Heat 1 | Thruxton | 12/04/71 | Rondel Racing | Brabham BT36-Cosworth | 1st |
| Yellow Pages Trophy, F2, Final | Thruxton | 12/04/71 | Rondel Racing | Brabham BT36-Cosworth | 1st |
| **Spanish GP** | **Barcelona** | **18/04/71** | **Motor Racing Developments** | **Brabham BT34-Cosworth V8** | *Steering failure, retired* |
| Pau GP, F2 | Pau | 25/04/71 | Rondel Racing | Brabham BT36-Cosworth | *Water pump drive failed, retired, classified 10th* |
| ADAC Eifelrennen, F2 | Nürburgring | 02/05/71 | Rondel Racing | Brabham BT36-Cosworth | 5th |
| *Daily Express* International Trophy, Heat 1 | Silverstone | 08/05/71 | Motor Racing Developments | Brabham BT34-Cosworth V8 | 3rd |
| *Daily Express* International Trophy, Heat 2 | Silverstone | 08/05/71 | Motor Racing Developments | Brabham BT34-Cosworth V8 | 1st *(1st on aggregate)* |
| **Monaco GP** | **Monte Carlo** | **23/05/71** | **Motor Racing Developments** | **Brabham BT34-Cosworth V8** | *Crashed, retired* |
| Hilton Transport Trophy, F2, Heat 1 | Crystal Palace | 31/05/71 | Rondel Racing | Brabham BT36-Cosworth | *Metering unit failed, retired* |
| Hilton Transport Trophy, Final | Crystal Palace | 31/05/71 | Rondel Racing | Brabham BT36-Cosworth | DNQ |
| **Dutch GP** | **Zandvoort** | **20/06/71** | **Motor Racing Developments** | **Brabham BT34-Cosworth V8** | **10th** |
| Rouen GP, F2 | Rouen | 27/06/71 | Rondel Racing | Brabham BT36-Cosworth | 3rd |
| **French GP** | **Paul Ricard** | **04/07/71** | **Motor Racing Developments** | **Brabham BT34-Cosworth V8** | *Low oil pressure, retired* |
| **British GP** | **Silverstone** | **17/07/71** | **Motor Racing Developments** | **Brabham BT34-Cosworth V8** | *Run into by Oliver on grid, retired* |
| **German GP** | **Nürburgring** | **01/08/71** | **Motor Racing Developments** | **Brabham BT34-Cosworth V8** | **9th** |
| **Austrian GP** | **Österreichring** | **15/08/71** | **Motor Racing Developments** | **Brabham BT34-Cosworth V8** | **5th** |
| Swedish Gold Cup, F2, Heat 1 | Kinnekullering | 22/08/71 | Rondel Racing | Brabham BT36-Cosworth | 13th |
| Swedish Gold Cup, F2, Heat 2 | Kinnekullering | 22/08/71 | Rondel Racing | Brabham BT36-Cosworth | 13th *(14th on aggregate)* |
| Rothmans International Trophy, F2 | Brands Hatch | 30/08/71 | Rondel Racing | Brabham BT36-Cosworth | 2nd |
| **Italian GP** | **Monza** | **05/09/71** | **Motor Racing Developments** | **Brabham BT34-Cosworth V8** | *Transmission seized, retired* |
| GT Race, Heat 1 | Paul Ricard | 12/09/71 | Ford of Britain | Ford Capri 3000 GT | *c/d Surtees. 1st* |
| GT Race, Heat 2 | Paul Ricard | 12/09/71 | Ford of Britain | Ford Capri 3000 GT | *c/d Surtees. Transmission failed, retired* |
| **Canadian GP** | **Mosport Park** | **19/09/71** | **Motor Racing Developments** | **Brabham BT34-Cosworth V8** | *Spun off, retired* |
| Albi GP, F2 | Albi | 26/09/71 | Rondel Racing | Brabham BT36-Cosworth | 5th |
| **US GP** | **Watkins Glen** | **03/10/71** | **Motor Racing Developments** | **Brabham BT34-Cosworth V8** | **7th** |
| Rothmans Victory Race | Brands Hatch | 24/10/71 | Motor Racing Developments | Brabham BT34-Cosworth V8 | 8th |
| Torneio F2 Series Round 1, Heat 1 | Interlagos | 31/10/71 | Rondel Racing | Brabham BT36-Cosworth | 7th |

| | | | | | |
|---|---|---|---|---|---|
| Torneio F2 Series Round 1, Heat 2 | Interlagos | 31/10/71 | Rondel Racing | Brabham BT36-Cosworth | 4th *(6th on aggregate)* |
| Torneio F2 Series Round 2, Heat 1 | Interlagos | 07/11/71 | Rondel Racing | Brabham BT36-Cosworth | 9th |
| Torneio F2 Series Round 2, Heat 2 | Interlagos | 07/11/71 | Rondel Racing | Brabham BT36-Cosworth | 6th *(5th on aggregate)* |
| Torneio F2 Series Round 3, Heat 1 | Cutyba | 14/11/71 | Rondel Racing | Brabham BT36-Cosworth | 9th |
| Torneio F2 Series Round 3, Heat 2 | Cutyba | 14/11/71 | Rondel Racing | Brabham BT36-Cosworth | 5th *(6th on aggregate)* |
| Torneio F2 Series Round 4, Heat 1 | Cordoba | 21/11/71 | Rondel Racing | Brabham BT36-Cosworth | 14th |
| Torneio F2 Series Round 4, Heat 2 | Cordoba | 21/11/71 | Rondel Racing | Brabham BT36-Cosworth | 3rd *(10th on aggregate)* |

## 1972

| | | | | | |
|---|---|---|---|---|---|
| **Argentine GP** | **Buenos Aires** | **23/01/72** | **Motor Racing Developments** | **Brabham BT33-Cosworth V8** | *Fuel pump failure, tyre problems, retired* |
| **South African GP** | **Kyalami** | **04/03/72** | **Motor Racing Developments** | **Brabham BT33-Cosworth V8** | **6th** |
| Esso Uniflo Trophy, F2, Qualifying Heat 2 | Thruxton | 03/04/72 | Graham Hill/Tate of Leeds (Racing) | Brabham BT36-Cosworth | 6th |
| Esso Uniflo Trophy, F2, Final | Thruxton | 03/04/72 | Graham Hill/Tate of Leeds (Racing) | Brabham BT36-Cosworth | *Engine failure, retired* |
| Jim Clark Trophy, F2, Heat 1 | Hockenheim | 16/04/72 | Jaegermeister Racing | Brabham BT36-Cosworth | 12th |
| Jim Clark Trophy, F2, Heat 2 | Hockenheim | 16/04/72 | Jaegermeister Racing | Brabham BT36-Cosworth F2 | *Engine failure, retired* |
| *Daily Express* International Trophy | Silverstone | 23/04/72 | Motor Racing Developments | Brabham BT37-Cosworth V8 | 7th |
| **Spanish GP** | **Jarama** | **01/05/72** | **Motor Racing Developments** | **Brabham BT37-Cosworth V8** | **10th** |
| Pau GP, F2, Qualifying heat 1 | Pau | 07/05/72 | Jaegermeister Racing | Brabham BT38-Cosworth | 7th |
| Pau GP, F2, Final | Pau | 07/05/72 | Jaegermeister Racing | Brabham BT38-Cosworth | *Fractured oil line, retired* |
| **Monaco GP** | **Monte Carlo** | **14/05/72** | **Motor Racing Developments** | **Brabham BT37-Cosworth V8** | **12th** |
| Greater London Trophy, F2, Qualifying Heat 1 | Crystal Palace | 28/05/72 | Jaegermeister Racing | Brabham BT38-Cosworth | *Collision with Birrell, retired* |
| Greater London Trophy, F2, Final | Crystal Palace | 28/05/72 | Jaegermeister Racing | Brabham BT38-Cosworth | DNQ |
| Lottery GP, F2, Heat 1 | Monza | 29/05/72 | Jaegermeister Racing | Brabham BT38-Cosworth | 1st |
| Lottery GP, F2, Heat 2 | Monza | 29/05/72 | Jaegermeister Racing | Brabham BT38-Cosworth | 1st *(1st on aggregate)* |
| **Belgian GP** | **Nivelles-Baulers** | **04/06/72** | **Motor Racing Developments** | **Brabham BT37-Cosworth V8** | *Rear upright detached, retired* |
| Le Mans 24 Hours | Le Mans | 10-11/06/72 | Equipe Matra | Matra MS670-V12 | *c/d Pescarolo. 1st* |
| Rouen GP, F2, Qualifying Heat 1 | Rouen | 25/06/72 | Jaegermeister Racing | Brabham BT38-Cosworth | 8th |
| Rouen GP, F2, Final | Rouen | 25/06/72 | Jaegermeister Racing | Brabham BT38-Cosworth | 7th |
| **French GP** | **Clermont-Ferrand** | **02/07/72** | **Motor Racing Developments** | **Brabham BT37-Cosworth V8** | **10th** |
| **British GP** | **Brands Hatch** | **15/07/72** | **Motor Racing Developments** | **Brabham BT37-Cosworth V8** | *Crashed, retired* |
| Shell GP, F2, Heat 1 | Imola | 23/07/72 | Jaegermeister Racing | Brabham BT38-Cosworth | 11th |
| Shell GP, F2, Heat 2 | Imola | 23/07/72 | Jaegermeister Racing | Brabham BT38-Cosworth | 4th *(5th on aggregate)* |
| **German GP** | **Nürburgring** | **30/07/72** | **Motor Racing Developments** | **Brabham BT37-Cosworth V8** | **6th** |
| **Austrian GP** | **Österreichring** | **13/08/72** | **Motor Racing Developments** | **Brabham BT37-Cosworth V8** | *Fuel metering unit failed, retired* |
| Festival Prize, F2, Heat 1 | Salzburgring | 03/09/72 | Jaegermeister Racing | Brabham BT38-Cosworth | 4th |
| Festival Prize, Heat 2 | Salzburgring | 03/09/72 | Jaegermeister Racing | Brabham BT38-Cosworth | 4th |
| **Italian GP** | **Monza** | **10/09/72** | **Motor Racing Developments** | **Brabham BT37-Cosworth V8** | **5th** |
| John Player F2 Championship Final | Oulton Park | 16/09/72 | Jaegermeister Racing | Brabham BT38-Cosworth | 10th |
| **Canadian GP** | **Mosport Park** | **24/09/72** | **Motor Racing Developments** | **Brabham BT37-Cosworth V8** | **8th** |
| Baden-Württemberg Prize, F2 | Hockenheim | 01/10/72 | Jaegermeister Racing | Brabham 8T38-Cosworth | 5th |
| **US GP** | **Watkins Glen** | **08/10/72** | **Motor Racing Developments** | **Brabham BT37-Cosworth V8** | **11th** |
| John Player Victory Meeting | Brands Hatch | 22/10/72 | Motor Racing Developments | Brabham BT37-Cosworth V8 | *Gear linkage problems, retired* |

## 1973

| | | | | | |
|---|---|---|---|---|---|
| *Daily Mail* Race of Champions | Brands Hatch | 18/03/73 | Motor Racing Developments | Brabham BT37-Cosworth V8 | *Collision with Pilette, retired* |
| **Spanish GP** | **Barcelona** | **29/04/73** | **Embassy Racing** | **Shadow DN1-Cosworth V8** | *Braking problems, retired* |
| Spa 1000Km | Spa-Francorchamps | 06/05/73 | Matra Sports | Matra MS670-V12 | *c/d Amon/Pescarolo. Retired, engine* |
| **Belgian GP** | **Zolder** | **20/05/73** | **Embassy-Hill Racing** | **Shadow DN1-Cosworth V8** | **9th** |
| **Monaco GP** | **Monte Carlo** | **03/06/73** | **Embassy-Hill Racing** | **Shadow DN1-Cosworth V8** | *Rear suspension problems, retired* |
| **Swedish GP** | **Anderstorp** | **17/06/73** | **Embassy-Hill Racing** | **Shadow DN1-Cosworth V8** | *Ignition failure, retired* |
| **French GP** | **Paul Ricard** | **01/07/73** | **Embassy-Hill Racing** | **Shadow DN1-Cosworth V8** | **10th** |
| **British GP** | **Silverstone** | **14/07/73** | **Embassy-Hill Racing** | **Shadow DN1-Cosworth V8** | *Loose steering rack, retired* |
| **Dutch GP** | **Zandvoort** | **29/07/73** | **Embassy-Hill Racing** | **Shadow DN1-Cosworth V8** | *NC, water leak* |
| **German GP** | **Nürburgring** | **05/08/73** | **Embassy-Hill Racing** | **Shadow DN1-Cosworth V8** | **13th** |
| **Austrian GP** | **Österreichring** | **19/08/73** | **Embassy-Hill Racing** | **Shadow DN1-Cosworth V8** | *Broken rear suspension, retired* |
| **Italian GP** | **Monza** | **09/09/73** | **Embassy-Hill Racing** | **Shadow DN1-Cosworth V8** | **14th** |
| **Canadian GP** | **Mosport Park** | **23/09/73** | **Embassy-Hill Racing** | **Shadow DN1-Cosworth V8** | **16th** |
| **US GP** | **Watkins Glen** | **07/10/73** | **Embassy-Hill Racing** | **Shadow DN1-Cosworth V8** | **13th** |

## 1974

| | | | | | |
|---|---|---|---|---|---|
| **Argentine GP** | **Buenos Aires** | **13/01/74** | **Embassy-Hill Racing** | **Lola T370-Cosworth V8** | *Engine failure, retired* |
| **Brazilian GP** | **Interlagos** | **27/01/74** | **Embassy-Hill Racing** | **Lola T370-Cosworth V8** | **11th** |
| *Daily Mail* Race of Champions | Brands Hatch | 17/03/74 | Embassy-Hill Racing | Lola T370-Cosworth V8 | 17th |
| **South African GP** | **Kyalami** | **30/03/74** | **Embassy-Hill Racing** | **Lola T370-Cosworth V8** | **12th** |

| | | | | | |
|---|---|---|---|---|---|
| *Daily Express* International Trophy | Silverstone | 07/04/74 | Embassy-Hill Racing | Lola T370-Cosworth V8 | *Suspension failure, retired* |
| Spanish GP | Jarama | 28/04/74 | Embassy-Hill Racing | Lola T370-Cosworth V8 | *Engine failure, retired* |
| Belgian GP | Nivelles-Baulers | 12/05/74 | Embassy-Hill Racing | Lola T370-Cosworth V8 | 8th |
| Monaco GP | Monte Carlo | 26/05/74 | Embassy-Hill Racing | Lola T370-Cosworth V8 | 7th |
| Swedish GP | Anderstorp | 09/06/74 | Embassy-Hill Racing | Lola T370-Cosworth V8 | 6th |
| Dutch GP | Zandvoort | 23/06/74 | Embassy-Hill Racing | Lola T370-Cosworth V8 | *Clutch housing bolts fell out, retired* |
| French GP | Dijon | 07/07/74 | Embassy-Hill Racing | Lola T370-Cosworth V8 | 13th |
| British GP | Brands Hatch | 20/07/74 | Embassy-Hill Racing | Lola T370-Cosworth V8 | 13th |
| German GP | Nürburgring | 04/08/74 | Embassy-Hill Racing | Lola T370-Cosworth V8 | 9th |
| Austrian GP | Österreichring | 18/08/74 | Embassy-Hill Racing | Lola T370-Cosworth V8 | 12th |
| Italian GP | Monza | 08/09/74 | Embassy-Hill Racing | Lola T370-Cosworth V8 | 8th |
| Canadian GP | Mosport Park | 22/09/74 | Embassy-Hill Racing | Lola T370-Cosworth V8 | 14th |
| US GP | Watkins Glen | 06/10/74 | Embassy-Hill Racing | Lola T370-Cosworth V8 | 8th |
| | | | | | |
| **1975** | | | | | |
| Argentine GP | Buenos Aires | 12/01/75 | Embassy-Hill Racing | Lola T370-Cosworth V8 | 10th |
| Brazilian GP | Interlagos | 26/01/75 | Embassy-Hill Racing | Lola T370-Cosworth V8 | 12th |
| South African GP | Kyalami | 01/03/75 | Embassy-Hill Racing | Lola T370-Cosworth V8 | NS, *practice crash* |
| *Daily Express* International Trophy | Silverstone | 12/04/75 | Embassy-Hill Racing | Hill GH1-Cosworth V8 | 11th |
| Monaco GP | Monte Carlo | 11/05/75 | Embassy-Hill Racing | Hill GH1-Cosworth V8 | DNQ |

**Embassy-Hill Racing results, post retirement:**

| | | | | | |
|---|---|---|---|---|---|
| Belgian Grand Prix | Zolder | 25/05/75 | Embassy-Hill Racing | Hill GH1-Cosworth V8 | *Brise: piston failure, retired Migault: suspension failure, retired* |
| Swedish Grand Prix | Anderstorp | 08/06/75 | Embassy-Hill Racing | Hill GH1-Cosworth V8 | *Brise: 6th Schuppan, drive-shaft failure, retired* |
| Dutch Grand Prix | Zandvoort | 22/06/75 | Embassy-Hill Racing | Hill GH1-Cosworth V8 | *Brise: 7th. Jones: 13th* |
| French Grand Prix | Paul Ricard | 06/07/75 | Embassy-Hill Racing | Hill GH1-Cosworth V8 | *Brise: 7th. Jones: 16th* |
| British Grand Prix | Silverstone | 19/07/75 | Embassy-Hill Racing | Hill GH1-Cosworth V8 | *Brise: crashed, retired, classified 15th. Jones: 10th* |
| German Grand Prix | Nürburgring | 03/08/75 | Embassy-Hill Racing | Hill GH1-Cosworth V8 | *Brise: accident, retired. Jones: 5th* |
| Austrian Grand Prix | Österreichring | 17/08/75 | Embassy-Hill Racing | Hill GH1-Cosworth V8 | *Brise: 15th. Stommelen: 16th* |
| Italian Grand Prix | Monza | 07/09/75 | Embassy-Hill Racing | Hill GH1-Cosworth V8 | *Brise: accident, retired. Stommelen: accident, retired* |
| US Grand Prix | Watkins Glen | 05/10/75 | Embassy-Hill Racing | Hill GH1-Cosworth V8 | *Brise: accident, retired* |

Key:
NC: not classified
DNQ: did not qualify
NS: non-starter
DSQ: disqualified

**Graham Hill's F`1 World Championship placings and points tally**

| | | | | | |
|---|---|---|---|---|---|
| 1958 | — | — | 1967 | 6th | 15 |
| 1959 | — | — | 1968 | 1st | 48 |
| 1960 | 15th | 4 | 1969 | 7th | 19 |
| 1961 | 13th | 3 | 1970 | 13th | 7 |
| 1962 | 1st | (52) 42 with deductions | 1971 | 21st | 2 |
| 1963 | 2nd | 29 | 1972 | 12th | 4 |
| 1964 | 2nd | (39) 41 with deductions | 1973 | — | |
| 1965 | 2nd | (47) 40 with deductions | 1974 | 18th | 1 |
| 1966 | 5th | 17 | 1975 | — | — |

**Formula 1 World Championship placings lst-6th + Pole + Fastest lap**

| 1st | 2nd | 3rd | 4th | 5th | 6th | Pole | Fastest lap | Races |
|---|---|---|---|---|---|---|---|---|
| 14 | 15 | 7 | 9 | 7 | 8 | 13 | 10 | 176 |

# Index

716c